KENNIKAT PRESS

NATIONAL UNIVERSITY PUBLICATIONS

SERIES ON LITERARY CRITICISM

General Editor

EUGENE GOODHEART

Professor of Literature, Massachusetts Institute of Technology

GLENWAY WESCOTT:

The Paradox of Voice

Ira Johnson

NATIONAL UNIVERSITY PUBLICATIONS
KENNIKAT PRESS
Port Washington, N.Y. // London

GLENWAY WESCOTT: THE PARADOX OF VOICE

ACKNOWLEDGMENTS

Thanks are due to the following persons and organizations for permission
to use   excerpts and quotations from copyrighted material. To Harper
and Row, Publishers, Inc., for *The Grandmothers.* Copyright 1927 by
Harper and Brothers. Copyright renewed 1955 by Glenway Wescott;
Goodby Wisconsin. Copyright 1928 by Harper and Brothers. Copyright
renewed 1956 by Glenway Wescott; *The Pilgrim Hawk.* Copyright 1940
by Glenway Wescott. Copyright renewed 1968 by Glenway Wescott;
Apartment in Athens. Copyright 1944, 1945 by Glenway Wescott; *Images
of Truth.* Copyright 1960, 1962 by Glenway Wescott; To Harold Ober
Associates, Incorporated for: *The Apple of the Eye.* Copyright 1924 by
The Dial Press; *The Babe's Bed.* Copyright 1930 by Glenway Wescott;
"The Dream of Audubon" *The Best One-Act Plays of 1940.* Copyright
1941 by Dodd, Mead and Company, Inc.; To Appleton-Century-Crofts,
Meredith Corporation for *The Twentieth Century Novel.* Copyright 1932,
1960 by Joseph Warren Beach. To Sy Kahn for *Glenway Wescott: A
Critical and Biographical Study.* Copyright 1957 by Sy Kahn (Doctoral
Dissertation, University of Wisconsin 1957). To Twayne Publishers, Inc.
for *Glenway Wescott.* Copyright 1965 by William Rueckert. To New
York Times Company for "Record of a Friendship." Copyright 1966 by
New York Times Company; To The Viking Press, Inc. for *Craft and
Character in Modern Fiction.* Copyright 1940, 1941, 1956 by Morton
Dauwen Zobel.

Published by
Kennikat Press
Port Washington, N.Y./London

To
my wife,
Christiane

PREFACE

I am especially indebted to the members of my committee at Cornell University, Don W. Kleine and Kenneth C. Frederick, and to its chairman, James R. McConkey, for their encouragement and lively interest in this work as it developed in its earlier form as a dissertation. Especially I want to thank William J. Stuckey of Purdue University, who spent valuable Parisian time in giving the entire manuscript a sympathetic reading of the most helpful kind. To my old friends Bill and Wynne Pittman of Bloomington, Indiana, I owe thanks for special aid and comfort.

This work would not have been possible at all, however, without the daily personal assistance and encouragement of my wife, to whom it is dedicated.

TABLE OF CONTENTS

GLENWAY WESCOTT:
THE PARADOX OF VOICE

1

INTRODUCTION

During the 1920's, Glenway Wescott (born 1901) was generally considered by critics and discriminating readers as one of America's most promising young writers. Beginning at nineteen as an imagist poet, he published his second and last volume of poetry in 1925. His verse is of very little importance, showing a lyric impulse and a respect for the image which can be much more significantly examined in his first work of fiction, *The Apple of the Eye* (1924), a novel that appeared when he was only twenty-three. Three years later he published his second novel, *The Grandmothers* (1927). It became immediately a critical and popular success. And a year after that followed his only volume of short stories, *Good-Bye, Wisconsin*. Then, except for *The Babe's Bed* (1930), a long story brought out in a limited edition in Paris, and a handful of short stories, no fiction was to appear from him until *The Pilgrim Hawk* in 1940, thirteen years later. This short novel, although it is not as broad in scope as *The Grandmothers,* is unquestionably one of fine and nearly flawless execution, the perfection of Wescott's art. Anthologized twice after its debut in *Harper's Magazine* in 1939, and then published in book form, something of its durability can be inferred from its republication — in hard covers — twenty-seven years later.

There was, however, no second greater period of fiction to appear from Wescott, as *The Pilgrim Hawk* had seemed to announce. In 1945, at last, came *Apartment in Athens,* a war novel, but a didactic one, and inferior in some ways even to

The Apple of the Eye. After that, except for two rather tepid short stories, there was no more fiction.

In certain ways Wescott is of his time and place and in the mainstream of American literature. His beginnings as an imagist poet, his early appearance as a critic-reviewer in the pages of *The New Republic, Poetry, The Dial,* and other little magazines, his themes and his experiments with form in his novels and short stories which appeared before he had turned thirty, his years as an expatriate — all have their parallels to the production and careers of other American writers of the twenties. Contemporary criticism, although appreciative and optimistic about his career, was with few exceptions brief and ephemeral, predominately placing him as a regionalist, a chronicler of pioneers, a recorder of frustrated and rebellious lives wasted away in remote middle-western towns.

Yet, as William Rueckert has indicated, although *The Grandmothers* does, like *The Great Gatsby* and many other works of the time, make use of the "cultural myth" that was "a commonplace among American writers of the twenties," and is in a "significant and deeply rooted American tradition," it is, like *Gatsby,* more important for its intrinsic artistic value than it is as a socio-historical corpus. It should be added as well that *The Pilgrim Hawk* endures not by what has been taken for its subject or theme ("a great love story," is the critical commonplace), but by its achievement as one of the finest of its genre.

The work of Glenway Wescott is worth an even more thorough study than it has received. Despite the quality and the uniqueness of his sensibility, however, he is not a major American writer; this is not simply due to a certain narrowness of subject and limitation of vision (some major writers have been so handicapped). It is also that he appeared to have just those qualities needed for major achievement and to have started early and fast in that direction, only to disappoint; by the time he was forty-four he had stopped writing fiction.

The only book-length studies of Wescott are an unpublished doctoral dissertation of Sy Myron Kahn (Wisconsin, 1957) and William H. Rueckert's *Glenway Wescott* (1965). Kahn's study is of indisputable value: it breaks the ground for any further criticism of Wescott's work and is the only documented source for what limited biographical information is available. It considers everything that Wescott has published from the beginning of his career: poetry, reviews and criticism, fiction and non-fiction. Rueckert's book also covers all of Wescott's publications and his career; it adds much to the understanding of Wescott's art, being more concerned with technique and with critical approaches to fiction, and it recognizes that Wescott has a crucial artistic problem. Its insights are often trenchant, but no thorough explications are attempted. My book differs in scope, depth, and approach, particularly concerning technique, from either of its predecessors.

What follows is a critical study of all of Wescott's fiction with the intention of thoroughly explicating and illuminating each work to assess the techniques employed, their degree of artistic success and failure, and the relationship of each work and its technical attributes to Wescott's entire fictional production. Very special attention is given to techniques that reveal an explanation of Wescott's small production and early silence.

The Apple of the Eye is characterized by many techniques in the modern tradition, but especially by a limited though powerful and rhetorical narrative voice. Two serious flaws are evident: the novel's didacticism, due to Wescott's conception of *image* and *truth,* and the disparity between the omniscient narrator and the rest of the work. Consideration of these two problems are necessary in measuring Wescott's intention and achievement. It soon becomes clear that it is only when he is able to resolve them that his fiction achieves the potential it at other times seems to promise.

The Grandmothers to a surprising degree does fulfill that promise, fusing secondary themes with what are always to be Wescott's major themes, love and the self. Here Wescott has found a form that is not only amenable to his subject, but perfectly suited to his strengths — and his failings — as an artist. His great technical achievement is the development of a participating narrator, identical to the author's second (artistic) self,[1] inseparable from subject and form, and gifted with a voice able to exploit what is outstanding, the *lyrical* and *rhetorical* quality of his prose. Such a narrator nearly eliminates the disparity between voice and other elements, and it makes functional what in the first novel had been flaws — including the abstracting of *truths* from *images,* which now becomes essential to the narrator's rumination on the family of stories. Yet, rather than develop important techniques that would give him greater flexibility, Wescott was apparently, by means of the new participating narrator, able to make virtues of some of his rather pronounced artistic shortcomings.

The stories in *Good-Bye, Wisconsin* are experiments in several forms with varying degrees of success. In the title essay, Wescott announces his desire for a new "style," meaning the "objective" fiction he from then on thought he should write. However, the theme of the self, the concept of *image* and *truth,* and the technique of the participating narrative voice are so fused in Wescott's creative imagination and, apparently, so closely related to the author's personal self, that this fusion results in his only consistently successful form of narration.

What Wescott sought was a greater distance between the personal self and the second, or artistic, self. In *The Babe's Bed,* he attempts to put an end to the method of the participating narrator and to search out and destroy the psychological necessity behind it because he feels that the result is self-projection rather than what he calls *truth.* In this sense *The Pilgrim Hawk* is a rewriting of *The Babe's Bed.* Yet in neither work does Wescott recognize the contribution of his concept of *image* and *truth* to the very abstracting and generalizing he so deplores. A rationale that led to serious shortcomings in his other works, it is still retained in his attempt at an objective novel, *Apartment in Athens,* and significantly contributes to its failure. Neither does Wescott succeed in eliminating the narrative voice; in its emasculated form it is the second major cause of that novel's failure, which suggests, along with evidence in the essays, *Images of Truth* (1962), that Wescott is still strongly drawn toward the form in which he achieved so much. Although the ultimate reasons are probably deeply personal, Wescott's long fictional silence has been due to being drawn toward two opposing and irreconcilable concepts of narration and form, only to find himself immobilized between them.

2
THE APPLE OF THE EYE

The Apple of the Eye, Glenway Wescott's first novel, appeared in 1924, the first section of it, "Bad Han," having appeared in two parts earlier that year in *The Dial.* He was then twenty-three years old, but even at this early age, he had already produced one book of poems, *The Bitterns* (1920), and composed the contents of what would be his last book of poems, *Natives of Rock: Poems: 1921-1922,* to be published in 1925. He had also written book reviews for *Poetry, The New Republic, The Dial,* and *Broom.* Both the poems and the reviews are of minor importance and interest, and only rarely do they offer a genuinely pertinent insight into the author's novels and short stories.

The Apple of the Eye, The Grandmothers, Good-Bye, Wisconsin, a handful of uncollected short stories, and *The Babe's Bed,* more than half of Wescott's fiction and all of what is his first and largest period of production, make use of middle-western material. Yet to categorize Wescott as a regionalist, as some critics and reviewers have done, is to be short-sighted. It is in the essay, "Good-Bye, Wisconsin," which heads the book of short stories with the same title, that he directly confronts Wisconsin and the Middle West as a region, and it is here that he specifically documents his rejection.

The essay is important to the understanding of Wescott's attitude and its relation to his fiction and his career, but in his fiction the region is a secondary theme, although it often widens and extends its significance. The regional quality of *The Grandmothers* ceases to be only that, and what the novel implies about

7

the Middle West broadens to include the American past, its myth and its reality. Yet the major themes of love and the self are equally important; they are, as William Rueckert has made clear, themes that with consistent strength flow through all of Wescott's work. It is true that through 1930 one of Wescott's concerns is defining for himself the significance of Wisconsin in terms of his own vision, but it is never his only concern, and his control of it keeps his work from being simply or even pre-dominantly regionalist. "The versions of the meaning the Middle West had for Wescott," Sy Kahn has said, "are not so much shifting interpretations corrected by increasing maturity, but rather segments of rich evaluation. Wescott himself felt that his fiction of the twenties exhausted his knowledge of the Wisconsin material and marked the end of a phase in his writing." Kahn is accurate in evaluating the early Wescott as "essentially a lyrical creator of moods rather than a social critic, satirist or historian," a writer who "dramatizes the psychological impact of the land and rural life on his characters."

The Apple of the Eye is set in Wescott's native Wisconsin, specifically the kettle-morain region in eastern Wisconsin. It is a hilly, rocky, uneven country, where the farming is poor. It is generally unlike the Middle West with its fertile and lucrative plains or the Wisconsin of rich dairy farms and pleasant lakes. Yet the countryside in *The Apple of the Eye,* its weather, its flora and fauna, and its marsh are admirably suited not simply as setting, but as material for Wescott's prose with its symbolic textures and predominating tone. It is the land as much as the characters, and even more than the cultural attributes of country or town (for Wescott is very weak in rendering these), that both functions as a metaphor for the fecund vitality of life and aids in establishing the imaginative poverty, sterility, and frustration of the environment — one which the intelligent and sensitive hero, Dan Strane, parts with in disappointment and sadness, with tender and muted nostalgia. For the novel is primarily one of initiation, secondarily one of revolt from farm and town.

Structure and Theme

Book One ("Bad Han") is the telling of the story of Hannah Madoc, pagan and stoic, whose endurance and strength mark her as secular saint of life, whose qualities make her legendary. She, as well as the marsh, are established as major symbols that carry through the novel. Her legend, with its truth, transcends time and place and is told and retold in the next sections by Mike Byron and Jule Bier, anti-Puritan preachers. Her unquestioning acceptance of love, her survival of the loss of it, her conquering of despair, her salvaging of a kind of love and self-sufficiency at last are not achieved by adhering to a self-torturing ideal or code of conduct, nor by wrestling with a sense of guilt, but through acceptance, endurance, and the living of life as it is.

Selma Bier is also introduced in this section. The major thematic opposition in the novel to what Hannah represents is what Selma (aided by her sister Theodora Strane) represents: Puritanism. Wescott apparently has in mind the term as rather generally used by Van Wyk Brooks and other critics of the time, but he makes a more precise definition in a 1923 review when he speaks of "the evasion of experience. It has two phases: evasion by theory, in conduct and thought (Puritanism), and evasion by inability, through lack of intellectual machinery. The former may characterize the land of the Ku-Klux-Klan and 'Clean Books,' the latter is the mark of all bad literature." [1]

Book Two introduces Mike Byron, a wanderer who has been to the city and the state university. He is, as Dan Strane is to be later, a spiritual son of Hannah, and the first initiator and liberator of Dan, freeing him from the Puritanism of his religious heritage, his family and region. In Book Three Jule Bier, as second initiator, tells the legend of Bad Han, and in his sermon explicates the text for Dan. Bad Han then becomes his third initiator and his second "mother," and Dan as her spiritual son becomes like Mike and Jule an initiator and preacher when he tells the story to Mrs. Dunham, his third "mother." The process completes his understanding of the purpose of life — to live it — as well as discovering for him his vocation of story teller, one who transmits his sense of life through art.

Books Two and Three dramatize two of the possible outcomes when those indoctrinated in the "evasion of life by theory" are confronted with life itself. The romance of Mike and Rosalia takes place entirely in Book Two. It runs parallel to and is part of the process of Dan's awakening consciousness under the tutorship of Mike. Rosalia eventually dies (as does her mother later) of the very Puritan sickness Mike has spoken of, and from which Dan himself suffers. The separation of the flesh and the spirit in Rosalia is the more dramatic and pitiful. She is beautiful, physically and sensually ready and capable of passion and love. But her idealistic code (Puritanism), which she does not question, leads to anguish and frustration when the flesh and emotions are denied, to guilt and sorrow when they are not. In her ignorance and naiveté, her underfed and tortured imagination when she has "done wrong" — in contrast to Hannah — can only condemn her to pregnancy and death. She dies, ironically, "a virgin mother." Certain realities of life are recognized by the idealistic code only as evil, with no allowance for individual nature or situation; therefore Rosalia cannot follow the code and survive.

Dan Strane, the central character of the novel, represents the other possibility of the confrontation of life and theory: rejection of theory. But it must be achieved through a painful initiatory experience. Dan is faced, when first introduced in Book Two, with Methodism's formula of chastity, marital fidelity, and eternal reward. His imagination speaks otherwise, and so does Mike and Mike's behavior. Dan's vicarious experience of the romance between Mike and Rosalia leads to his major ordeal, for his idealizing mind, along with Mike's understandable reticence, induces him to see their romance as Ideal Love. Book Three traces his disillusionment with that ideal and with Mike's philosophy, his shocking, numbing discovery of death not as the wages of sin, but of the destruction of self due to the imposition of the rigid, life-denying code of Puritanism upon life. Before this all becomes clear to him, he goes through various stages of emotional and moral illness: hate and the desire to murder, the impulse to suicide, the self-loathing of sin and guilt, a numb half-life of sorrow, craving, repentance and enervation. After Selma's death, his recovery begins with Jule's telling of Han's legend, and his sermon. The retelling of the legend helps to give him a new conception of himself and it gives his own life form and meaning. His clash with his parents, although followed by reconciliation, is his last maturing step, and he is now free to go away and to live life. In contrast to Rosalia, a martyr to regional Puritanism, life and the capacity to love in him have won out over death.

Character and Theme

The Apple of the Eye is one of Wescott's minor works, yet as
a first novel it is worthwhile to consider its accomplishments and
its shortcomings for the insights it affords of the author's development, his later failures and achievements. Characterization
is certainly one of the novel's weaknesses. Of course, other
qualities such as dialogue, dramatic realization and general
conception, to name a few, are also pertinent to the characterization. But it is in the inadequacy of character in relation to
the development of theme — as epitomized by the statements of
Jule Bier and the concluding thoughts of Dan Strane (see plot
summary) — that they fall most short of their function. Measuring
them by the very moral framework that the novel insists upon
reveals not only their lack of verisimilitude and realization, but
the inadequacy and the moral confusion of the novel as a whole.

Not only is Hannah Madoc, as she is presented in the first
section of the novel, meant to be realized as a character, her
whole story is intended as a legend which sustains one of the
thematic polarities of the work. Her story is more successful as
a separate unit than when it is considered as performing its
larger function. As an anti-Puritan saint she must serve as the
perfect example of "how to live." That the moral implications
of her life will be found wanting in Puritan terms is not only
to be expected, it is necessary, and consequently she serves
again and again as a contrast. She takes love when it comes
without question and survives the loss of it after going through
a period of despair. Her ordeal is unlike Rosalia's or Dan's, for
it is not the torturing inner conflict due to an ideal code or
sense of guilt; it is the process of overcoming anguish and
despair, the victory of self through acceptance and endurance.

Hannah's father dies as a direct result of injuries sustained
when Hannah in self-defense shoves him off the front porch.
There is never a hint that she is sorry her father is dead, nor
that she is sorry that she is the cause of his death. She is careful not to inform the examining doctor that her father did not
fall, but was pushed. As for her later concern, we are given
only this passage in chapter two, and nothing more:

> But Hannah did not care (that a German family
> now occupied her farm), nor did she think of her
> father. Never since that violent night had she gone

> through the elements of the scene to take blame upon
> herself or to shift it to his dead shoulders. She realized
> that no one else knew, but went past the memory on
> tip-toes; as she had walked down the lane in childhood
> past a certain gate behind which the air was poisoned
> and the grass defiled by the carcass of a horse or sheep,
> and hurried swiftly on, unstricken, irresponsible.

The promptings of her conscience are in other words simply an ignorable bad smell. Perhaps the choice of the word "irresponsible," rather than, say, "unresponsible," is a clue to a moral contradiction never resolved. Hannah, like Stephen Crane's Frederick Henry, solves her moral problems by ignoring them. Crane's intention, however, is ironic. It is one thing to recognize one's guilt and to avoid hurting others or judging them too harshly (as Mike and Jule suggest) in order to achieve a certain stoicism; but it is another thing to deny that it exists.

Hannah's extra-marital affair with Jule Bier is acceptable as consistent with the anti-Puritan theme, and the fact that neither Jule nor Hannah attempt to take it up again after his marriage, it is implied, is not because of conventional morality, but because of the injury it would cause Selma and Rosalia. What of Hannah's prostitution, from which she is saved by Selma and Jule? One critic, at least, has concluded that Wescott approves of it.[2] This assumption is hardly justified, although prostitution is not viewed as a sin in the conventional sense; and it is Hannah's "resentment, pointless and humble," at the loss of love, not a deliberate wallowing in evil, that leads her to it.

The fact is that Hannah's characterization, although perhaps the most convincing in the book, will not sustain the weight of meaning it is intended to have for the novel as a whole, and it is insufficient to bear constant reference and repetition as an example of life as it must be lived. Her easily willed amnesia concerning her father and the part she had in his death seems mere moral insensitivity. It is especially so when considered with what else we are given of her. Her good works and the legendary quality she has for her neighbors are not enough. That she lives an isolated and anguished life is pitiful, perhaps, in view of the fact that her single idea is to be near Jule. But it seems to spring from a kind of numb simple-mindedness. And her self-sufficiency results in a most restricted life in every way; she has no friends, and, we are told, desires none. Yet she is

unbearably lonely. Her life is one reduced to its barest minimum — with only the sight of her lost love sustaining her — but
without the joy or hope of any fruition, or, as far as we know,
of any sense of moral, spiritual, or material accomplishment.
Perhaps conceived of as a kind of latter-day Hester Pryne, she
is, compared to Hawthorne's heroine, emotionally starved and
simply dull. There is no moral struggle here (she has no background to provide it, not even the Methodist church-going one
of the other characters) simply because she is not aware that
there could be one.

   In the early part of the novel, Jule Bier's "automatic" following of his father's desires in marrying Selma Duncan is understandable in terms of his background, his unawareness that he
loves Hannah, and his awe of Selma — the same awe he still
retains three years later when, "silent, in surprise and wonder"
that she knew of his affair with Hannah, he genuinely feels
"satisfied" that "she has triumphed again" when she suggests
rehabilitating Han. Although he appears from time to time,
nothing more is evident of Jule's character until he takes on the
role of spiritual father to Mike, and afterwards, to Dan. His
character not only suffers because he serves a didactic function,
but because the "philosophy" he is made to expound reveals the
inadequacy of the thematic conception, the very moral framework of the novel. After relating the legend of Bad Han, Jule
tells Dan (although defending Selma as a "good woman" who
is a victim of religion) that if he had married Hannah, his
daughter Rosalia would not be dead now. Even at this moment,
and in his grief, neither he (nor Dan) consider his contribution
to the fate of Hannah and the death of Rosalia. The reason he
did not marry Hannah is never faced in the novel after the
beginning. Jule himself never morally measures his motivations
for marrying Selma — his obedience to his father's ambitions.
As for the anti-Puritan sermon intended to sum up the theme —
even if we accept it as biased and overgeneralized because of
the character's clumsy inarticulateness, two things show moral
confusion: the reliance on Han as a good example, and Jule's
ignoring of his own share in the outcome of events. Hannah is
seen as exemplar not only because she has no sense of guilt,
but also because she "never blamed anybody; she knew everybody did what they had to." This seems merely a back-handed
justification by Jule for his leaving her. The cause of Rosalia's

death is her "strict" upbringing, yet there is every indication
that Jule left that upbringing entirely to Selma. As for Jule's
reference to people "in the old country" being different, it is
merely confusing, and the comments on education and brains
muddle the issue, although both are "in character." The difficulty is partly that the passage is primarily didactic, and is
consequently bound to shrink and warp whatever successful
experience the novel has been able to evoke; partly that Jule is
the wrong character to deliver the speech; partly that it reveals
an inadequate conception of character and moral framework.

Jule's remarks on Mike continue to show the same kind of
shortcomings. As Kahn has pointed out, Dan Strane's actual
and vicarious experience leads him to a kind of valid working
philosophy between the extremes of those held by Mike and
Selma. But no critic has seen that Mike's religion is tested too
and found wanting; it is never clear to what degree this is
intentional, but contradictory intentions also appear. Mike's
pagan idealism is an oversimplification and although he recognizes the "sickness" of Rosalia's religion, he is as unable to convert her as she is to convert him. He too needs the practical
guiding advice of Jule Bier before he is forced to leave Rosalia
with sorrow and regret, an outcome he has not foreseen. And
he is, of course, never aware of the tragic outcome of Rosalia's
impasse. Although it is hardly stressed — it is de-emphasized by
avoiding any kind of reference that could imply such — his view
of life has only in theory taken account of others. Although he
believes "our duty is to be happy," he too suffers, and although
he believes that "the main thing" is to be "good to each
other," the results of his love for Rosalia confounds such simplicity. In the test of experience, human relations prove his
approach an unworkable ideal, as much an "abstraction" as
Puritanism. Yet it is by his intentions that Mike is judged and
found guiltless by Jule. This may be understandable enough.
However, the impression is deliberately given that Mike is
essentially following the same desirable acceptance of life as
Hannah. And Jule's statement about Mike, that Rosalia's death
is not his fault, and that "people do as well as they can," is
intended to exonerate not only the young man, but his philosophy. In this novel, orthodox religion and those who have it
receive the only blame.

Mike himself is believable as a sensitive young man of a

certain type, but he often appears unintentionally loquacious and sometimes ludicrous because he is made to serve, through dialogue, the function of a pagan preacher. Rosalia never comes to life as a person, for in the scenes of her romance she is nearly mute, capable of only the conventional romantic utterings — believable enough, perhaps, but only the subjective passages on her are successful, and they show, from a distance, only a frantic struggle below the level of rational thought. She has not been realized before that. As for her "tragic play" patterned after Ophelia, it is the greatest single failure in the book. Selma Bier, who begins to take on some identity when she is first presented scenically in the third section of "Bad Han," although very important conceptually in being the counter to Hannah and Mike particularly, remains almost entirely a figure at the edge of some other character's consciousness. Nothing she does from then on is given in dramatic terms — not even her death or funeral, about which there is only an expository paragraph concerning her significance. Dan's mother, Theodora, like Selma, begins strongly with the relation to her son of her sheep-shearing courtship. But it is rendered mostly through Dan's sensibility and becomes part of his characterization. After that, although she is the opposing force to Mike's influence, there is only an occasional pious line or demand for a pledge of chastity which is simply disguised exposition. One difficulty is an unintentional Laurentian ambivalence toward Dan's mother on the part of both Dan and the author. Although it is the mother more than the father who has applied the moral pressure, it is the father who is made the cruel and arrogant voice of parenthood at the end. The father's sudden manifestation at this point is startling, for it is very likely that the reader has forgotten his existence long before this. His appearance as a young man in the sheep-shearing scene, where he is a type only vaguely realized, seems to have nothing to do with the final and only scene in which he has identity. We know he exists because at one point Dan identifies him with crudeness and animality as opposed to the sensitivity of his mother, but otherwise there is only an offhand reference here and there. He is curiously not even mentioned as one of those present at grandfather Duncan's funeral.

It is likely that the unsuccessful characterization of the parents is related to the underground homosexual theme that runs through the novel. Mike Byron serves as Dan's initiator, perhaps the most important one. Dan idealizes Mike's love for Rosalia and feels betrayed by him when he thinks Mike is responsible for Rosalia's death. Nevertheless, he is emotionally attached to Mike not only as initiator but as a substitute for his father, who has remained remote until his near-rejection of Dan at the end of the book. The strength of Dan's feeling for Mike Byron makes what is portrayed as Dan's sexual immaturity seem an unconscious disguise on Dan's part, a repression of sexual love for Mike. This is nowhere expressed by the author overtly, but Dan's lack of sexual interest in women, despite his age, and his abysmal failure in even the simplest initial moves with Phyllis Dunham and with the prostitute in Milwaukee — both make his uninhibited good-bye kiss of Mike suspect. The suppressed significance seems contained, however, in the symbol of the male fireman — which Dan perceives as a vision at the moment he is unsuccessfully solicited by the prostitute, and after which he sends her away.

Dan Strane is, of course, the major character, and he is the most convincing and best-realized. The whole final third and much of the second section is directly concerned with his process of maturing, his growing break with his parents, family and home, "country" or region, and religion. It is here that Wescott's prose is able to serve its most sympathetic function; even though his character is not realized in very objective terms — it is hard to think of him except as a sensibility — what effectiveness there is in the final section depends on the successful rendering of the subjective life of Dan Strane. Other aspects of characterization are so intimately related to the problem of point-of-view and narration that they will be considered later in this chapter.

Symbolism: Structural Rhythm and Symbolic Texture

Like so many first novels of the young and talented, *The Apple of the Eye* suffers from too many flaws to call it either significant or an artistic success, but it reveals a remarkable talent and although there was a tendency to place it without further insight into the "revolt from the village" category, there was also a general recognition of Wescott's talent as "fresh" and "promising." Kahn has summed up the contemporary critical reaction:

> In *The Apple of the Eye,* Wescott demonstrated a narrative dexterity that marked him as a promising talent in a decade rich in literary ability. The novel attracted serious critical commentary, first in newspaper reviews and later in critical articles. Novels set in the Middle West were frequent to reviewers in the twenties, but the briskness with which they reacted to Wescott's novel attests to its finish and power. Reviewers were in accord in announcing that Wescott's talent was fresh and that his novel gave a valuable dimension to the image and myth of the Midwest. In *The Apple of the Eye,* as in subsequent works which further defined the meaning of Wisconsin, he exercised a relentless fidelity to his vision of the region, making technique and style the slaves to his truth.

Certainly many critics mentioned Wescott's "style," by which they usually meant his prose, or use of language. But sources of what they felt as "finish and power" likely rest on certain qualities of technique in the modern tradition of fiction, such as a patterned (as distinguished from plotted) ordering of events, for design itself, or for mythic implications; a consistent arrangement of related images for symbolic texture; and a use of major symbols.

Important events, in *The Apple of the Eye,* are in their proper seasons. The arrangement of events with careful attention throughout to the season in which they take place allows for a paralleling of them with the emotions of the characters and gives a cyclical rhythm to the novel. The cyclical rhythm not only evokes "a sense of life controlled by basic natural rhythms," as Kahn has indicated, but it is also appropriate to the pagan-stoic philosophical basis of the theme. In addition, without being obtrusive such rhythm results in mythical overtones of death and rebirth appropriate to the events in the novel.

In "Bad Han" it is October when Hannah's father dies, and she spends the winter at hard work in Boyle's tavern, waiting and developing an outer toughness to protect her inner life. In April she meets Jule, and their romance flowers in the spring and grows to maturity in the summer. In November she moves to Mrs. Balker's farm, and the winter is divided between dreary

cold work during the day and the warm secret meetings with
Jule at night. In mid-winter he tells her he is to be married.
Three years later it is again April when Jule and Hannah meet
and he comes to take her back to her farm, where her new
life begins. Her activities move with the seasons through the
years. In the end, she, like her father, dies from a fall, and in
early autumn.

It is early spring, years later, when Book Two begins and
when Mike Byron, at the time of the funeral of Grandfather
Duncan, first takes an interest in Dan and falls in love with
Rosalia. In late spring the friendship between Mike and Dan
takes on a new dimension with Mike's telling of the story of
Bad Han; by "voluptuous" mid-summer Dan is vicariously
living the romance of Mike and Rosalia, which has now reached
its full development in passion and frustration, and at summer's
end Mike departs. It is an end, too, of Dan's maturing summer. Rosalia is distracted and frantic through autumn, when all
is dead to her, and dies in an early winter storm.

In Book Three, it is for the third time April, when Rosalia's
body is discovered (like her pious grandfather she is buried in
the spring, a year later), and when Dan begins his descent into
the psychic depths from which he is to emerge reborn as a
young man and incipient artist. It is during the August harvesting that Selma Bier, ironically, dies, and that Dan is given
again the life-renewing legend of Bad Han and the secular
sermon which contains the key to his new growth. Then it is
October once more, and a new life (as for Hannah in the first
chapter) is to begin for Dan Strane. It is an end and a beginning and the seasons once more have completed their cycle.

The life of the characters follows the cycle of the seasons for
man is of the earth, or, in the words of Mike, "only flesh."
The death of the old (in mythical terms both the sacrificial
figure and the "Holdfast" figure, symbol of the *status quo*) to
make way for the new is evident in the death of Hannah's
father, Grandfather Duncan, and Selma Bier. Rosalia's death
as a victim of Puritanism makes possible Dan's rebirth and
leads to his ordeal and purgation. Hannah, as a kind of secular
saint, lives on after her death in legendary form.

The major symbol in the novel (barring Hannah) is the marsh.
It is to some extent a cumulative symbol, taking on additional
meaning with repeated usage, and it is a many-faceted or

revolving symbol. That is, what it symbolizes depends on the context, but often on the character acting within the context as well, who may, or may not, be aware of its symbolic quality. As a symbol, the marsh is all-pervasive, and gives unity to the novel. As a part of the nature imagery it also aids the rhythmical structure. Early in Book One it is, like Han herself, "fecund but useless, a lure for the listless eye," and at the end of the first chapter, immediately after the death of her father, the marsh symbolizes for Han the life she will live as she turns "her face toward the marshes of frost and water, toward the sharp-husked seed and stony leaf." At the end of chapter five, when Han has agreed to go back to her farm, the marsh has much the same quality as her fated existence: "She lifted her large face, as if she could smell the sour marsh wind." In her first days after her return to the farm, she looks at the marsh:

> She saw nothing but vast husks and dead pools. There was a faint sound of hidden movement — of water bubbling through the sod, of sap in the spiny stalk, and shoots in the dead clump. ... The marsh earth seemed fatigued, and bitter that, within its age, this youth surged. Hannah sighed as she put her parsnips over the stove.

Here the marsh becomes, as in the very first example, like her. During the first years on the farm she tries to forget her loneliness in temporary affairs that only increase her yearning:

> In the night a brief quaver of revelry came from her house, little and helpless in the loud sigh of grasses erect in water, of branches overlaid by branches — the wide fecundity unused and unbeloved.

And as she becomes an "old woman in her middle age":

> Beyond — vast, strange, and dramatic — spread the marsh, Hannah's companion. Its spotted pools palpitated; its grasses flickered and troughed; on the horizon its narrow wiry-stemmed trees rose and fell like flails. Flocks of birds flew over it, their pale breasts turning; the air divided into bundles of their cries. It required no labor; it held out the lure and responsibility of no harvest; it obeyed no law. It twisted and it stormed, without repentance; it gave what was taken from it without complaint.

Not only is it her companion, the marsh is again a symbol of
Hannah herself, and her life. On the morning of her death,
with Jule beside her, she looks for the last time at the marsh:
"Autumn had fallen on the wide, harvestless acres; a stern
brilliance of sumach, of nosegays of blood-red wild leaves, of
berries and rosehaws, of stripped mahogany and silver wings."

In Book Two the marsh takes on new meaning. Before associated with Hannah, her psyche, and her life, the qualities
already given it of lawless, unrepentant nature and "wild fer-
tility," are put to new and wider uses. It is between spring and
summer and to Dan, at that season hovering between childhood
and maturity, the marsh seems ominous, malign:

> But in the north the marsh lay, again distinct and
> ominous, more contrasted than in spring, when its
> tangled anarchy, the effect of its prodigious swales and
> pools, its subtle sadness, its malignity, were spread
> over the land.

On the way to the picnic at the lake, the afternoon that the
romance between Mike and Rosalia begins, the two lovers-to-
be walk with Dan past the marsh. It is an image implying
latent sexuality; and Rosalia's fascination forecasts the sexuality
of their affair to come, and its quality of waste.

> They passed the marsh, Rosalia stared into the florid
> waste—the grass thick as hair, the crude foliage, the
> flaring blossoms, the thick roots with fringes of little
> roots. It seemed to fascinate her.
> All the way Mike, holding the reins idly in one hand,
> fixed his eyes on her, luminous with a kind of quiet
> laughter. When she looked up, they became very blue,
> and seemed to urge her to share his excitement.

In chapter four ("Delight and Tears"), Mike has taken
Rosalia with him to hunt for strayed cattle in the marsh, where
the seduction scene takes place. The marsh as they enter it is
ominous, mysterious, sexual.

> The vegetation grew still more prodigal; stagnant
> odors rose. Over the infrequent flowers with scant petals
> and coarse calices, rarely visible insects issued their
> nasal tones. Slowly the normal woods gave way; the
> swamp in sinister magnificence reared around them.

*   *   *   *   *   *

A bird plunged into the heart of a tree, leaving for a moment an opening, where the leaves shivered heavily. The cry of another pierced the air. The road was steep. Mike watched his feet keeping time with Rosalia's small feet, dimly aware of some symbolism in its direction, pressing deeper and deeper into the dim wet forest.... blunt logs led down to the pools, opaque with slime, separated by wiry grasses and banks of caked mud. The hoods of the skunk cabbages were dry. There were grottos of trees, dead and swelling vegetation, the swales and sink-sands.

Not only Rosalia's seduction, but her death in the swamp is foreshadowed here too. And after the seduction under the haw-thorne tree, her sense of shame and guilt is felt by Mike, the effect of the marsh on him adding to its symbolic quality:

Now she wept without restraint. Tears came to his eyes. He glared helpless about for an escape from this misery and shame. Over them looked the tree, over it looked the hills, over them loomed the sky. There was the tainted water with its greenish surface. There were the stagnant vistas, and the trees wallowing in plants. Between them and him lay the sobbing girl.

Rosalia imagines herself pregnant in chapter five ("The Virgin Mother"), feeling that the rest of her life will be shame and that she will be driven from place to place, homeless. In her anguishing mixture of erratic emotions the marsh takes on meaning for her:

She liked the marsh best. The slime, the roots, the bright berries, some of which were poisonous, the slug-gish brooks, the small creeping animals, the ponds, the kettles, the sink-holes, the dying farms were sympa-thetic. She felt as if she were saying good-bye to all the landscape, and leaving the marsh last because it was most like her life at the end.

In the next state of her progress toward death she is dis-tracted; Ophelia-like she wanders the marshes — and the haw-thorne tree, scene of seduction, takes on ironic significance for her (the passage is also a sample of the use of the flora symbolically):

The next day her parents went to Rockhill; and she

returned to the marshes, to busy herself like a child
with tragic play. She picked the strangest leaves—
pennyroyal, and sumach, and bittersweet, some wiry
sprays of crimson berries, and tufts of autumn blossom
—using her lifted skirt for a basket. Then she went to
the old hawthorne, the one like a canopy, and decor-
ated the grass beneath it with loose bouquets and
garlands, making a festive bed, with a pile of berries
for a pillow—singing as she worked, "Oh where and
oh where is my highland laddie gone?"

Finally, in a passage too long to quote here, the swamp,
over which the early winter storm gathers, becomes the scene of
her death, storm and marsh paralleling the hallucinatory child-
birth that is simultaneous with her death.

In Book Three ("Dan Alone"), as Jule and Dan are led to
Rosalia's body in the "bad place" in the marsh, Dan notices
the ambiguously cheerful hawthorne flowering, and as they
approach the body the implications are appropriate:

Fresh grass grew in water; last year's grass lay in
water, hairy strand upon strand. But slime floated on
many pools. They skirted dangerous mires. Livid gouts
of gum oozed from the scabby bark of the tamaracks.
There were flowers colored like a snake, yellow and
green.

Then, in the summer, weeks later when Dan next views the
swamp, it is a grave:

From the hill-tops Dan saw the swamp; the terrible
multitudes of trees, the bloated thickets, the stubs, the
streaming grasses. Here and there cattle looked em-
bedded in the green and brass, and the black and blue
shadows. To the boy it was an enormous grave, a
bizarre grave, heaped with dead, everlasting flowers. A
paroxysm of abhorrence overwhelmed him.

After Selma's death during the August harvest, when Jule has
sought Dan's aid as a farm hand, the quality of the marsh to
the boy parallels his mood and his harvesting of experience. It
sets the stage for Jule's confidential talk and message:

The never-harvested marsh had the appearance of
harvest. All the bitter greens grew mellow. Autumn
colors drifted over the tangled, fertile, but fruitless

acres. These colors and the overheavy, drooping forms were mournful; but there was no turbulence. One night the harvest moon pushed cumbrously out of its heart, and ascended, rough and orange, giving little light.

Finally, the marsh, like the symbolic seasons, completes its cycle. Dan has absorbed the meaning of the legend of Bad Han from Jule, Mike and experience; he finds rapport with Mrs. Dunham and is soon to find his vocation. His anguish and sorrow has mellowed some, and he sees in the marsh an association of Han's life and his maturity:

> He dreamed of her wandering in the marsh. ...It was a place for her. With her strange face and short hair, her beauty must have been curious like its beauty. Both she and it were old and not old. She was unlike other people as it was unlike other fields. It had no harvest. She had no child.
>
> She was not dead in his dream of her, but still walking here. Not walking as a good spirit, caring for people, bringing them good fortune, but simply walking. She had not cared for Rosalia. Rosalia had died in her marsh. Perhaps during her life she had told people what to do, and helped them, and made them happy. But now she had nothing to do with these things.
>
> Now she had nothing to do with life; but life resembled her. Had it ever been good to him or bad to him, or to Rosalia, or to anybody? Its purpose was to go on, just to go on.

So much attention is given here to tracing the major symbol of the marsh for several reasons. It shows the use in Wescott's first novel of the *revolving* symbol, a technique which was to reach its perfection in one of his finest works, *The Pilgrim Hawk*. The marsh is also part of his general use of nature symbolically in *The Apple of the Eye*; and finally image and symbol are an intrinsic part of his prose style, shortly to be discussed.

Aside from passages on town life, which are at a minimum, the whole environment, the very milieu of the book, is rendered in terms of the natural surroundings of the region. Flora and fauna are the material for metaphor and image (some of the latter non-functional). Sometimes they are used to evoke emotions, thoughts, or attitudes of the characters; at other times the implications are outside either their consciousness or emotional range. The marsh is a major symbol; of lesser rank is the hawthorne tree, and there is the characterizing symbol of the white rose for Rosalia:

> The beautiful girl crouched before a white rose, her dress lifted above the ankles. Over the polished stem of green, the painted thorns, the notched, glossy foliage — the miraculous blossom floated, porcelain-white. The fragrance floated upward to her face, cool and languid . . .
> Rosalia's eyebrows were frail and exact, like the arc of the edge of a petal. The iris of her eyes was formed of filaments of blue on a blue ground. Her nostrils thinned to an ethereal whiteness. . . . Where her pale skin vanished under her dress, the whiteness whitened; and every motion diffused through it the ghost of a tint. She moved with a grace almost sinister.

And in a moment Mike appears:

> There was a certain languor in the motions of his muscular legs in the faded khaki trousers. Between his long brown fingers he twirled a rooster feather.

The rooster feather, here to indicate male sexuality, is part of a profuse pattern of bird imagery used throughout. Sometimes the characters seem aware of the implications, sometimes not, and although used in various ways (often figuratively as a kind of dramatic comment) its connotations usually concern the inner life and are frequently related to love or spiritual freedom. In the very first scene, in the sky above the marsh, Hannah sees "the herds of water-fowl in insubstantial letters on the sky" as though the course of what she will experience is still to be spelled out. When her life has taken the pattern it is to keep for years until her death, she wanders the countryside:

> The great bitterns retreated upstream, their peaked noses declined between their hunched shoulders. Hannah followed them, and they jumped squawking into the twilight and took refuge in the black, thin trees. She lay down in the warm, rasping grass; and the bitterns returned, three and three in military order, turning their heads to discover her with a row of eyes like the eyes of a fish.

The word-play on bitterns reinforces the symbol.[3]

On a typical night during her courtship with Jule, appropriate birds form a kind of chorus, aided by flora, for sexual-romantic overtones:

> The darkening air seemed crowded with pendant calices and stamens, which set in motion sweet draughts. In the feathery tree-tufts some little birds sang, vesper sparrows and phoebes.

The scene is not without its foreshadowings, with turkeys roosting "in a dying tree against the light," while in the sky in "eccentric triangles a bat flapped over them." When Hannah informs her employer's wife, Mrs. Boyle, that she has had to repel Mr. Boyle's advances, and the wife laments that a man doesn't like a woman who is always having children, a bird is used ironically to punctuate the conversation: "The two women sewed. A cockerel rose on his spindle legs to crow discordantly." The settled comfortable existence of Jule and Selma Bier is also subject to the same kind of comment; as they ride in a buggy from the station, "a mud-hen sat on the corrugated surface of the mill-pond, rocking, gyrating." In the midst of the lyric passage concerning John Strane's sheep-shearing and his courtship of Theodora, told by Theodora to her son Dan, but with details imagined by the boy, there is, among others, an ironic implication: "sparrows darted and vanished, chirping. On a dim shelf a female pigeon vomited down the throats of her young; others swelled and chanted amorously." Outside, the "lonely bird going up" perhaps parallels Theodora's emotions, and in the same paragraph, "An ivory rooster printed the mud with his starlike feet, murmuring to his hens" seems to objectify in dramatic miniature what is happening, with nice juxtaposition of the ideal (*ivory, starlike*) expectations and the reality. In lush midsummer on the afternoon the romance between Rosalia and Mike begins, "Birds with ruddy feathers and sharp bills came out of the hearts of top-heavy trees to the shaggy edges, and embarked on the air." In the "voluptuous summer" when Rosalia is still rejecting Mike because of her beliefs, "Amid the heavy beds of green," and other burgeoning vegetation, there are "the panting fowls with wings outspread, the gloomy, dust-blackened men struggling with the crops—Rosalia was like an echo of spring.... She seemed to brood upon, and always to

reject its coarse, convulsive luxury..." When Mike is leaving
and bidding Dan good-bye, birds are used for a simile: "They
spoke, and faltered; and the incomplete sentences faded away,
like the speech of birds in the inpenetrable trees getting ready
to sleep." At the crucial time when Rosalia feels abandoned by
Mike, and desperate, there is a passage paralleling her situation:

> She paused by the reedy lake. The water was at once
> bleak and soft. From one shore a hell-diver moved out,
> so light that the beating of its feet under the water
> made its breast shudder upon the waveless surface. It
> moved with a slight buoyance, as if to meet another
> bird, knowing that there was no other, but going out
> nevertheless to meet it, marking the lake with a resolute
> line as it swam. There was no other bird visible. At last,
> it was alone in the exact center of the lake, and seemed
> for a moment to turn and hesitate. Then swiftly and
> smoothly it sank into the water, leaving a very faint,
> circular ripple, which swelled like a bubble and vanished
> like a bubble breaks. Rosalia knelt on the shore, and
> stretched out her hands, and dropped them with a
> splash into the water. It startled her by its coldness;
> and she rose and walked quickly home.

The next day, Dan finds her walking down the marsh road in
her frenzied distraction, and asks her what she's doing in that
"dreadful place."

> The girl laughed softly. "Don't you know that it's
> my home? I saw," she added, "a dear little mud-hen,
> and she couldn't find the other one."

The behavior of wild fowl and hawk, as part of the "Profane
Spring," help set the tone for the beginning of Book Three, and
the frank, untroubled laughter of Phyllis Dunham makes Dan
"think of the cry of the water-bird." The beginning of the last
chapter ("Departing in Peace") symbolizes and forecasts Dan's
freedom and departure, its primal and mythical nature:

> Suddenly he saw moving there a company of shining
> forms. It was a flock of wild geese, flying extremely
> high, going south. They were grey, and would have
> been invisible, but their wings in motion glittered when
> they caught the light. He heard them honking. One
> above the other, tier upon tier, they moved slowly like

a troop of angels. The light faded; and the grey geese
sank into the sky, leaving there a lonely solemnity,
into which their faint clamor still fell.

Crows form a special category, it seems. They first appear in
the novel just before the death of Hannah's father, and they
early indicate the marsh as a place of potential death—"Silver
upon their jagged wings, crows alone went through the funereal
trees." They are present when Hannah first spades her garden
upon returning to the marsh farm where she will live out her
life and die:

Then she spaded the garden. When at dusk the old
crows loosed their wings in the lustre of the sun toward
the roost in the oaks, one third of the garden lay
black like plush.

The gathering crows are what lead to the discovery of Rosalia's
body. They last appear as part of the final twilight panorama
(after the flight of geese) as Dan views the countryside. The
tone is nostalgic; although he does not yet know he is to leave,
Dan knows that one great experience of his life is over:

Over one end of the porch, wilted wild cucumbers
rustled. Crows appeared over the hills, and crossed
the valley in a straight line; their heavy bodies sank a
little in the air, and were lifted again with each stroke
of their wings. One croaked to another. The silence
was emphasized by their voices, the solitude by their
diminishing and vanishing forms, like birds of jet.

In Wescott's work as a whole the use of birds for symbolic
purposes reaches its profuse extreme in "The Dream of Audubon, Libretto of a Ballet in Three Scenes." In the final paragraph, Wescott sums up the symbolic meaning he has intended
in the ballet. Among his concluding lines are the following:

We are all hunters; and our heart's desire, whatever it
may be, is always somehow a thing of air and wilderness, flying away from us, and subject to extinction in
one way or another.

Rueckert has said that this passage "states one of the major
themes of *The Pilgrim Hawk* and is one of the keys to the bird
symbolism in all of Wescott's work." As shown in the above
quotations, it often takes a close examination to see what is

symbolized in a particular scene or work (birds do not, for instance always represent the "heart's desire"), and how it is an intrinsic part of the symbolic texture of the prose. In *The Pilgrim Hawk* rather than the entire genus being exploited for its symbolic potentialities, the Pilgrim Hawk (as individual bird and species) becomes a many-faceted or revolving symbol, and is the ultimate development in that technique which is first evidenced by the marsh and bird symbolism in *The Apple of the Eye*.

The techniques examined here, the use of imagery to create symbolic texture as an intrinsic quality of the prose, to build cumulative symbols which through their numerous facets of implication can be said to be revolving because they can be turned from one facet to another for meaning — either through recognition by various characters, or through the awareness of the omniscient narrator alone (although he is evident always, even when the character is aware) — form a major aspect of Wescott's art, a positive one, which even in this early novel is impressive, and which justifies serious attention to the work in spite of its shortcomings. These techniques are one aspect, one quality of his distinctive prose style.

Prose, Point-of-View, and Narrator

Wescott's prose style is one of careful diction that achieves a finely-chiseled quality and a surface of meticulous finish imparted alike to landscape, animals, and human figures. It is the source of much of the regional quality of the novel. Wescott's Wisconsin is a land where "the shocked corn" stands "in the fields like a village of barbaric silver tents," where "squawking bitterns" wade "into the air, their interlaced quills golden as rust and granite blue" and the crows have "square notched wings like ragged sails." In nights with "fence posts black as ebony," the "sweet smelling milk" beating in the pail at milking-time leaves "a faint tube-shaped mist in the black air."

There are large and small panoramas:

> Like the breaking of a dream, spring vanished. The pearl air, and the moisture and the melancholy richness, and the corollas of wet wax, and the tart aromas, and the languorous dew, and dusk falling all afternoon, and

the mist — their season was over. Disappearing, they un-
covered a bright land in rectangles of graduated green,
with trees immobile in straight lines like fountains of
vegetation. Meadows of small flowers in flat colours —
mulein, mustard, blueweed, and sweet clover; crowds of
bees, glistening and mechanical. It was June, the morning month, trodden by bronze cattle, horses of mahogany. Slowly, the eminent, poised sun arose, and
sank deliberately.

The sky swung like the top of a tent as the wind
rose up to rain.

The light lay in soft close plumes, and the sky was
like a spray of aster.

Hannah crouched on logs and stones, and watched
the round enameled turtles dry and fade, and swim
again. A heron heaved into the sky, its long, lacquered
legs scoring the green bay.

Such passages are on nearly every page of the novel. Less
frequently is it evident that the earth is inhabited by men and
that villages and towns exist. But they too seem one with the
landscape and imbued with the same rhythm:

Men in blue shirt-sleeves and overalls stalked about
the little pyramids of manure in the fields, now melted
and soft, scattered it loosely over the earth, or as the
buggy passed, leaned their stubbly chins on the handles
of forks.

The young people did not dance gracefully. Labour
had moulded them too gaunt, too heavy, too strong.
The heel predominated in the movements of their feet.
They stooped. Their arms hung as if weighted. Their
faces became vacant as if they were sleepy. They clung
drowsily. Sometimes the men stared curiously into the
face of one with purple lips which was full of a wistful
animal melancholy.

The houses on both sides of the road, brick and
clapboard, were surrounded by picket fences and ever-
greens. A little sad deer of iron with slant iron eyes
stood among frugal dead grasses. Near him a woman in
billowy skirts of grey calico floated over the ragged
snow.

> The sun rose in a stately manner; the dew vanished.
> At noon the day like a yellow rose opened wide, fold-
> ing the land in the rustle of its petals. Horses trotted
> crisply in the fine light — buckskin, dappled, roan, bay,
> and black — drawing carriages to and from church.

The adjectives and adverbs, although profuse, are chosen
with precision, the lushness often given by the modifying phrases
and clauses. The sentences and paragraphs so carefully carved
and fitted together, slow and even halt movement, giving a
static effect, for there is a shift required from image to image.
If action is involved it is nearly always slow, and the effect
one of turgidity. Even the horses (in the last example above)
trotting "crisply" do so "in the fine light" in which the movement is immersed and framed. It is further confined and slowed
by the rather expository "drawing carriages to and from
church." The verbs and participles are often turgid, often sensuous, and alike in their quality of slowing the action they
describe. The minor figures seem part of the very rural earth
and landscape, their lives moving with the same primordial
rhythm as the livestock. The major characters vary from this
norm, Hannah, of course, being closest to the earth, and to the
marsh in particular.

The prose is flexible enough in weaving image patterns and
creating symbols, or when its purpose is lyrical expression concerning the countryside or evoking subjective states in the characters. Often, as Kahn has so aptly expressed it, the characters
"seem bewitched into dreamy, somnolent states, particularly
when they are in love or when they feel extreme emotions of
pleasure or grief. Sometimes a whole group of people seem
spellbound." "Emotional shock," he adds, "throws minds into
static states and shock is frequent in the minds of Wescott's
characters." Rosalia is given as the most obvious illustration of
this, her suppressed passion for Mike indicated by her sleep-
walking, and later the trauma she suffers from abandonment
and imagined pregnancy takes the form of "lassitude and finally
immobile exhaustion in the marsh." Dan Strane lives under an
emotional anaesthesia after helping to bury Rosalia, his summer
"drugged," his emotions "frozen," and his spirit "torpid," and
previous to that the experience of the two lovers, Mike and
Rosalia, "mesmerizes him." Kahn calls attention to the combination of imagistic landscape and "description of stasis" that

creates "a hypnotic atmosphere, and impression of life in a trance."

However, the lyric, disciplined, imagistic prose of sensibility — which is Wescott's notable achievement so early in this first novel — is markedly limited, inflexible and awkward when it comes to two important elements: creation of scene and dialogue. Except for Mike Byron, a sometimes garrulous mouthpiece of romantic sensibility, the other characters are not only awkward of speech but inarticulate. What is worse, the dialogue is strikingly unrealistic and often unauthentic — by forfeit, for the idioms common to region and time are remarkably few, and the result is a limp and emasculated standard American English. The dramatic potentialities of situations — for characterization, for thematic tension or clarification, and for other purposes — are rarely if ever imaginatively realized, especially in confrontations of character with character. Here, for instance, is the entire scene at the end of chapter four of "Bad Han." Jule Bier has come to rehabilitate Han, has taken her to dinner, and they have returned to her room in a disreputable house. It is one of the dramatic culminations of the novel; Hannah up to this point does not know Jule's intention.

> Then he told her, slowly and methodically, what he wanted her to do. Curiously, not upon her face, but beneath her face, there was an amazed and excited expression. She looked old, untidy, and goaded by petty troubles. The menacing yap of the poodle bounded up the stairs.
>
> "...You were always a good hand at a garden and you could keep a cow."
>
> "The farm is so heavily mortgaged. It might be hard..."
>
> "I've plenty of money since I got married." he said.
>
> Her eyes widened. "Does your wife know about this?"
>
> "Yes, she does."
>
> She took his brown hand in her strangely pale hand, her fat hand covered with showy rings. She had assumed that the strangeness of a new wife had worn away, and he had come back to her. Now a new and difficult concept thrust itself into her thought. She saw in it an opportunity to cling to him, the only opportunity to cling to him. She fondled his hard hand.

Her stare was stern. She breathed heavily. To his simple vision everything seemed insubstantial; the flagrant paper flowers, the lace, the litter, the envelope of cheap red satin, the overabundance of her flesh — all hanging loose, ready to be stripped away.

She lifted her large face, as if she could smell the sour marsh wind.

This is by far one of the better realized scenes. Its shortcomings are obvious. Rather than "the absence of flamboyance," having "the suitable effect of suggesting suppressed emotion or explosive feeling held in check by Puritanical decorum," as Kahn insists, there is a disappointing limpness.

Is it true, as Kahn and other critics suggest, that "rather than through dialogue, it is in the description of the countryside that Wescott renders the emotions of his characters"? A close scrutiny for the answer leads directly to Wescott's use of point-of-view and narrator, which is the most important key to both his powerful and impressive prose and to his fundamental failure in this novel.

It is more accurate to say that description is a *substitute* for the rendering of emotion. Here are the first two paragraphs of the novel:

The sun settled into the tawny marshes. Lean cattle with large bony heads came down the lane to struggle around the water trough. Summer was falling from the thin trees.

Hannah Madoc stirred the fire. For two hours she had waited for her father to return from an election in Beeler. Supper was ready to set on the table. She sat by the window, hungry and resentful, preoccupied with the marshes, a broken, dominating brightness. The snarled grass mile after mile piled by the wind, the thick sunlight in cups of white water, the herds of waterfowl in insubstantial letters on the sky.

The language is obviously not, and not intended to be, that of Hannah. In fact, during the entire novel she does not once *say or think*, literally, in words of her own, anything at all about the countryside. It is doubtful, if she is looking at the marshes, that she would think, or even feel, that they are "tawny," and a farm-girl familiar with livestock, she would not be given to thinking of their heads as "large," and "bony."

As for the summer "falling from the thin trees," that is an impressionistic concept entirely beyond her. The second paragraph begins with information she may be aware of, but the statements are not intended as her thoughts. "The broken dominating brightness" and the rest of the paragraph is in language and concept not hers. However, since we are informed that she is "preoccupied with the marshes," the emotional tone established is one with which Hannah is in accord, and the reader identifies Hannah with the mood. It is in such scenes, with character in isolation, that Wescott is most successful with this method. Often, however, the difference in language and tone of the description from that of which the character would be capable is so great that they cannot be joined in mood. This kind of disjunction is even more pronounced in some scenes where there are two characters in some kind of situation. Here are Hannah and Jule arriving at a rural summer dance:

> One night in August they went together to a dance at Silver Creek. The Sabbath had been a hot recess in the frenzied harvest. Men moved hammocks and chairs under the pale dried trees, and sat in their shirt sleeves, wiping their faces, speechless. At intervals the locust *pricked the air with his minute scream. The world twisted about, and the boiling fields turned into the shadow of night.*
> The little mare tipped her ears forward and backward. *The hills were little horns of warmth pointed into the amber sky.* As it faded the quaggy hallows filled with musk and fog, *which eddied in circles past her pink distended nostrils.*
> "It only took us forty minutes to come," Jule said, holding out a thick silver watch. Hannah jumped over the wheel. "I'll wait for you in the cloak room."
> (Italics mine)

What are the thoughts and feelings of Hannah and Jule as they arrive? Is their emotion "rendered" through this evocation of countryside and physical atmosphere? First of all, we are not informed that we are in the minds of either Jule or Hannah, and although we may assume that they may be aware of their surroundings, it is in no such terms or concepts as given in the italicized portions. Their actions and words do not indicate so. We are not at all sure that their emotional response is in tone with that established by the prose; and on the other hand, if there is a contrast, and there sometimes is, there seems to be no irony evident or intended.

The point-of-view here, and throughout the novel, is omniscient, and the language and all its qualities (except for that of dialogue) are those of the omniscient narrator. In this passage the point of observation is far outside, and, one may say, above that of the characters. The concern is with the matter of *distance*, the gap between the material viewed (countryside, people, or thoughts and feelings of character in isolation or dramatic action) and the means of viewing, which are here the omniscient narrator who quite deliberately colors with his vision everything seen, and what is very important, makes himself known in terms of *voice*, the accent or tone of the language which implies the attitude behind it.

Sometimes the narrator seems to lessen his distance to give us the thoughts of his characters. The following concerns Jule's thoughts of Hannah, then moves to his father:

> He treasured her as part of himself. He did not brood upon her or idealize her. As his flesh thickened and concentrated in a solidity of health, his imagination roved unsatisfied.
>
> And he was driven by his father's passion, by the old man labouring in a frenzy of mortification. He (the father) could not forget that he had eaten cast-off turnips and cabbages, that his son's life had been preserved by charity.

It is more accurate to say not that the distance is *lessened*, but that the narrator has *focused* upon Jule's thoughts, then his father's. For the expository statement, the recognition that Jule "did not brood upon her and did not idealize her," and the relationship of imagination to flesh, is the narrator's and in his words, and the perception about the father also his. It is also typical that when the focus is on thought or attitude, exposition or analysis or generalization, the language is pithy and aphoristic, the *result* of insight — rather than the following of the flow of thought.

These passages on Hannah are typical:

> She became an old woman in her middle age, feeding her fowls, pushing a wheelbarrow of corn for her cow,

or resting on her porch in the bent, evening sunlight. The tokens of August enclosed her: a few ribbed pie pumpkins, a festoon of sweet-corn seed tied by the husk, black crests of dill like feathers in the yellow air. Her short grey stiff hair gave her head a square stolidity; her crooked eyebrows bent over two pits, from which thrust her hard, straight gaze; her broad cheeks hung from the cheek-bones and were veined with minute red threads. She smoked a pipe, and the smoke swung upward and hung in the air.

To her simple eye nothing was degrading, nothing evil, everything formed a single difficult pure coil, moralless and pure.

There is no question that the first selection — a summary which turns through static image into a tableau — is evidence of a clearly marked distance; the second, on Hannah's subjective, is after all just as far away, abstracted and captured in an aphoristic image. The distance remains at this degree throughout Book One, and it is not lessened in the second and third sections, which are much more concerned with the subjective states of Rosalia, Mike, and Dan. Rosalia, in her frenzied state lost in the storm that leads to her death, feels thus:

As she became accustomed to the darkness, she could discern horrible forms, slightly blacker than the mass of night; spikes thrusting at her face, huge shrouded bodies, and immense shadows, weakly upheld, which balanced over her and threatened to fall. If she had been able to think, she would have recognized them as fence-posts and trees, hillsides, houses and barns. But her experience, all her memories were obliterated by the onslaught of anguish and terror, by the pain which meant to her, being a mother.

Although the images given are those imagined by Rosalia, control-words such as "became accustomed" and "could discern" help maintain a definite distinction of distance, an awareness of the narrator, especially emphasized by the statement, "If she had been able to think..." The sensibility of the narrator may seem closer to that of Mike Byron and Dan Strane in a passage such as the following on Mike:

Was her will stronger than his? He blamed his own extreme excitement. His physical violence had

> threatened her, before her mood was ripe. He felt himself humbler and wiser. *Magnificent and faint, her loveliness rose up in his mind to dismay him.* In the clinging cotton, adrift in the watery darkness like a spurt of moonlight. (Italics mine)

But again, the distance is not lessened, but rather the *focus* is steady. The italicized portion, for instance, is not a *rendering* of Mike's mental experience, but an aphoristic somewhat paradoxical statement *about* what he experienced, rounded off in the next statement by rendering through imagery.

Often the distance is even more apparent:

> But partly for the boy's sake (Dan's), and partly to cast over his experience, for a few moments, a glamour which would hide his disappointment from himself, he (Mike) avoided any reference to Rosalia's misery, or to his increasing sense of something intolerable closing down upon him and stifling him. He perfected what had happened, as he spoke, like one who knows that he soon will have nothing but memories.

The following passage, even though very concrete and focused on Dan's thought, maintains distance by such genteel words as "lean" and "coarse" and "untidy," and the passage is (very often the case with Wescott) a *summary* of his impressions, regulated and commented on by the narrator.

> But the girls he knew were not beautiful. Their throats, their breasts were lean or coarse; they wore their hair in untidy nests over their ears, and stared at him with avid, watery eyes. Their men had hairy wrists and chapped mouths; and when they walked, their clumsy legs pounded the ground.

The omniscient narrator in this novel is all-pervasive. Armed with the impressive but nevertheless sometimes inflexible quality of Wescott's prose, making himself evident, making himself heard through the quality of voice, he is the very medium through which everything is experienced by the reader. Though the focus may vary, the voice always maintains a distinct distance. There is, of course, nothing wrong with such a technique in principle. But artistic success will then depend upon the success of the narrative voice. It is evident that characterization, realization of dramatic potentialities, and rendering of subjective states are often not successful. Yet the prose itself and the power of the voice is what makes the book more than the ordinary first novel.

Kenneth Burke, in an early and generally lauditory review,[4] senses that there is some such opposition:

> It is a book almost exclusively of emotional propulsion. Indeed, it even becomes a drenching in emotions, those softer, readier emotions which we designate usually as "feminine," an experience purely of "delight and tears" (to borrow from one of the chapter heads) and it is thus a kind of revival in letters, an atavism, albeit a revival which is done with such force, such conviction, that one is caught unaware, and before he knows it is deeply involved.

Such "emotional propulsion," "drenching in emotions," and "force" and involvement come not, as we have seen, from effective dramatization, characterization, rendering of thought and detail, but from the power of the narrative voice. Burke goes on:

> His book, if it makes few demands upon the intellectual equipment of the reader, is a profoundly appealing piece of emotional writing, or one might better call it an emotional experience. ... for one is left in possession of the story's overtones much as one is left with the overtones of some dream or some actual event which has occurred in one's own life.

The hypnotic quality of characters moving through a dream, commented on earlier, is, as Burke indicated, to some extent the effect on the reader as well. There is a link, after all, between such effects, between the writing being "emotional" and it making "few demands upon the intellectual equipment of the reader," even though Burke does not overtly connect the two. Further, he objects that the novel does not "widen the field of our 'aesthetic perception,' particularly in the important discovery of symbols which adequately summarize for us the emotional and ideological complexities in which we are involved." It is true that the force of Puritanism, as such, is certainly not felt in the novel. Part of this as we know is certainly the result of shortcomings in character, drama, scene and dialogue, or perhaps more accurately, in what Wescott is unable to achieve with the narrative voice and prose. So excellent for evoking countryside and making image and symbol for the pagan polarity (seasons, weather, flora, fauna, marsh and birds) it can do little to make us realize the opposite force. But certainly the effect of being left with the overtones of dream was the author's intention. Kahn has stated that Wescott thought of himself as writing a prose akin to poetry, imagistic in style, rhythmic and characterized by the cumulative patterns of images as symbols and the weaving of motifs. Spellbinding was one of the ends in view. "The poet's purpose," as Wescott stated in one of his early reviews is "to put the reader under a spell or a series of spells."

Ruth Suckow, in perhaps the most perceptive contemporary comment on the novel, although praising certain aspects of it, had this to say:

> This novel, in its impulse and method, inclines rather toward poetry than toward that vital concern with character...the basis of pure fiction. The sureness of the characterization seems to rest upon thoughtful consideration and not so much upon that minute and intuitive understanding of people as people that usually makes a born writer of fiction. The characters are human qualities — purity, chastity, sensuous joy, the primitive — rather than human beings. But what the book lacks in the sense of intense intimacy and of deep human relish for the spectacle of life it perhaps gains in a poetic simplicity of conception.

There is, as Miss Suckow senses, an opposition between poetic "impulse and method" (including the engaging quality of prose and voice) and "vital concern with character." That the characterization "*seems* to rest upon thoughtful consideration" points to the constant distance and detachment (most evident in the careful generalization and aphoristic statements) that the narrative voice maintains. The result is that the characters are abstractions. The "minute and intuitive understanding of people as people" is not supplied by the narrative voice, and it is not supplied by any other means. Although praising the book's "fine sense of form," Miss Suckow is also aware that

> The preoccupation with form exacts its penalty, however, in a certain static quality. Each sentence, each

paragraph, and part is so careful, so complete, that it tends to halt the movement instead of becoming an integral part of it.

In other words the prose (and hence voice) works against those elements of form we consider as motion: narrative itself, and scenic movement. But that is not all:

And there is, too, a certain remoteness or isolation in the quality of the author's vision which often gives the effect of someone standing a little too much apart and seeing with a distinct but at times unrelated view; so that we get, not quite as much a vivid participation in the thing itself as a fine and truthful but rather too personal vision of it.

It is the narrator, of course, that Miss Suckow identifies with the author's vision; and the power and evidence of the voice which is a vehicle for that vision, partly by means of constant distance, does make itself felt almost as a personality—but one, Miss Suckow feels, that is "unrelated" and "too far apart" (too much distance), consequently "too personal."

The narrator in *The Apple of the Eye* is not a character, not a narrator identified as a person who tells the story. The rhetoric of the narrative voice is not an *investigating* rhetoric, because the voice even when generalizing or analyzing is above all a recorder of impressions, a creator of tone, intensely attuned to spellbinding rather than ruminating, considering, drawing distinctions, and clarifying. It is a detached voice, always maintaining a distance, but varying in focus. It is our only means of seeing, of perceiving what occurs and how it occurs, even when it is focused closely on the sensibility of a character. The use of this narrative voice is responsible for many of the novel's fine attributes, allied in technique with the symbol- and image-making resources of the prose.

Nevertheless, there is a disparity between the narrator and other elements of the novel. The attention to the qualities which will make for spellbinding seems to be at the expense of "intellectual demands," particularly characterization, dramatic realization, and adequate confrontation of the two thematic polarities that should take on a form of believable life. It is at the expense of a moral vision complex enough, and realized enough, to justify what the narrator insists is the theme; for he does insist, in aphorism and generalized statement or through a substitute, didactic dialogue. It is this disparity that at the very beginning of his career is one of Wescott's fundamental artistic problems. By it his intention and achievement can be measured. It is only when he is able to overcome it that the result is fiction of the highest quality and significance.

3
THE GRANDMOTHERS:
A FAMILY PORTRAIT

Three years after his first novel appeared, Glenway Wescott published *The Grandmothers: A Family Portrait,* upon which much of his literary reputation rests, fulfilling, essentially, the predictions of those who had seen him as a writer of great promise. The novel was a popular as well as a literary success, winning the Harper Prize Novel contest of that year. It is his greatest and most successful fictional exploitation of middle-western material.

But *The Grandmothers* is not simply another of those regional novels lauding the strength, endurance, foolhardiness and clever-ness of the pioneers and sentimentalizing their dull lives; nor is it simply a part of the "revolt from the village" protest move-ment of the time.[1] Wescott, as Sy Kahn points out, unlike "Ruth Suckow, Sinclair Lewis, or Sherwood Anderson, seeks for meaning not in the present but in the past, in the enigma of old women's tales." It is a rejection of the geographical frontier for a "migration to the frontier of imagination by which the past is reconstructed, organized and understood," increasing the spiritual territory of the American artist. Through him America may come to a similar self-awareness.

The novel ceases to be a regional work and becomes one of the reality and myth of the American past, of its meaning, in other words, to the modern pioneer, one who seeks to find and clarify the self — in this case, Alwyn Tower, expatriate and artist. His concern with the past is what sharply distinguishes

41

Alwyn Tower from the expatriate protagonists of Hemingway, Fitzgerald, and others.

Pioneering and expatriatism are important themes in *The Grandmothers,* but not the leading ones, for they become interrelated to and fuse with the greater themes of love and the self.

All of this would mean little if Wescott had not made a great technical advance since *The Apple of the Eye,* finding a form that almost perfectly suited his subject matter, theme, and particularly his strengths and failings as an artist. There is little point in retracing what one suspects at first glance and what Kahn has discussed: the influence of Henry James, Marcel Proust, Stephen Crane, Joseph Conrad and Ford Maddox Ford. The discussion remains somewhat general, however, and except for Proust, slights what is probably the most important aspect of such influences, that of point-of-view and narrator. Any serious writer of fiction in the twenties or after is likely to show the influence of these writers and of others of equal importance; Wescott, too, was in the mainstream of the modern novel. But it is significant that he experimented in his own way with whatever he learned from his predecessors with "original and stunning results."[2] He not only produced a worthwhile novel, but he found a form that responded to his hand and served as a crucible for his given material.

The first two chapters of *The Grandmothers* introduce Alwyn Tower, the character through whose sensibility — via the third-person-limited point-of-view — everything is perceived. Since Alwyn is also the protagonist, these chapters serve as well to introduce both the subject of the novel and its method. Alwyn in time-present is an American expatriate living in Europe; in the second chapter there are two short glimpses of him in the Austrian Alps and on the French Riviera (La Turbie), symbolic heights (towers) from which he recalls and narrates all the rest of the events in the novel which take place in time-past in America.

He remembers the earlier Alwyn and his fascination with the past — specifically the lives of his ancestors, generally his region and his country. It is a fascination which obsesses him still, and it is the energy behind his re-creation, with the aid of memory and imagination, of a family chronicle, one that allows him to ruminate on these histories and to perform the necessary aesthetic act to give them meaning. His purpose, from his personal physical distance in time and place and his imaginative aesthetic distance in Europe, is to make what appraisals and judgments he can (chapter 15), so that with the meanings — the "truths" — obtained he may benefit from the knowledge directly in finding his own identity. The multiple meditation, evaluation and re-creation is, as well, a means of exorcising the "personages in rocking-chairs, the questionable spirits leaning over his cradle, (who) had embodied not only the past, but the future — his own wishes and fears." The haunting quality of events and person-ages is dispelled by the aesthetic act. The result is that Alwyn — it is obvious now that he is the artist that Dan Strane of *The Apple of the Eye* hoped to become — is no longer possessed, but left with "this family of stories which he could not have remembered, but seemed nevertheless to remember." His destiny after this, like Dan Strane's, is to encounter life and to live it.

As a character in the novel, Alwyn appears from time to time in the past in his relationship to members of the family, as well as in the fictional present from which he narrates. It is clear that he is not only a character-narrator, but the protagonist, for his artistic act is that most significant adventure, the discovery of the self.

Chapter one presents Alwyn as a small boy (recollected, we discover in chapter two, by the later Alwyn in Europe) who is compelled to question and consider anything that might clarify the mystery of the lives of his present family and his ancestors. Objects, events, phrases or stories, especially from his grand-mother Rose, all have symbolic potential for him; the bow-legged table with its "lace tidy" holding the family Bible, the portraits in one frame of the Fireside Poets, "equally complacent and almost equally muffled by untidy beards," gazing "across the room at a pair of enlarged pictures of Alwyn's grandparents in middle life," the conch shell faintly echoing breakers, "as if heard across the great width of America which separates Wis-consin from the sea. It seemed to the boy that in the same way every object in those rooms echoed the forces which had once been at play around it, very faintly, from a distance of years instead of miles. ...The long series of passions which has in the end produced himself." There are the daguerreotypes, the hair-album of Serena Cannon, the box of arrowheads, and the countryside which was once a wilderness, and is for Alwyn as well the "wilderness of history and hearsay, that distorted landscape of a dream which had come true before it had been dreamed," now "buried under the feet of modern men, and the ripening crops." All of these evoke a familial, regional and national past.

The second chapter further shows us the mind of the narrator at work, as in Europe he meditates about his "knowledge of America and his family." Here he generalizes about what are the three overlapping subjects of the novel: (1) The Towers as individuals and as a family (2) America (3) Alwyn Tower himself, as a Tower, a middle westerner, an American and an individual.

> He did not quite like their suffering, their illiterate mysticism, their air of failure; but he understood them, or fancied that he did. It did not matter whether he liked them or not — he was their son.
>
> Among them, of their marriages and love affairs, there had been born a composite character, the soul of a race; something so valuable that one recognized it only as an atmosphere, a special brightness, or a peculiar quality of the temperaments and customs and fortunes of Americans; as if it were the god of place — half invisible .... Whatever it was, it was the hero of the stories that he knew, the tales of his grandmothers. By comparison with its dwelling place, Europe seemed only the scene of a classic play continually repeated; for a moment only .... But there was that moment in every day of Alwyn's life.[3]

Alwyn then considers the historical essay, "as it were, a short biography of America," that he wrote when he was nineteen. It deals with the motives, actions, beliefs, and myths of the pioneers and their descendants, and touches on, through general statement, many historical and cultural forces, some of which become forceful motifs in the novel: the causes of early migration and its effects on later beliefs; what America symbolized to the pioneers and their consequent disillusionment; their worship of a God *"who was poverty," "the precept by which poverty would be changed into wealth; He was a law."* There are the effects of narrow Protestantism on love and artistic expression; the development of the "laughing race of the earth," to whom "unhappiness was treason" and where "no tragic arts flourished;" the link of youth-worship, matriarchy, Momism and success-worship.

The pioneer theme, or theme of hope, is a major one. Alwyn thinks of his ancestors as repeatedly moving West "into every corner of the continent:"

> ...and each migration repeated, with a little less religion and a little more weariness the pilgrimage which had brought them there: disappointed men, going further, hoping still...
> At last there was no corner where wealth and joy might be thought to dwell. ...At last those pilgrims who had failed to discover their heart's desire had to look for it in heaven, as it had been in Europe, as it had always been. Disillusioned but imaginative, these went through the motions of hope, still pioneers.[4]

Although he believes his essay true of America, Alwyn has doubts about it being true of America as a whole; he then writes "a character sketch, enumerating the traits of his relatives." Again it is a series of broad generalizations which will be clearly illustrated by what follows: the Towers' doubt of their own visions, their talent and aptitude for music and culture of which they are suspicious as a weakness; their love of country and hatred of cities, their thoughtfulness, lack of shrewdness, and ill-advised imaginations; their consciousness of being unrewarded for their virtues by the recognition of material success —"They believed in democracy, hoping that it would reinvest with power those who deserved it"—their awareness of a dim aristocratic background that fortifies their sense of grievance.

> ...they were not menials, but deserved a sweeter fate; life was unjust. This conviction was inherited by every young Tower, from father to son; and in that inheritance younger son shared equally with elder. A grievance was their birthright...[5]

In exorcising the ghosts, in ridding himself of his childhood, and in attempting to put an end to the grievance which is a birthright of the Towers as disillusioned "perpetual pioneers," Alwyn must "back-trail"—move East rather than West, become an expatriate, and consequently a pioneer in an entirely different sense. Alwyn's necessity for back-trailing in this sense is, as Rueckert has said, "the central truth contained in the Tower's composite family portrait and chronicle."

The twelve central chapters, the bulk of the novel, are stories

of two generations of the Towers: the pioneer generation that
came to Wisconsin from New York State in the 1840's — Alwyn's
grandparents, great aunts and uncles — and the second generation, his father and mother, uncles and an aunt. Between the
stories of one generation and another, at the middle of the
book, is chapter 8, "The Dead," which dramatizes in microcosm something like the process of the novel taking form,
although with minor figures, as dim portraits and daguerreotypes are commented on cryptically by Alwyn's grandmother.

The final chapter, entitled "Conclusion. Another Moving. His
Grandmother Tower's Deathbed," ends the work by completing
the experience of the narrator as he continues the self-exploration
that he has conducted in terms of his family history, by now
drawing numerous conclusions at the levels of the Towers,
America, and himself by means of some major metaphors drawn
from the themes. The chapter centers around three actions: (1)
the migration of the Tower family to another farm; (2) the dying
of Rose Tower; (3) the action of narrator Alwyn's mind producing prolific generalizations as he assists in the moving, and later
as he watches by the deathbed.

Grandmother Tower looks forward to the "short but momen-
tous journey" of death, willing and ready to go, sorting and
marking her belongings to leave behind. Yet it will take her
months to die and in the meantime the family moves to a new
ugly house on a smaller, more profitable farm near the town of
Brighton; for the old one, which has been sold, "had not kept
its many promises." Out of the Northwest territory, "royally
vast and fertile in large part," Henry, "unwisely aristocratic,"
to whom "beauty and prosperity looked alike," had picked
"merely the loveliest piece of land he had ever seen," half of
which lies on a stony hilltop, much of it forest and swamp.

Alwyn and the hired man, Karl, set out with two teams
drawing a loaded manure-spreader for the new farm, the others
going by automobile or following them by carriage, a modern
migration with small hopes. The Towers are the last of the
original pioneer settlers, Karl being representative of the frugal
penniless Bavarians and Saxons who have taken their place.

At nightfall the caravan is far from its destination. Alwyn,
meditating on what pioneering times were like, takes a turn in
the road which he belives to be a mistake, comparing himself
and his search to that of the pioneers, pitying the "race of

religious, childish, energetic tramps that they were—because he himself had gone astray on a road he did not know."

He is led to speculate on the use he can make of his knowledge of his ancestors, on writing about them, on his grandfather Henry's failure at biography due to his fearing to lift the reticence which "disguised the pity of his life." Alwyn determines not to have a tragic life, "so that he should be able to tell about it if he wanted to."

The lights of the town of Brighton appear, and Alwyn knows that he has been right about the crossroads after all, "though of a third generation, a better pathfinder than he knew."

Months later Alwyn sits up with his dying grandmother Rose through the night. Meanwhile his grandmother Duff is dying too, she who asked of him:

> "How is my young sweetheart? Now, tell me the news of my young man. Is he getting on well out in the world?"
> No one else had ever said that; no one, alive or dead, had thus made a place for him in the story.

Her words are "like the saying of an oracle, to be interpreted two ways; in a play on words, a menace or a promise" and Alwyn is led to think of his analysis and investigation of the familial past as a kind of incest, and extensive metaphor clarifying for him, in generalities, this creative act which leads to a defining of the self.

Taking the word *mother* to mean "that which produced one" and recognizing that "the desire to understand was, after all, desire," those who go back "do so in imagination to what had produced them, their hope, anxiety, and interest went back. Against the law. The weak went back. The strong returned," to go forward again, backward and forward, "two continual motions of the imagination making up that of their lives." Thus, with acquired experience as an aid, one is able "to build one's continual bridge from the past, across a sort of abyss into the dark future..." and to discover "why they had fallen again and again into the dark. Knowledge gained by breaking the law." Wisconsin too is his sweetheart, even though he has not had the pioneer's experience, not his fear of God, nor yet had children, nor lived "by the sweat of his brow."

Nevertheless, "it had been true love," and (in an involved

metaphor) the result is his "weak, incalculable manhood,"
which is like "a newborn child."

He wonders if he can profit in life from the past, if he can
keep his heart from breaking, at least "until he was ready to
die." His birthright is a patrimony "of the knowledge of life,
of skeletons in the closet, or precepts which had led infallibly
to resignation or disappointment, handed down to him in his
turn."

He then conceives of life as a fugue, his being one which will
repeat his ancestors' with "materials more closely and differently
combined," the "materials determined in advance; certain human
limitations, American characteristics, family traits," the sur-
prises being "the rhythm and order of the combinations."

> And his own, if he did his work well, ought to resemble
> a fugue, without a break (that is without disaster) from
> the beginning to the end, without violent emphasis, each
> element in perfect relief, played without loss of memory
> or unsteadiness in either hand: counterpoint of their
> appetites, their frugality, cunning, vanity, idealism, and
> homesickness.... And the phrase at the end?

Speculating on what his life will be like, that he will perpetu-
ate "the so-called warfare between the sexes," that he will
unite the traits of the two grandfathers, and realizing that he
will have to "compromise between his talent for poverty and
love of wealth," he hopes it will not be the same compromise
his Uncle Jim has made.

When James Tower arrives with news that his mother-in-law,
Mrs. Fielding, has not long to live, Alwyn thinks of her as his
"third grandmother," (actually she is the fourth, counting
Wisconsin), and that she is "representatively tragic." His generalizations extend from her to Chicago, Wisconsin, the West, and
America. Following are excerpts from a passage extending over
three pages:

> An old, pampered heroine of a great period of the
> nation's history, that of the birth and infancy of
> wealth; proud of herself as a proof that it had been a
> success. Alwyn believed that it had not been. She and
> her house had given him a history lesson.
> ...Neither Chicago nor Wisconsin had justified its
> existence.... It seemed able to do, more and more

powerfully, only two things; grow rich, and complain. The country lives had been no more than self-supporting; in his mother's words, no worthy gifts to the world had been made.... Across the Mississippi Valley the barbed-wire fences lay like the staves of music paper on which there were scarcely any notes.... It had not kept its promise, so it was still the promised land.

Represented by Mrs. Fielding, in great towns like her town, the West had taken its first step toward a civilization; it had been a step in the wrong direction.... Would it not have to fall back upon the past, upon the poor God of poverty and His remnant of pioneers, unchanged though dying out?....

Avid company of failures, out of date, behind the times, perhaps timeless. Ethically, socially, above all financially, they had made little progress; in modern methods of pretending to be happy, of pretending to have satisfied on earth their hearts' desire, they had made none at all. Pioneers because their unhappy dispositions unfitted them for everything else....theirs was the only glory, such as it was.

The Middle Ages of America (not middle-age, but youth) were coming to an end... Too soon, the holiness was going out of the land. There were modern inventions for warming the heart, and certain fires with too bitter smoke had been allowed to go out — except upon old-fashioned, unattractive hearths. And perhaps, if America was to justify its existence, to be justified for the massacre of redskins, the broken white hearts, the destruction of the city called Tenochtitlan or something of the sort — the children of those hearths, reared in, embittered and half-intoxicated by the smoke, would have to do the work. And they might be ready for any outlawry; ready to betray, for the work's sake, those whom they would continue to love even more than they ought; to betray the west to the east in the warfare between the two in order to gain for the former the advantages of defeat as well as victory; to betray their native land as a whole for some characteristically native land of their imagination...the sons of the men who thought they had failed... Stronger than their fathers.... The future of America, if it was to be worth troubling about, depended on them.

> Flattering and terrifying himself by his thought, according to his family's habit of mind, Alwyn shrank from the responsibility of being the hope of his native land.

He realizes then that he "would probably need to know those original beginnings, which, as he had persuaded himself, were unchangeable among his relatives, perverted among his countrymen, unchanged in him." It is at this point that the young Alwyn writes the historical essay that appears in chapter 2. His grandmother Duff dies; he continues to watch over the other grandmother, feeling now that he has been too long a kind of detective, that the "futile unweaving and reweaving of the evidence" is vain, and a kind of shame because he has broken "an instinctive law for Americans: that of being infatuated with and interpreting the past," the punishment for which is "a kind of expatriation though at home," in "a land of the future where all wish to be young; a land of duties well done, irresponsibility, of evil done without immorality, and good without virtue." The missing virtues are the offspring of memory, which America does not have because there is no past worth remembering, and no tragedy, which is considered a kind of treason. "Memory was incest . . ."

John Craig arrives from the west and Rose Tower has her last surge of strength. John (Evan) tells her of visiting the grave of Leander, and she replies, "I always loved him best." Then she tells the former Tower, "You were always a good boy, Evan," and he is greatly moved. The last actions, though casually told, are appropriate: the invitation of Evan, asking Alwyn to visit him (he has his chance to go West); the arrival of Leander Orfeo Craig, with whom Alwyn has an affinity at once, the young man being unlike a member of the family "or even an American;" and the last ceremonial gesture of his grandmother: "Children, get out the photographs."

Alwyn is aware of the "ghosts" of local history which have troubled him for years, and would leave them behind gladly, but feels "he would have need of them all, gods or pioneers or whatever they were, to lead an entire life. . . . Out of pride he wanted to be able to love and praise them all, even the last one. . . ."

The Matriarchy Theme

One of the most important themes in *The Grandmothers* is announced in the essay Alwyn wrote when he was nineteen.

> The whole country had one symbol: a very young man, always at the beginning of a career, always beside his mother. For she had taught him to revere success and taught him its maxims. He would never forget that when she had been at his side the mirage seemed real and not far away; he would never again be so happy as he had been, under her spell. So young wives imitated the mothers of the men they loved. America became a matriarchate.

The women the Towers marry, Sy Kahn has pointed out, are "less imaginative than their men," and better equipped "to understand adversity and disappointment":

> The need in the defeated Tower men for direction and support, for emotional shaping and fulfillment, makes them particularly susceptible to forceful, active and unsophisticated women like Rose. Consequently, in their husbands there is at worst a loss of manhood and at best domestication; both the men and the children become heavily dependent upon them.

Rose Hamilton loses her first love, Leander, not simply to the memory of his brother Hilary, but to his mother, when, upon his return from the war, he stumbles into his mother's embrace. She later shows maturity in marrying his widowed brother, Henry; Rose is throughout the novel a vivid character, spontaneous, alive, and direct in contrast to her husband and to the Tower men who are idealistic, dreaming, and melancholy.

But what of the nameless mother of the first generation of Towers? The scene of Leander's return, one or two other vague references, and Henry's praise of her as a tribute to "pioneer mothers" in his fragment of biography (49 ff.) are curiously all we know of her. The results evidenced by Henry, Leander, Hilary, and Nancy, are not happy, although no critic has noticed the vagueness of this particular mother, nor expressed any curiosity or awareness about her contributions to the unhappiness of her offspring. Perhaps it is not very surprising, in a way, for any references to or implications of her responsibility, except for those cited above, are missing from the book. Although Kahn too, seems unaware of her shadowy nature, his generalization seems valid:

> The Tower women make the family circle a formidable bulwark against outsiders. It also intensifies family relationships and introverts the young so that more than not they are unable to find satisfaction or security outside its walls. As children the Tower brothers (Alwyn's father and uncles) 'were afraid of girls and preferred each other to their friends.' Later the taciturn, dreamy, visionary men glorify their mother.

The domination takes various forms. Nancy Tower manages finally to thoroughly defeat and emasculate her husband, Jesse Davis, leaving him at last with little more than a drift toward death. Unlike the women who marry Towers, however, Nancy's victory is not the result of brusque energy, resilience, and even stoicism; it is her nervous energy born of guilt and violated sensibility, an "infernal though unconscious cleverness," that allows her to revenge "herself on 'life's gross gestures' by making madness breed madness." There is, as well, as Kahn has noted, "a hint of latent incest" in the relationship between Henry and Nancy, though they do not consciously recognize it. The close ties of the family, he emphasizes, breed a pride, isolation and loneliness, and a "powerful, though muted passion" among the family members.

Although we know nothing of Harrison Tower, whom Alwyn's great-aunt Mary Harris marries, Mary is more masculine in terms of character than some of the Tower men. And, like Marianne and Rose, she is one whose dominating characteristics are not destructive, but positive. Her courage, daring, and fortitude, and her ability to dominate to some extent her first husband, Cleaver, are the traits that save her life and bring her home to Hope's Corner. She apparently never loses these traits, as her final tour of Europe indicates.

Alwyn's aunt Flora, of the next generation, though certainly no exact counterpart of Nancy, is in her way afraid of the aggressive men who court her, and her "cleverness" consists of using the mores and ritual of courtship to wear away the morale of her suitors. It is also a means of refusing to face her urges to sexual love, and of punishing herself because she feels such urges. American 19th century Protestantism with its Puritanistic code, and her family's religious prejudices, sanctify this pattern. She withdraws from love and life, finally into death itself. Flora, to a great extent, like Rosalia of *The Apple of the Eye,* is a victim of regional Puritanism. But she is also an example of a woman who fails in her unconscious attempt to dominate, a failed matriarch.

James Tower's story carries forward several themes. He follows the Tower and the American pattern of frustrated artistic cultural expression and thwarted dreams which result in disappointment and failure. Although "lucky" because he is educated to break away from the life of physical labor on the farm, he is reduced to a kind of family servant of the Fieldings, of the *haute bourgeoisie.* He is corrupted by a life of ambitionless ease and luxury; the course of his religion parallels that of American Protestantism in an urban materialistic world, becoming first a "cheerful modern" faith, then a disguised matriarchy, one in which the dowager mother's house becomes a "sacred establishment," "a sort of private chapel to the glory of motherhood, which is the source of the glory of God." He is minister to the worldly needs of a family of females.

Mrs. Fielding is the supreme matriarch who

> rules her domain like some savage, ruthless queen and personifies the power of mid-western materialism. She is the ruling matriarch whose wealth assures and increases her dominance of the family. Along with her daughters, she succeeds in debilitating and thoroughly corrupting James as both minister and man. Thus in Chicago, as in the country, the old hopes and heroic deprivations and gestures of the pioneers have dwindled to the routine of servitude.

Her reign, as Alwyn sees it, is what followed pioneering as the cities of the West take their "first step toward civilization; it had been a step in the wrong direction."

In Evan Tower several themes reach their most pronounced emphasis, love and expatriation being the most important. More aware of his search for the self than any of the Towers except Alwyn, Evan is also a kind of supreme bachelor who attempts not only to leave national but family ties. His falling in love with a domineering woman ends the search for the self. Suzanne is European, and it is, ironically, her idea of America — the

American Dream—that defeats him as much as anything else. "It was America she wanted, America she loved in him."

In certain ways Evan represents the young American male in his loss of self in his life, in his necessity, after a brief futile rebellion, to "join the regiment and march with the rest;" the young American male whose marriage is over before it has begun, love having "run its course," who escapes several kinds of tyranny only "to play the tyrant to himself." But it is submission to the domination of Suzanne (who is clever and conniving besides) that makes such self-tyranny necessary. His life in one end of the house with his cowboys ("the boys"), while his wife lives in the other (like Nancy Davis), is symbolic of one pattern the American marriage can take. And, like so many Americans who have buried the self, he hopes it will come alive again in his son.

The chapter on the relationship between Ira and Ursula Duff presents Ursula as the most wronged of this pair, and the most sympathetic. Yet the combat between these two that continues for years in a painful and furious deadlock has its beginnings early in the marriage when Ursula energetically campaigns to reform her husband. She succeeds, but the rest of their lives, as a result, is devoted to his revenge and her retaliation.

As for Marianne, Alwyn compares and contrasts her to Flora, seeing that they are "equally anxious to be perfect" and that they are submitted to the same courtship pattern of young virgins and their suitors, but that Marianne is the converse in suffering no conflict between her wishes and her ideals. Flora is a Tower, and like the Tower men, is enervated by Tower characteristics and disappointing failure. Marianne, like the other women who marry Towers, contributes to marriage energy and strength of character.

The marriage of Marianne and Ralph is the only one in which there is no self-destroying friction between partners. Ralph is typically a Tower in many ways, and the equanimity of his married life is not due to any masculine domination on his part but rather to his wife's feminine flexibility, generosity and selfless love, aided by her "happy" religion that is a "miracle of energy and peace." Marianne is not typical of the women who dominate the American male.

> She is rather a perfect expression and symbol of
> America's best qualities and potentialities, the one

faultless blossom on the thorny stalk of American Puritanism. Her powers complete rather than enervate her husband; her energy impels rather than overwhelms her children.

The theme has its variations and its relation to others. Early in the book but in the fictional present, expatriate Alwyn observes a drunken forty-year-old American sailor on the Riviera sobbing "I want my mother! I want my mother!" as he is hauled off by the shore patrol. Near the end of the novel the former expatriate and Westerner Evan Tower comments that Chicago seems to him a "woman's town." Rose's brothers, also pioneers, represent a different breed of men from the Towers. These hunters, trappers, and unregenerate males declared, when Rose was young:

> "Pretty soon, smart fellows like the Towers'll spoil this country. Make a woman's country out of it, just like Kentucky. We're goin' to git out then, west."

Alwyn does not, of course, idealize the Hamilton men, nor men like Jesse Davis, and Cleaver, all of whom have a certain masculinity in common; but in America, civilization, he is aware, means to a large extent feminization. (The matriarchial theme is related to the polarities of masculine and feminine sensibility discussed later.) Mrs. Fielding is a symbol of the resulting matriarchy. The link between matriarchy and the pioneering past and decline of religion is set forth by Kahn.

> With the pioneers' perpetual migration and repeated disappointments, and with evangelical religion coming to a dead end as it paralleled the loss of hope, women and mothers more and more took up the burden of optimism and decided, and substituted, in a similar way, for the God that had failed men. God's moral laws and the awe and veneration due Him were unconsciously changed for obedience and subservience to her strength and dicta.

Pioneering, Expatriatism and Love

The Grandmothers is not simply a regional work, and it is about pioneers and pioneering in the largest and most complex sense. As Rueckert emphasizes, citing Joseph Warren Beach, it is true that what impresses Alwyn is "the abortive idealism of these strenuous lives, the fundamental melancholy deliberately ignored, the fanatical Puritanism, the spiritual pride and failure,"[6] and equally true that "the myth of America of the 1920's" was "a commonplace among American writers and part of the intellectual atmosphere of the time." This common atmosphere results, he indicates, in resemblances to many works in this particular respect.

> Most of the male Towers, for example, are James Gatzes (living in Wisconsin instead of North Dakota) who yearn to become Jay Gatsbys, to spring newborn from the platonic conception of themselves. They are all would-be aristocrats of the imagination, perpetual pilgrims and pioneers, always ready to set sail by ship or prairie schooner for the fresh green breast of the new world of their imaginations. They live in a perpetual hope's corner, the fallen and frustrated idealists of the new world who are unable to "renounce the dream," "the voyage of yearning," " 'the divine delusion.' " When Brooks speaks of America as an "impoverished civilization" in which things were "old without majesty, old without mellowness, old without pathos, just shabby and bloodless and worn out," it might just as well be Alwyn Tower in one of his meditations on the condition of America — or Wescott himself speaking in the essay "Good-Bye Wisconsin." But there seems little point in simply documenting these similarities of idea, of phrase, and, more significantly, of style and tone; the important fact is that the myth, which is inherently powerful, was pervasive and that Wescott's use of it, which was certainly profound and thought out, places the novel in a significant and deeply rooted American tradition.

But, as Rueckert concludes, these ideas do not account for the "power and originality" of either Fitzgerald's novel nor Wescott's.

Since the true subject of the novel is the meaning of the composite family portrait to the narrator, the importance of the pioneering theme (or any other theme) is what Alwyn makes of the generalizations, the truths, he has abstracted. Whereas the Towers have found that America has not kept its promise — that "wealth would be exchanged for virtue" — what Alwyn Tower searches for is self-knowledge by his investigation of the past. Alwyn hopes to escape their disillusionment, bitterness, disappointment and the Tower grievance by being a pioneer himself, but with a difference, his path not geographical and exterior, but psychological and inward. He will continue the heritage of pioneering in order to fulfill his responsibilities and achieve his destiny, by the labor of searching the past and by creation in art. It is not only a personal task so that he may go forward in his own life, but a mission to scout out as well America's future. Like his grandmother Rose, he will bring to life fragments of history to tutor the new generation. Thus the pioneering experience is drawn into a major metaphor (as part of the aesthetic act) that contains for Alwyn the usable truth in his liberation of the self.

He is not able to perform this complete aesthetic act until he is in his tower of Europe, from which he can look back with personal and aesthetic distance. To get there he has had to reverse the pioneering movement, geographically and psychologically, to "back trail" and move from the West to the East, to betray his country for "the native land of his imagination." In this way the second major metaphor is drawn from the expatriate theme, which is illustrated particularly by certain characters. Mary Harris is not only " 'the greatest of pioneer women' " but in one sense an expatriate herself, for it is "abroad" on the Missouri frontier that she discovers her real home and through hardship and danger returns to the locus of her past and self represented by Hope's Corner. She illustrates the point that all pioneers, all the Towers, are in the same sense expatriates, from England, from New York State, and often from Wisconsin, for pioneering and expatriatism are forms of the search. The Tower heritage of a sense of grievance comes from their failure to gain in the new world what they feel they lost in the old, their wealth, cultural leadership, and gentility, and it is this, Kahn concludes, that leads to their introversion and withdrawal.

> Isolated from the aristocratic life of their ancestors and never quite at home in the new world, they remain spiritual expatriates, who, like Flora, feel "the homesickness of a spirit which had not felt at home anywhere." They substitute family ideals and pride for the talents and aspirations that a hostile fate and indifferent society have left unfulfilled and unrecognized. Thus

membership in the family rivals citizenship in a nation.
(One might recall Alwyn's thought at the beginning of
the novel. 'He had no native land — he had a family
instead.') Rejection by or abandonment of the family
is particularly painful for a Tower, when allegiance to
it has been particularly ardent.

Evan Tower illustrates the pitfalls and dangers of expatriation.
Evan loses the self (Evan Tower) in a false self (John Craig),
ironically turned into an expatriate in his own country by the
myth, the promise of America that obsesses Suzanne. His greatest error is his attempt to erase the past, to destroy it, rather
than to understand it; he erases rather than defines himself.
Expatriatism is a form of pioneering, but in Alwyn it is not a
retreat but an attack, a move toward new experience. At the
same time he feels he will be punished by banishment, the loneliness and guilt of an outcast.

It can hardly be overstressed that only in the larger, and
hence metaphorical sense is pioneering the subject of the novel,
and that its major themes are love and the self. Both of these
are related to every other theme, it seems, intertwined, and
sometimes indistinguishable; the two favorite subjects for Alwyn's
generalities are love and the Towers as idealists, and of course
in love they are idealists, and pioneers in search of the self; and
love, like America, often does not keep its promise. Nearly
every Tower for one reason or another suffers as a victim of
love.

Henry Tower, the precursor of the line, also sets the pattern
in love upon which the others will play variations. It is the loss
of his young wife, Serena Cannon, that determines the rest of
his life, makes it seem unimportant. She seems to represent not
only the romantic ideal, but, as indicated by her name, an
ideal serenity of life that can only come through reciprocal love;
and perhaps her maiden name, Cannon, with its connotations
of religion and law, also suggests that sexual love carries the
secret of the virility of life itself. Henry loses hope and even
interest in the future when he loses Serena. His loss shapes his
life, drains it of all energy, makes him morose and introspective.
It importantly affects his attitude toward his family and helps
in this way to shape their lives as well. He cannot enjoy "the
laughter of his sons" and leaves "their troubles ... to his wife.
They were her children." What is this but a lack of love? No

character, including the analytic Alwyn, ever draws together Henry Tower's relationship to all the other characters, nor tallies the results. The significance and even the fact of his lack of love for his sons is somewhat obscured. Evan feels closer to Leander than he does to his own father, and loves him instead, and it is Leander's faulty advice that fortifies Evan's impulse to desert and consequently ruin his life. Even in his old age Henry never consents to see, let alone forgive, Evan, even though he knows he ought to, because "he never forgave anything." Henry relegates Ralph to a life of poverty and labor on the farm; he is Ralph's "fate." James is doomed to the ministry; Henry successfully crushes his chances for love (with Irene Geiger) and for individual development. He forces his sister Nancy to do her "duty" by her husband, until she is driven nearly to madness. His change of mind reveals that his love for her has some incestual overtones. Later he ruins Jesse Davis's chance for love and happiness with the widow he intends to marry in later life. As for his daughter Flora, Henry is the most unbending of anti-Catholics, imploring her never to marry a Catholic on his deathbed, and contributing much to her rejection of her lover and her death. He even alienates the young Alwyn, irascibly abrogating his agreement to pay the boy for capturing cabbage moths. He passes down a dominant trait, for Alwyn never forgives him. The cost of Henry's disappointed love and hope for himself and others seems endless. Rueckert quite accurately associates Serena with "the native land of the imagination" which is always around the corner for each Tower, briefly glimpsed and then lost, and which each spends his life unsuccesfully, to find, implying that love and the ideal are one.

Mary Harris, the adventuress, marries three times. In contrast to Nancy and Flora, she is able to use conventional marriage to save herself, although twice it nearly brings disaster. It is "out of vague necessity" on the Missouri frontier that she marries Dr. Brandon, but when he is murdered and her very life is in danger, her bold and courageous proposal of marriage, a deliberate offering of herself to Cleaver, is what saves it. It is her great love of place, Hope's Corner, which symbolizes for her the North, her country, a home and a family that is no longer there, that gives her courage to survive dangers and Cleaver's brutality. She at last finds genuine love in Harrison Tower, and lives happily the rest of her life with him. She is capable of pioneering — of at last finding love — because she is capable of a certain kind of action. She can confront and transcend her losses. No stage in her life, no event or series of them arrests her for all time in a spellbound state. She is not a Tower.

Rose and Marianne, who also marry Towers, resemble her in this respect. Although she is at first rejected by Leander, and never really understands the Towers, Rose is brought to life again by marriage to Henry. Because of her own resources she is able to overcome the loss of Leander's love, the death of two children and other disappointments. In middle life she has achieved a workable stoicism, but her love for her daughter Flora is so great that when the girl dies at 29, Rose's faith and strength are shaken. It becomes clear to her from then on that life has no importance. Because the middle-aged James is so different from the boy she knew, she half forgets that he is her son, and years after Evan's desertion she welcomes him but has little interest in his life. Shortly before her death, however, the news that he and his son Orfeo are coming give her a last surge of strength; she tells Evan for the first time that he was "always a good boy," and she is stimulated to get out the photograph album for the last time.

Marianne, as indicated in the discussion of the matriarchal theme, stands as the supreme example of the ideal achieved, in life and in love. Nancy Tower's story may seem to depend more exclusively on personal psychology, on the special case of the sensitive inhibited girl who is capable of love but finds its sexual expression repulsive. But the inflexible codes of 19th century America nearly doom her. She is driven by both families to accept a married woman's role. It is only Henry's love, which allows him uncharacteristically to change his mind, that saves her. Flora in the second generation suffers similar difficulties. The inhibitions and prudery of American Protestantism with its particular emphasis on the revilement of the flesh is a powerful force. She is immobilized by the opposite pulls of physical passion and spiritual passion associated with chastity. Like Rosalia of *The Apple of the Eye,* she is a victim of the Puritan split between the body and the soul, and typically for the Towers, between sensuality and a kind of moral or religious severity. She resembles them all, we are told, in her fear, prudery, timidity, and indecision. Anti-Catholicism in

Henry and the community prevent her last chance of marriage.

In spite of his pioneering-melancholy, Ralph Tower does achieve his Serena in Marianne. Perhaps it is partly due to luck, for his shyness and ineptness in courtship nearly cost him a love which is to sustain him his entire life. However, in his love for his children he carries on some of Henry's character. In true American fashion he is impatient and disapproving of Alwyn's sensibility (which resembles Leander's), of his distaste for hunting and taxidermy, and although it is muted in the novel, there is love lost here — indicated by Alwyn's being closer to John Craig (Evan) than his father, as Evan was closer to Leander than his father.

Ira and Ursula Duff are the converse in their relationship to Alwyn's parents; love has become hate, a passionate trap symbolized by the pair of locked antlers. It is typical of love's paradoxes that out of this relationship should come Marianne, the most successful lover of them all.

It is in James especially that the love and matriarchy themes cross. First James is unable to keep from sacrificing love — and artistic expression as a form of self-discovery — to the dictates of the family and to American prejudices against art. For James, love becomes submission. His defeat by the family, specifically Henry and Ralph, sets the pattern for him to marry Caroline Fielding and live a life of submission to her and to her mother. Rather than submission to God, through love, he capitulates to middle-class materialism and luxury ruled over by the matriarchal goddess, Mrs. Fielding.

Evan Tower, a kind of ironic converse of his father Henry, dooms himself, not because he loses his loved one, but because he finds her. Perhaps love as a blind passion is the best way to describe what Evan illustrates, or love as fate. But actually Evan illustrates more of the aspects of love than any other character. He sees it as a trap, feels it as a lonely, frustrating passionate yearning that makes one sorrowful and stupid. He discovers that lovers are fools, lovers are helpless, and that love is "madness." He escapes love as homosexuality, however, when he deserts Marbury and the "family of sailors."

Two of the important motifs that are part of the general love theme are homosexuality and incest. The relationship of Leander to Hilary combines both. On that fateful night that splits Leander's life in two parts, he recognizes the latent homosexual nature of Hilary's love and his own response. He continues to repress his impulses, at least in Wisconsin. By paralleling the Evan-Marbury relationship with that of Hilary and Leander, the themes of the expatriate, or outcast, and that of homo-sexuality are made to imply each other. Leander thinks of him-self as an outcast, and in a sense most of the Tower men, and Nancy and Flora, are outcasts because of their sensibilities. The Leander story is an illustration that homosexuality is one of the forms that sensibility can take (Evan avoids it) in an Amer-ican society that is generally hostile to the cultivation of it. The novel delineates a sharp American polarity between the "masculine" and "feminine" traits. Sensibility (including artistic sensibility) is considered feminine, or at least effeminate, and insensibility, even brutishness, is considered masculine. Generally speaking the Tower men are, in varying degrees, at the feminine-sensibility pole as opposed to the masculine-insensibility pole, as represented by Rose Hamilton's family, Jesse Davis, Timothy Davis, and Cleaver. The Hamiltons (who say the Towers make America a "woman's country") must be considered, with their like, in this polarized relationship to the Towers to give a basis for accurate broad generalities about the American past, as Alwyn obliquely implies in chapter 2. Wescott thus successfully confronts what had remained an underground theme in *The Apple of the Eye.*

Within the Tower family such sensibility takes various forms and results in individual problems. Ralph Tower seems to rather curiously combine the polarities in his gift for delicate preserva-tion of animals shot down in the hunt. In Hilary and Leander it takes the form, repressed or not, of homosexuality. In Evan it takes the form of a disgust with an internationally insensitive and aggressive America, the war, and the family; in James it appears in his susceptability to female domination (as it does in others) and in his musical ability. It is represented by musical ability too in Henry, who surreptitiously plays his flute, in Hilary's girlish tenor, in Flora's tremulous song. Flora is so strongly pulled both ways by polarities that she cannot survive; in Nancy sensibility takes the form of disgust with the physical aspects of love, perhaps for much the same reason. Her close affinity with Leander is that both are repelled by the "mascu-line," the crude, gross and insensitive.

As for incest it is only in the relationship of Leander and

Hilary and of Leander and Timothy that it is overtly implied, although hinted at in milder form between Henry and Nancy and Leander and Evan. Incest is of course a form of love, and what it emphasizes here is the claustrophobic nature of the Tower family relationships, their sensibility seeking love within the isolated family, a situation which is partly due to their idealism, pride and aristocratic pretensions.

Alwyn carries forward the strain of Tower sensibility. It was thwarted in Evan because he tried to erase the past, and as artistic expression it was thwarted and corrupted in James, but in Alwyn (who reminds Evan of Leander) it takes the form not of homosexuality or a delicate garden of herbs, but reaches its consummation in the discovery of the self through artistic expression. It is only through love, passionate love, that this is accomplished. The love theme, with its varying motifs, is drawn together into a third major metaphor, that of incest, in the concluding chapter.

In the final chapter of the novel the major themes become material for generalization (as they have throughout the work), and material as well for a cluster of major metaphors, by which Alwyn procures the necessary knowledge of his heritage to help him attain his separate selfhood. The conclusions, the "truths," are evident to the later Alwyn Tower, who, after his back-trailing expatriation to the tower of Europe, recounts an earlier Alwyn undergoing the beginning of the creative and recreative process that will result in the liberation of the self and his creation of the family of stories we have just finished reading.

As previously stated, Alwyn thinks of his investigation and analysis as incest, a key metaphor that clarifies the creative act of defining the self. Alwyn, like Dan Strane, takes the word *mother* to mean "that which had produced one." Curiosity, desire to know, is the motivation for the act of passion which is the penetration of the past, involving various kinds of incestuous love for the members of the family, including his three grandmothers—Rose, Ursula and Mrs. Fielding—the region— his "sweetheart" and "grandmother" Wisconsin—and his country. All of these are mothers and grandmothers. He has loved them as a child, and now as a man, in memory, which is for Americans, incest.

Out of this "true love.... not altogether sterile, illusory as the relation had been" is born knowledge, "just enough knowledge to live on...and it was the mother of the weak, incalculable manhood which, within and protected by his immature arms, lay like a newborn child." In other words, out of his incestuous passion for knowledge (already his own offspring by incest) of family, region and nation is born what amounts to his new, or second self (his grandson by incest), Alwyn Tower the artist. It is this Alwyn of incestuous ancestry who by his incestuous mating with memory and imagination, becomes the father of the "family of stories," which is the novel. The writing of the novel is also then a passionate act of love. One can think of the family metaphor, or the sexual-familial metaphor as one that encloses the whole process in the final chapter, a "fictional geneology," as Rueckert says, "with elaborate commentary, of this new self." As such, it is not so much a portrait of the Tower family as it is Alwyn's self-exploration and self-portraiture in terms of his family.

Perhaps two points should be re-emphasized: that the family chronicle is one of perpetual pioneers who have all failed, who, dreamlike in their individual towers, hoping in Hope's Corner, never find their Serena in the native land of their imaginations; that Alwyn, as the concluding chapter indicates, succeeds exactly where they have failed, and escapes their destiny. He now hopes (conscious of the word's irony) that his life, combining the now known family traits, will resemble a fugue, perfectly played, counter-pointing the family's appetites, their frugality, cunning, vanity, idealism, and homesickness. Now apparently finished with the task which has been his passion, and having exorcized the ghosts and spirits and "glad to leave them behind," he is still wary of an arbitrary rejection that would obliterate the very knowledge he has gained. "But he felt that he would have need of them all, gods or pioneers, or whatever they were, to lead an entire life... Out of pride he wanted to be able to love and praise them all, even the last one...."[7]

Character, Structure and Theme

The novel can be considered structurally as a time-arranged family album framed by the introductory and concluding chapters, the portraits arranged in roughly chronological order according to the birth-date of each character, one row (the first half of the book) for the first generation, another row (the second half) for the second generation, with a cluster of remote relatives and acquaintances ("The Dead") between them, and a large double-portrait near the bottom frame of the maternal grandparents, the Duffs. But such a view of the structure is superficial and of only limited use. The profuse generalizations throughout the novel lead to the broader generalizations developed in the conclusion. It is here, too, that the several themes find their synthesis in a broad family metaphor. They serve also as strands binding individual characters and chapters to each other, each character to the family, and the family and regional chronicle to the American past. The primary structural principle is that of the narrator. He is not only the primary structural principle but the primary formal one, and the highly successful fusion of form and function in this novel rests on the successful use of the narrator and voice, which will be discussed later in this chapter.

Characterization was one of the major weaknesses of Wescott's first novel, particularly characterization in relation to the development of theme. There is no question about *The Grandmothers* being far superior in this respect. For each of the dozen major characters upon which so much depends is adequately conceived for the purposes of the work. There is no sense here of the moral confusion, of the lack of verisimilitude, and faulty realization that so flawed *The Apple of the Eye*. There are no characters like Hannah, Jule, and Selma who seem inadequate to the thematic intentions of the author. For one thing, no single character is meant to carry as heavy a thematic burden as Hannah Madoc, even though the characters in the second novel are generally more complex. No single character is intended to be a secular saint. Rather it is what may be learned from all of these lives, as they are made material for the investigating, ruminating, contemplating mind of Alwyn Tower, as they are recreated out of memory and imagination, that provide the "truths" by which he learns to live.

One of the flaws of the first novel was its didactic quality, and the character of Jule, and to some extent others as well, suffered from carrying out this function. There is nothing like the baldness and inadequacy of Jule's thematic speeches in *The Grandmothers*. The didactic quality, or rather what sometimes threatens to become that, is performed by the narrative voice of Alwyn Tower. The kind of generality and aphorism that in the first novel were emanations from the omniscient narrator are here made by Alwyn too, but they are the product of one identifiable mind, and functional in the fullest sense, for it is the overseeing mind that must draw what conclusions there are, and this mind is the book's subject.

Wescott's fondness, even insistence, upon making generalities, upon carefully turning aphorisms and driving his "truths" home with specific statements is still with him. The difference, a great one, is that in his second novel the results of this fondness are in principle justified by the subject and form. Yet a question of degree is aesthetically important; there is an excess of generality in the final chapter, inadequately relieved by the concrete situation of Alwyn weaving them from his meditation. The generalities are not closely enough derived from, and hence vitalized by, memorable concrete events in the family of stories. The same is true of another large inert section entitled "The Religious Faith of the Family" (in chapter 11). The fact that it is tied to Marianne and her religion does not obscure the lack of events or details of character; we cannot visualize — for we are given no chance to — Marianne acting in ways that would give rise to the generalities; we are cheated of this and left with abstractions.

Apparently, in Wescott's view, at least in his practice, *truths* are necessarily abstract and general.[8] *Images* are concrete — an entire story may be an *image* — and *images* have to be, it seems, converted to *truths* before they can be mentally digested and then made use of, and it is the *use* of these *truths* that justified the creation of the *images*. This concept of *image* and *truth* applied in both of the first two novels is a curiously pragmatic and utilitarian view of art and human sensibilities, and one that would seem antithetical to Wescott's values generally in life and in art. It is a concept which works well enough in *The Grandmothers* and is central to the book's conception. The excess of generality is not enough to constitute a major flaw. But, in *The Apple of the Eye,* the concept is central to its failure, and it becomes a major aesthetic problem in Wescott's career.

Two related shortcomings in *The Apple of the Eye* which directly concerned unsuccessful characterization had to do with the inadequate quality of, and scarcity of, dramatic scenes and dramatic confrontations of character. Again there is a great gap between the two novels, at least in *effect*. Certainly a more mature and complex conception of character in the second novel makes a great difference. But what of the actual scenes and confrontations? True, there are many more of them, and they are certainly of higher quality. But one reason for there being many more is that there are many more characters. The "album" form has given some critics the mistaken notion that the novel is simply a series of short stories. Nevertheless, it is true that there are certain characters whose biographies are almost entirely within a single chapter, which, with little or no change, could stand as a separate unit: those of Mary Harris (chapter 5), Nancy Tower (chapter 6), Evan Tower (chapter 12), and Flora Tower (chapter 13). The single fragment on Ralph Tower (chapter 11) is not enough for a story as given. Others require one chapter and at least part of another: Leander (4,7) James (9,11), Marianne (10,11) and the Duffs (10,14). Rose and Henry Tower, the progenitors, require large portions of more than two chapters, the bulk of Henry's biography needing three, and Rose requiring significant slices in several besides the first, last, and chapter 4. Such an accounting gives a false impression, of course, for there are numerous small incidents, lines of dialogue, shards of scenes, and summary references — sometimes a mere line or two of information — pertaining to one character but appearing in the story of others. These cross-connections of character are ligaments that help bind the individual to the family, as in a similar way the particular and abstract "truths" link them to the family also, and the family to the pioneers, and the whole work to the region and America.

The relation of this particular kind of structure to character is that the concentration, the focus, is upon one character at a time, even though the treatment may be broken into two or more pieces and separated. The character's sensibility is rendered through the narrator's sympathetic voice, and his character is structured in summary-narrative form (Ralph Tower is the only one whose character has little narrative shape). Because of the album form, and the high degree of selection and concentration, it is possible for the author to avoid any but the most critically necessary confrontation of character and dramatic scene. This technique is more like that of *The Apple of the Eye* than at first appears, because there it is a part of an unsuccessful work; but in that novel too one character at a time received primary focus, with other characters often existing only on the fringe of his consciousness — with a resulting lack of confrontation. What is inadequate in the first is justified in the second by the form, accomplished through the use of the overseeing mind and voice of the narrator. The narrative technique, the means of rendering character, however, is *essentially the same*. Even though Wescott has improved greatly in the execution of such technique, scene and confrontation are skimpy, and succeed mainly by virtue of being enclosed in the language of the commenting narrator. The successful narrative voice has the effect of making virtues of the author's shortcomings. There is also, due to lack of scene and drama and detail, more often than not a blurring effect on characterization whenever a character appears outside the chapters mainly devoted to him.

Symbolism: Structural Rhythm and Symbolic Texture

In *The Grandmothers*, Wescott continued to work in the symbolic tradition. The patterning of events to appropriate seasons, with a consequent paralleling of them with the emotions of the characters for cyclical rhythm and mythic connotation is of lesser importance to the novel as a whole, however, and it is evident only in certain of the portraits.

There are only a few retrospective lines about Nancy Tower's marriage to Jesse Davis, but the pattern of her marriage and near madness has some parallels to nature's cycle. Spring and summer intensify in her the emotional poles of love and repulsion. One November she is taken to an asylum. The next October, suffering another crisis, she runs away from Jesse to the Tower home for good. By spring, "a miracle" (rebirth) takes place and she is never again "eccentric."

Except for the fact that she dies and is buried in autumn, the cycle of the seasons has no importance in the story of Mary Harris. Perhaps it is that she is willful and courageous, and much less subject to the domination of such "natural" forces and repression than Nancy. But Flora, like Nancy, is a contrast to Mary Harris, and in her story the seasons, in spite of her name, are never once indicated, and there is no floral symbolism except for the association that Alwyn makes of her and the smell of attar-of-roses.

The narrative of Marianne follows the pacing of the seasons closer than that of any other character. Her childhood is ended when she is baptized in the June of her sixteenth year. In the spring of her nineteenth year she meets Ralph and falls in love with him. She suffers unrequited love through the summer, in the fall attempts to end that portion of her life by going away to college and then in the winter starts to teach school. During that winter she starts her unhappy relationship with Paul Fairchild, is engaged in the spring, and during the summer suffers from indecision, inertia, and from the long battle against his attempts at seduction. By autumn she has given up hope of happiness, and at last the dramatic break with Paul occurs, and before long she is married to Ralph Tower.

The novel, with its complexity of subject and form, need not count on such rhythm, and if every story followed the pattern perhaps the repetition would be overdone. But it is difficult to see the basis for excluding Flora from the pattern.

The cumulative symbol and the revolving symbol are used throughout. Bird-imagery, an important pattern in the first novel, appears again, becoming the most important symbolic texture. Imagery of birds—the eagle, the passenger pigeon, birds of prey (8), and the turkey (25)—aid the historical-cultural vision that Alwyn has of America. It is used as a part of a larger tableau of the night of the soul, or rather the absence of birds signifies loss of hope, or of spiritual freedom (15); again related to spiritual freedom, birds signify the homing instinct in the portrait of Mary Harris (72,77,93). They appear in Marianne's story as an ironic comment (188), as part of an extended metaphor on the emotions (193), as the symbol for a character (323-324), and as dramatic action commenting on character (198).

Although effective, these references are relatively few when compared to the number for any one symbol in *The Apple of the Eye*. The most significant use of the bird as a symbol appeals in the chapter on Leander. In conjunction with Leander's symbolic garden, woodcock and garden in this chapter provide the most forceful use of flora and fauna imagery in the novel. The garden that Leander has so carefully cultivated symbolizes the inner life he has nurtured and cultivated, especially in the delicate odor of the herbs, which "the whole garden resembled" as the earth was "forced to whisper a nervous poetry." Full of sexual imagery, the symbolism runs the danger of being merely ludicrous at the close of the following passage.

> He separated the plants, each one perfect of its kind, by artifically arid spaces, and covered the roots of the Ophelia rose with a pavement of pebbles. Two moss roses appeared to bleed from their own thorns. There was a mourning-bride thrust full of stamens, one or two flame-throwers, a moonwort and a rock of arabis. In the autumn, on the brown dusk, a day-lily with its pale face of a frightened boy, went to sleep.

The question is whether the personification of the lily as a "frightened boy" — immediately reminiscent of Hilary — is not, after all, simply sentimentality. The use of a *lily* to personify this particular boy is unfortunate in its naiveté, since in American slang the word has connotations of homosexuality. And in view of the fact that Wescott has shown himself capable of punning on the names of birds,[9] it is equally unfortunate that he chose a woodcock as his central symbol here. These are minor oversights, however, in a highly successful chapter.

The singularity of the woodcock from its kind, its sense of being safe and loved, the thought of Leander that only he and Hilary would be moved by such a shy creature, the secretive almost "supernatural" quality of the bird's coming and going, carefully freight the bird as a symbol of the capacity for precious and rare love. The dramatic events that follow — with the lusty Irish female Iris sensing unconsciously the whole relationship, and her insistence on having its feathers for her hat (Wescott knew his Freud) — lead to the dramatic destruction of the bird by Timothy, the accomplishment of his freedom from Leander, and Leander's angry despair as, in a rage, he destroys the now autumnal garden which had reached perfection.

The other major use of birds as a symbol is in conjunction with Ralph Tower's taxidermy, the products of which the young Alwyn has too much sensibility and imagination to appreciate. Ralph's chloroforming of the snow owl causes Alwyn to awaken from dreams of "that hand passing gently over his

own face." The owl again here like other birds seems to signify one's inner nature, the self which Alwyn fears will be suf-
focated by his father and the attitudes and values he represents.
In the final chapter, Alwyn, thinking of writing about his
family, fears he might be "doing no more than his father did
with birds and animals: spreading them out and cleaning the
bones (the drier, the better they would keep); choosing a single
attitude for each one and wiring it as firmly as possible; arrang-
ing them in groups as lifelike as groups of lifeless bodies could
be." His hope is to catch the animating spirit, in other words —
not "single attitudes" or simply a series of them.

Animal imagery as a symbolic texture is quite limited, with
only occasional appearances, such as that of the bull for Timothy, the most important animal symbol being the horse. It
appears most frequently and as a sexual symbol in the chapter
on Flora. Her first suitor, Richard Wallace, drives "the most
violent and shining horses in the country." After rejecting him
she declares to herself that she loves him, feeding apples to
the "feared and adored colt Oboe," who releases a "cry of
love and hunger" when he sees her. Her next suitor, the
Catholic Dr. Ruhl, who is in his thirties, drives "less fiery
horses" and goes through the same movements of seduction,
but with the intention of being repulsed, to test her chastity.
The sexual potency of Jesse Davis is also symbolized by a
horse. As Kahn has recognized, there is an appropriate cor-
respondence between the man and the type of horse that symbolizes him. Kahn has also indicated the similarity of Wescott's
use of such symbols to those of D. H. Lawrence, although he
does not note the horse her mother rides in the dreams of
Marianne. The least effective of all the symbols in the book,
because it is so patent and so contrived, is the pair of locked
stag-horns used to signify the relationship of Ira and Ursula
Duff.

Flower imagery is not as profuse as in *The Apple of the Eye,*
since there is not the creation of a total environment rendered
in terms of the region. But the technique, when it appears,
is the same. There are the characterizing symbols of the cinna-
mon rose for Rose Tower, the perfume of attar-of-roses for
Flora, and more complex, swamp orchids in a hirsute hand,
signifying Nancy's ambivalent attitude toward Jesse and love.

Leander and Ursula Duff, after his return from California,

are drawn together by their love of flowers. They exchange information and even spend a regular hour or two "in rather formal talk" of flowers, which seem here to be a means of conveying to each other the quality of their sensibilities. And Leander himself dreams not of the California mountains breaking open in gold, but turning into a rose, a rather standard signification of love.

Just as there was the hawthorne tree in *The Apple of the Eye,* there is here the mountain ash associated with the flowering of love, this time between Rose and Leander.

One image of some importance that Wescott uses is not taken from nature — the circle — appearing in various forms but always signifying the family circle, and the relationship of it to the individual involved. The first appearance helps clarify later ones.

> As he remembered his childhood, it seemed that much of it had been spent in the center of a carpeted floor, and all about in a circle of rocking-chairs there had been women and men — grandparents, and their friends, and old cousins, and great-aunts, and uncles, and behind each one a life had extended into the past like a corridor — poorly lighted, long corridors winding away in every direction, through reticence and forgetfulness, to their youth; and in the ring of rocking-chairs, the child for whose existence all the corridors had come together, had shivered in the gusts of emotion which blew vaguely down them, and tried to understand the strange syllables which echoed from one life to another.

This is a key image, Kahn notes in citing this passage and a number of others, carrying "an increasing burden of meaning as the story develops" — in other words, a cumulative symbol. And Wescott is able to manipulate it for complexity, as the above passage indicates.

> It is the passion of Alwyn's life to define the circle and to explore the long dark corridors, fearful and ominous as they may be...The labyrinth of corridors threaten the searcher with an endless maze of vicarious experience so that his own life may be lost in theirs. Furthermore, as each corridor is lighted and the past becomes less of a mystery, remaining with-

in the circle becomes a kind of security, a bulwark against an unknown future or perplexing world.

The circle, Kahn continues, is a kind of "treacherous security" to those like Alwyn, who are given to introspection and grievance, for it may lead them to exhaust their powers in investigating the past. The cost of breaking the family circle is heavy, both for those who fail (Nancy, Leander, Flora, Jim) and those who succeed (Mary Harris, Evan). Alwyn succeeds too in breaking through the circle. "In a test of strength it is he who ultimately encircles his family; the novel is a history of that ordeal." The image appears when Nancy is pressured by the Davises and Towers to return to her husband. The perfect marriage of Ralph and Marianne is like a circle. The fate of Flora — to be trapped within the family circle — is symbolized when Leander slips on her baby fingers Hilary's ring. Tattooed on Marbury's arm is a blue heart within a circle which, as the chapter develops, stands for Evan's situation as an outcast and is in contrast to the circle of the family. It also emphasizes the secrecy and permanency of his isolation.

There are images that work symbolically but are not part of a pattern: the symbolic act of Alwyn's in the second paragraph of the book of trying to find the foundations of the cabin which had been his father's birthplace; the forget-me-not wallpaper of his grandmother's bedroom; the discarded gravestone, now face down, used as a doorstep; the symbolic position of Alwyn in the heights on the Riviera and in the Austrian Alps (Europe as his tower), and many others. There are such scenes as the one in chapter 8, when the grandmother and the graveyard are brought together in their symbolic functions (reminiscent of a similar scene in the first novel, when Mike first tells Dan of Han's legend), and with Rose as transmitter and preserver of past values. As indicated earlier, the first chapter emphasizes that objects, events, phrases, and stories all have symbolic potential for Alwyn, and it is this quality of his mind as narrator throughout the novel which is so important in weighting images and events with symbolic power and consequently drawing from them the meaning or *truth*.

Prose, Point-of-View and Narrator

The prose style of Wescott in his first novel was one of the most striking and distinguished characteristics that announced the appearance of a new talent. Its strength lay in its capacity for creating symbols, weaving image-patterns, and evoking subjective states of characters, a prose both disciplined and lyric. Yet its limitations were marked, particularly in its awkwardness in the creation of scene and dialogue. The remarkable distance between the "promising" first novel with its many shortcomings and the finely-wrought *The Grandmothers* has already been indicated in the discussion of structure, character and theme. The improvement is just as remarkable in the author's prose, and in his solution of the fundamental problem of point-of-view and narrator which had been intrinsic to important failures in the first novel.

Although one does have a sense that these characters, particularly those of the first generation, are of their region and time, such a result depends upon many factors contributing to the character-portraits rather than the placing of them in large and small panoramas of nature so profuse in *The Apple of the Eye*. Such prose descriptions with the quality of set-pieces are non-existent, and when landscape or images of nature appear, they are directly functional either to the narrative, scene, or evocation of character. The prose that most resembles (but with improvements) that of the earlier Wescott appears in the chapters on Leander, serving to weave symbolic texture of garden and bird; on Nancy Tower, as an aid to evoking her sexual ambivalence; to some extent in the courtship of Marianne. But even here such prose is more immediately and directly functional and rather than lush, as in *The Apple of the Eye*, it is comparatively pruned and lean.

In creation of scene and dialogue discernable improvements are evident. In dialogue there is a general sense of improvement, but upon examination it is less than expected. There are no ludicrous or garrulous passages, and hardly an awkward turn of phrase. The improvement is a kind of negative achievement. No outright blunders are evident. The dialogue is not markedly unrealistic; on the other hand, it is not realistic either. There are a few attempts, but only a few, to capture native American idioms of that time and place, and usually the attempt is a bit awkward. Typically, instead, there is something like the following. Marianne is talking to her son Alwyn, who has asked, "Who is Mr. Craig?"

His mother hesitated for a moment. "I don't know why you shouldn't be told. You are old enough now to keep the family secrets. You have heard us all speak of your father's younger brother Evan — he is Mr. Craig. He changed his name."

Among all the utterings of these native mid-westerners there is not one "he don't," rarely, if ever, an "I guess," and never a "golly," a "gosh," a "darn," or a "damn," and never those corn-belt favorites, "real good" and "real fine." There is a remarkable lack of ear not only for vocabulary, but for the syntax of idiomatic speech. The above is a long speech; usually dialogue is confined to a few words or a line. The improvement in dialogue is mainly due to its unobtrusiveness. It is not typical, nor realistically accurate. It is ordinary.

As for the potentialities of situations, the rendering of them scenically, the improvement is certainly more evident. There are no limp or flaccid scenes which were so common in *The Apple of the Eye,* and whatever is rendered seems necessary. Below is a key scene from the chapter on Mary Harris, which is typical of the key scenes (including the ordinary dialogue). Her husband dead, her life in danger, Mary realizes she must go north at any cost. She approaches Cleaver, a man she has never seen, but who has a wagon and is going north.

She stopped at the top of three steps which descended to the yard. There was a man on his knees by a great wagon. Her courage failed, and she steadied herself a- gainst the trunk of a cottonwood. He was greasing the wheels. She saw the neglected curls running down the back of his neck under the coat collar.

Then he stood up; from the top step Mary realized how tall he was, and caught a glimpse of his face: the soft forehead, the rough sideburns, the moist, bad- tempered mouth. Then she unbuttoned her high collar and folded it back on her shoulders. Lifting her head, she descended; very softly the crinoline brushed the trunk of the cottonwood.

"You are Mr. Cleaver?"

He breathed heavily through his mouth and nodded.

"You are going north?"

"In the morning."

The most important question was the hardest to ask:

"Are you going alone? Are you married?"

The moisture in her eyes, her nervous mouth, her im-
modest throat, had an appearance of passion. So he
forgot that they were strangers and did not notice that
she scarcely looked at him.

"Will you take me with you?"

He flushed and drew himself up to his full height.
She had won. They walked behind the stable along a
little path. She told him her name and story, making
the story less tragic, lest he cease to be flattered. He
said nothing about the war; apparently he had intended
to leave before it broke out. They made plans; they
might have been lovers. He kissed her. Mary had never
been kissed by a young man, but his breath was musty
with drink.

He let her walk back alone in the dusk. There was a
moist place on both her sleeves above the elbow — the
axle grease from his hands. Without wanting to die she
wished that she were dead; but even the journey north
would come to an end.

The scenes have not the inflexibility, awkwardness and limitations which in *The Apple of the Eye* made themselves intrinsic to
the very qualities of the prose. There is not the slackening of
necessary thematic or dramatic tension that so often occurred in
the first novel. If, as happens from time to time, it appears that
some of the genuine dramatic possibilities in confrontation of
character with character are avoided, the form, as we have
mentioned before, allows for highly concentrated scenes, the
narrative pace forces one to read on, the pace of course being
in the control of the narrator.

The scene cited above is typical in its condensation. Even
though it is as close to a fully-developed scene as all but a
half-dozen in the novel, it has a truncated quality. Such details
as the softness of crinoline brushing the cottonwood are necessary for evocation of Mary's assumed attitude and Cleaver's
impression of it in one of the most significant moments in
Mary's life, but the rest of the action and detail can be
summarized.

The number of scenes per portrait varies. The section on "His
Father" has no scenes whatsoever. The chapter on Nancy Tower
has several. But generally speaking, the bulk of the remaining
prose of which the novel is composed is either summary narrative, or some form of exposition. The narrative, like the scenes,

is condensed. Days and months and even years may be omitted. Scenes are reserved for the most crucial moments. Often there does not seem to be room for analysis or presentation of the fine points of character, and the narrator, who apparently knows all, often prefers to generalize rather than probe. The dramatized scenes are as a rule toned for evoking the significant effect of occurrences on the sensibility of the character, as in the last paragraph in the quotation above. For instance, here is a scene following a shorter one in which Leander makes it clear to Rose that he cannot marry her.

> In that moment she knew what life was made up of; she would never forget again. As if from a great distance, by transference from someone else's thought, she knew that Serena was delirious—it was the doctor who was walking up the path—there was work to be done.
>
> Two days later Henry came. He was too late; Serena could not speak. After the funeral Rose went home, thinking that the rude cabin would never give her up again.
>
> At the end of the month Leander went to California. Henry Tower was living alone with his little son, and one day asked Rose to marry him. She felt as if she had been dead, and in an apparent eternity of lazy hunters, their gibes and quarrels; and suddenly, in the widower's melancholy voice, permission to return to the earth she loved was granted. Leander had not wanted her, but she was acceptable to the Towers.

What could be given in dramatic scenes—the return of Henry, the deathbed, the funeral, Rose's return home, Leander's departure, events leading up to Henry's proposal, and above all the proposal itself, are given in the briefest possible summary narrative. But the first paragraph and half of the last (more than the rest of the passage altogether) are concerned with Rose's feelings, and the significance of them to her life.

Finally, the prose of *The Grandmothers* shows a new improved flexibility and imaginative quality displaying a fresher eye for symbolic implications sharply expressed—for example, those excerpts from the chapter on Henry Tower:

> It (his alpaca jacket) held the shape of his body and soul; the sharp angle of the sleeves at the elbow meant irascible vitality; the empty pockets, poverty and indif-

ference; the imprint of the stooped shoulders, fatigue;
and the contradictory flare of the collar at the back,
pride. His beard was parted in the middle, and fell on
each side of a large bone button in his shirt collar; his
rheumatic hands were clenched; and wherever he went,
he seemed to be elbowing aside invisible people in his
way .... His clear, wide-open eyes were often indiffer-
ently unfocused, as if the eyes of his mind were
downcast.

The same qualities are apparent in much of the figurative
language, particularly the extended metaphor, such as the
following:

For the memory of another is like a ship which one
sees coming down a bay — the hull and the sails separating from the distance and from the outlying islands and
capes — charged with freight and cutting open the waves,
addressing itself in increasingly clear outlines to the impatient eyes on the waterfront; which, before it reaches
the shore, grows ghostly and sinks in the sea; and one
has to wait for the tides to cast on the beach, fragment
by fragment, the awaited cargo.

Numerous examples could be cited from almost any page in
the book. What is manifest here is a mind of greater complexity, insight, and sureness of expression than before. Certainly
some of this is due to the adoption of a means of narration
that allows such a mind clear expression.

The fundamental single difference in technique that is most
responsible for the advance from the artistic failure of the first
novel to the high degree of artistic success in the second is that
of point-of-view and narration. The limited third-person narrator-character, or, to use an easier term, participating third-
person narrator, is inseparable from the unique form of the
book, first of all, and the success of that form. Such a narrator,
who is a character narrating for the purpose of discovering and
releasing the self, is the very principle of the structure: the early
establishment of the narrator's mind and sensibility, and his
aesthetic objectivity in the fictional present, the threading of
themes, motifs, and generalities throughout the portraits that are
a combination of memory and imagination, and the concluding
rumination and analysis, all these work for the synthesis of what

the narrator has learned. Everything in the novel, then, is directly a result of the narrator's mind at work.

To recapitulate some of the ways that the use of such a narrator contributed to Wescott's improvement in technique: (1) what might have been obtrusive didactic passages are now heard in the generalizing, truth-seeking, truth-giving voice of the narrator, and are, in principle, functional; (2) aphorism, epigram and broad generality become functional for the same reason; (3) scarcity of dramatic scene and character confrontation — much less evident in *The Grandmothers* — is now justified because of the larger number of characters, the necessity of conveying a single life in a short space, and narrative pace. In addition scenes can be truncated, and narrative becomes often summary. Points weakly dramatized can be reinforced by exposition. (4) The inability to focus on more than one character at a time, with the result that other characters are out of focus or on the fringe (related also to lack of dramatic confrontation), is disguised by such a narrator, who is presumably in search of what "truth" each character in turn has to give him, and by a deliberate structure which makes single focus compatible. At the same time, the author's *forte* of rendering a single sensibility at a time is effectively emphasized.

The prose descriptions in some passages are, as in *The Apple of the Eye,* a substitute for the rendering of emotion. Often it is for purposes of establishing a tone with which the character's mood is in accord. But there is a significant difference. With Alwyn as narrator recalling and recreating the character and his world, there is no longer the disparity between the language and tone of the description and that of which the character would be capable.

As for the problem of distance: it was observed in *The Apple of the Eye* that although the omniscient narrator shifted *focus* on his material, including characters, his distance remained steady, relatively far above and outside his characters, even when rendering the subjective states of Dan, Mike, and Rosalia. The same is found to be true in *The Grandmothers*. The great difference is that such steady distance, allied with other inadequacies of the narrator and prose, contributed to numerous flaws in the first novel. In *The Grandmothers,* such distance is quite justified and qualified by the characteristics of the narrator-character, who although all-powerful, must recreate from mem-

ory and imagination, which seems to necessitate a certain distance. He is relating events after they occurred, from another
point in place and time. In addition, thus removed he can as
well include his own comments, feelings, and thoughts at those
moments in the past, then make new comments on them from
the fictional present. He can judge not only the other characters,
but the earlier Alwyn as he now sees him. The distance is appropriate — so much so that it seems necessary — to the form and
theme of the novel.

Wescott still fails to render often the actual thought and
emotion of his characters and is given to aphorism, paradoxical
statement, image and metaphor, exposition, and summary — all
about such feeling and thought. But the emotional *forte*, the
spellbinding quality of the prose and the narrative voice, partly
because of the vast aesthetic improvement of other elements and
the superiority of the mind that it reveals in this second novel,
and with the aid of a consistently effective nostalgic tone, is
more spellbinding, more powerful than ever. Critics have again
and again emphasized the lyric quality of the prose and narrator, attributing it to the predominant theme of the self, or
even more often to the imagistic quality of the language, and
and finding its source sometimes in the emotion of the narrator. True, Wescott is still a "lyrical creator of moods."
But once one is aware of this, it seems just as useful and
accurate, especially considering *The Grandmothers* and the mature work, to define an equally significant quality as rhetoric.
For image, metaphor, and especially aphorism and generality
are at the service of a narrative voice, rhetorical in tone and
function, concerned with investigating, capturing, communicating, and even persuading the reader not only of the actuality
and the importance of the fictional events, but with *truths,* with
abstractly stated concepts.

There are, in other words, with the advent of *The Grandmothers,* clearly two qualities of Wescott's prose (if we may
lump characteristics around two terms) and his narrative strategy,
both capable of spellbinding: the *lyrical,* with its imagistic,
symbol-making, mood-creating quality, and the *rhetorical,* that
of the ruminating, investigating, clarifying mind adept at aphorism, epigram, and organization of generality and abstraction.
Both of these qualities were incipient in the first novel, the lyric
quality particularly well-developed. But not until *The Grand-*

mothers, with the development of the narrative voice in control of the character in third-person, does Wescott find a technique so suited to his subject and artistic intentions.

In *The Apple of the Eye* the author's vision, identified with the omniscient narrator, made itself felt nearly as a personality, but one that, as Ruth Suckow put it, was "too personal," and "unrelated" because of too much distance. In *The Grandmothers* due to the development of a successful narrator and consequently a proper form, not only are a number of weaknesses of technique nullified or overcome, but the new narrator, a proper vehicle for that vision, is also felt as a personality. But of course he *is* a personality, a character in the novel, and his vision will necessarily be personal. His "unrelated" quality either thus disappears or makes itself felt as the proper aesthetic distance the narrator needs to perform his function.

There is no longer the disparity between the narrator and other elements of the novel. Rather than the narrator's qualities being at the expense of "intellectual demands," it is the primary means of satisfying them. Wescott's moral vision, his insight into the complexity of individuals has developed greatly too. Unquestionably, part of this difference, at least, is due to a narrator who is no longer separated from other elements in the novel, but is the very dynamic principle on which its form relies.

Thus, three years after the publication of his first novel, at the age of twenty-six, Wescott seems to have overcome most of his fundamental artistic problems by the development of a complex narrator, with the result that *The Grandmothers* is a novel of significance and artistic achievement.

Not that Wescott has now become the flawless novelist. Certain shortcomings and limitations remain, discernable under the surface of *The Grandmothers.* He still has a weakness for the didactic, related intimately to his curious concept of the dichotomy of *images* and *truth,* mentioned earlier, and his insistence on separating the two is evident in both novels. In each, near the end of the book, the protagonists extract *truths* from the images of which the rest of the novel consists. In *The Apple of the Eye* the result alone would be enough to make the novel a failure. In *The Grandmothers,* however, such a method is intrinsic to the very subject and form. The danger is that Wescott takes the concept as therefore valid in principle, rather than appropriate for that particular work.

There is, in *The Grandmothers,* still evident a profusion of generalities. Although many of these are the very stuff of the novel, there is still an excess. First, they are deadening and inert when given in long, sustained passages of exposition. Second, they often enough have little basis in events or even concrete details anywhere else in the book. Both of these faults are apparent in the passage on "The Religious Faith of the Family" and parts of the concluding chapter. The fact that they are the result of Alwyn's cogitation will not remove the curse.

When, in addition to the above, one considers that certain of the artistic ineptitudes, shortcomings, and flaws in technique were not so much met head on and overcome by practice as they were circumnavigated, avoided, or camouflaged by the adoption of Alwyn as narrator and the particular form (inadequate dialogue made unobtrusive, the fondness for the truncated scene, a heavy reliance on exposition and summary narrative, a minimum of dramatic scenes and character confrontation which with the habit of focusing on one character at a time blurs characterization), one is almost convinced that rather than developing other important techniques which would give him greater flexibility, he has used the new narrator to make virtues of some of his artistic vices. One must not ignore the solid achievement of *The Grandmothers,* however, how superior it is in many ways to the first novel, and how in its own right it is among the best novels of its time. But it is necessary to call attention to difficulties that might otherwise be overlooked, those which provide a basis for recognizing the causes of further achievements and failures.

4

GOOD-BYE, WISCONSIN; THE BABE'S BED; AND OTHER STORIES

Good-Bye, Wisconsin, which appeared in 1928, one year after *The Grandmothers,* contains the title essay and ten short stories, written for the most part between 1924 and 1927.[1] If, as Kahn states, the stories were "lyrical and impressionistic dramatizations of the explicit reactions and grievances which appear in the lead essay," and "illustrate the reasons he (Wescott) cannot stay in Wisconsin," they would be simply regional works. Rueckert is more accurate in pointing out that though "all the stories are set in Wisconsin and are bound to the region by virtue of the details of the physical scene, only a few are regional in the usual sense of the word; most of them could have taken place anywhere in the Midwest or in any rural community; and some of them could have occurred anywhere." Three of the stories are regional in that they have as their material the lives of "uneducated farm people," "treated as representative types of the region." These three, "The Runaways," "Prohibition," and "The Sailor," are regional portraits in the same sense that "Bad Han" is. But both "The Runaways" and "The Sailor" are concerned with flight from the past and expatriation and can thematically be grouped with another story, "The Whistling Swan."[2]

In "The Runaways," Amelia Fox, who does most of the work on the failing, hopeless farm of her drunken father and lazy complaining mother, is released from a life of complete drudgery by the death of both parents. Unattractive, ignorant, slow of mind, she marries her male counterpart, Nick Richter. They set the old farmhouse on fire for the insurance money (so ineptly that they have no chance of collecting) and leave for the city, where, fascinated by two women they meet from a carnival, they join what to them is the glamorous troupe; years later they are still with them.

For Nick, the barker at the "Gay Paree" show, "the carnival had not been his salvation." And Amelia, the show's ticket-taker, now wrapped in layers of fat, is "soothed by movement, and noise, gorged with excitement...satisfied." Both, however, have "learned that rómance is for those who see, never for those who do, and underpaid as a profession."

"The Runaways" is one of the lesser stories in the book. As for its being representative, it cannot be considered a straight piece of regionalism; none of these stories can. Although the symbology is often trite, and what seems to be the point—a moral one—is hammered home, some of the smaller symbolic details, so grotesque, are superb in their implication of moral vacuity and decay, and there is a constant unifying tone. Kahn says that the story "implies a criticism of expatriatism," but it is rather of expatriatism-for-the-wrong-reasons. The "Gay Paree" show is not "the reduced shabby symbol of Paris itself." It is a symbol of the debased romantic concept of Paris in the minds of such as Amelia and Nick. It is not so much a "warning to artists, adventurers, and dreamers who would take flight," as a parable of pseudo-artists, unimaginative adventurers and dreamers of the tawdry dream. The stupidity and naiveté of Nick and Amelia are different in degree only from the failure of wisdom in the much more intelligent who believe salvation can be found in erasing the past and seeking valueless excitement. The contrary example is, of course, Alwyn Tower of *The Grandmothers*.

Terrie Riley, the protagonist of "The Sailor," another ignorant semi-literate, also attempts to escape hopelessly depressing surroundings. But Terrie, who joins the Navy and spends some time ashore on the French Mediterranean at Villefranche, learns something different about life. Returned temporarily to Wisconsin after his hitch, he attempts to communicate what he has learned to his brother, Young Riley.

His formless accounts are entirely concerned with his drinking bouts and adventures with prostitutes in Villefranche. His vocabulary is pitifully inadequate; abstractions and generalities are beyond him. Yet in the supposedly formless pattern of his main adventure he senses a wisdom that for the most part eludes his grasp — hence the ironic symbol of the tattooed letters on the back of his fingers spelling out "Hold Fast." He tells of Zizi, the prostitute he asked to marry him, of his discovery of her involvement with the lesbian Minette, and the consequent complications of their triangular relationship. Feeling emotions he never felt before he, "thus, bit by bit, had become civilized, like a foreigner." As he performs his chores on the farm, Terrie's brother, Young Riley, listens and understands nothing: to him it is only a tale showing his brother's failing for liquor and wild women; he, himself, is one indication that such complexities in sex, passion, love, and hence the emotions that go with them cannot occur in Wisconsin, and, supposedly, America. Although he has had enough of women and drink, Terrie feels a "thirst...he would have to quench." He is "lonesome for temptation and regret, for sharp contrasts, for distinct good and evil — in other words, for Europe — but at the same time hated these things from the bottom of his heart because they had made a fool of him." The story rises above being a regional portrait to successfully explore the themes of love and expatriatism in an imaginatively compelling way.

"The Whistling Swan" does not deal with rural regional types, but in its themes of expatriatism and love and their relation to the region, it is like "The Sailor." The expatriate, Hubert Redd, is an artist, a composer, and in further contrast to Terrie Riley he is literate, educated, sophisticated and fully aware of the pros and cons of life in Europe and America. He has been called home after several years in Europe by his wealthy patrons who have subsidized him, but who withdraw their support because they disapprove of his morals and feel he isn't a satisfying enough bet in the talent lottery. In his small Wisconsin hometown he tries to decide whether to return to Europe or to marry his childhood sweetheart, who ceaselessly and uncritically praises him, and settle down to a teaching job in Wisconsin. His sweetheart is the actuality to whom he has addressed his letters of romantic idealism; his return has revealed to him the faults of his work and the limitations, he thinks, of his talent. Kenneth Burke perceptively summarizes the climax and comments on the method:

While walking in the woods, with a gun and his indecision, he comes upon a swan, which startles him and
which he shoots almost before thinking. Indecision van-
ishes. He will remain. In the shooting of the bird, felled
in a flutter of expert prose, he slays a portion of himself, that portion which was drawing him to Paris.
Wescott suggests — we are at liberty to complete the
psychology. An aspect of the hero's self is externalized,
and he slays it. The event may be taken, not as the
cause of his reversal, but as a paralleling of it. That
which occurs within, by dark and devious channels of
decision, he duplicates without as the destruction of the
swan. Following the symbolic elimination he is prepared
to remain, to marry and let our gentle girl become in-
dispensable to him.[3]

It is not simply the death of the swan that has such importance, but its death cries, which Redd can hear although he
cannot see the bird:

There was a terrific splashing. Then it screamed. He
had thought they were dumb, all the swans, he had
thought they were dumb. The scream went on and
changed and did not stop. In despair at dying, it
whistled, whistled, and took its breath. Broken open, a
heavy stream of music let out — but it was the opposite
of music. Now husky, now crude, what were like clots
of purity often, the rhythm of something torn. Greater
beating of the wings, greater agony of the splashes,
whipping, kicking. He was being made to hear what it
would have been insufferable to see.
    Hubert squatted on the wet shore and began to cry,
but stopped because the sound of his voice was ludicrous. He did not want to see what was left of the
swan. It was mere fright that had made him kill it, but
if he had not been frightened he would not have heard
its cries. He felt a sick satisfaction, definite jealousy of
the dead bird, an extreme feebleness, a great haste.

There is ambiguity in the ending, for although Redd's decision
is to stay in Wisconsin, the death of his expatriate urges have
brought about an inner demand to rise above Wisconsin in the
creation of ideal music or to remain dumb. But the swan's
death song makes the whole ending ambiguous. Was Redd's
sobbing in the woods the death song of his own creativeness?

Apparently all written before 1928, the stories in *Good-Bye, Wisconsin* deal with much the same material and themes and are similar in technique to what is found in the first two novels. The two major themes continue to be love and the self. Expatriatism, one of Wescott's major themes, is, of course, a special variation of the theme of the self. The three stories that deal with it, when combined with statements in the essay, present, Kahn says

> Wescott's fullest statement on the problem of expatriation. The theme appears in both the earliest and the latest stories Wescott wrote during the twenties (also "The Runaways" appears first in the collection and "The Whistling Swan" last) and indicates the importance of this idea in stimulating Wescott's imagination. As we have seen, the problem has no easy solution — actually no solution at all. The rewards of flight and life abroad are ambiguous and dubious. Disillusionment replaces innocence; new appetites stimulate new hungers. Whether one is a Redd or Riley, there is no resolution, merely an exchange of values that are apt to leave one more restless than before — or nomads, like Amelia and Nick. And the individual decision, if we are to judge by these examples, is not arrived at wisely, judiciously, but through circumstances, moods, and obscure collisions of ideas and reactions in the back of one's mind. In any event, the blessings of expatriatism are mixed, the damnation subtle and diabolical.

The difficulty is that generalizing about "the problem" often is at the cost of the specific insights of the individual stories. Any statement about the theme in general in Wescott's work cannot ignore the expatriate-narrator of *The Grandmothers,* Alwyn Tower, and the expatriate stories here cannot be taken as the "fullest statement" of this aspect of Wescott's theme of the self. It is through Alwyn Tower's expatriatism, his back-trailing, that he is able to achieve the necessary distance to judge his heritage and find the self. His is not "a Redd or a Riley," or "like Amelia or Nick," and he is the only really successful expatriate, the only one who could find the self through expatriatism alone. Although Amelia and Nick "expatriate" in the unconscious urge to find the self, they fail because they are capable of nothing but a tawdry dream. Terrie

Riley is superior to them in discovering that life is complex (and painful and pleasurable); and although he is not capable of enough insight to grasp his ambivalent feeling toward Europe (life), or do anything except try to quench his thirst for it, he is alive. To say that "merely an exchange of values" is involved is inadequate. As for Redd, there is the ambiguity of the ending and more important, the event of the slaying of the swan does, as Burke says, parallel the slaying of a portion of himself. Burke does not go on to say what the portion is, but it is obviously that portion capable of "taking flight," and capable of at least one song at death. It is out of "mere fright" that he kills it. Alwyn Tower and Hubert Redd are the only two expatriates who are artists and are the most pertinent to Wescott and his career. Alwyn Tower, the author's second self in *The Grandmothers,* is for Wescott the path taken, and Hubert Redd, so similar in background and sensibility, the path not taken, his eventual destiny remaining ambiguous.

It should be emphasized that both "The Sailor" and "The Whistling Swan" combine expatriatism and love as themes: in the first the two themes are of parallel importance; in the second, love is subordinate as a theme to expatriatism and the self. "The Sailor" is really the better story, although "The Whistling Swan" is concerned with the artist, with a mature and intelligent protagonist, and makes use, as will be considered later, of Wescott's favorite technique of narration.

Old Riley, the central character of "Prohibition," is, like the fathers of Bad Han and Amelia Fox, a drunkard, with the characteristics of the village drunk of small-town fiction. Riley is not melancholy, dangerous, nor frustrated, nor is he the crushed idealist. It is simply that sober he finds life dull. "Alcohol saved him from the mediocrity of the world." His drunkenness is "injurious to others," because it "furnished the community with a token of its inner desperation." He leads his two sons, Young Riley and Terrie Riley (whose later life is depicted in "The Sailor") to follow him in drink and carefree revelry— until his vice leads one winter to the freezing and amputation of both hands and feet, after which he leads a happy existence in his bed, drinking through a straw the whisky with which his wife provides him. His fate sobers everyone else, however. For the first time, his wife stirs from her sloth as Young Riley stops drinking to work hard at making the farm a paying thing, and

Terrie is allowed to join the Navy. The prosperity of the farm turns the Riley daughter's boy friend into a suitor and husband. Everyone, including Old Riley himself, is much happier than before.

This is the only piece written by Wescott that is comic in tone: "The Runaways," which uses a similar kind of grotesque detail, is merely sad. It is the monotony, the sobriety and lack of humor of a prohibitive society that is obliquely criticized here. It drives the older brother and Terrie, particularly, to drink, for drink makes the world "bright and distorted," and it is this that Terrie seeks in other lands: "that shining, deformed appearance even in broad daylight when he was sober." Only after his father's death can Young Riley, not as imaginative, find comfort in the more orderly dullness of hard work. It is only Terrie who seeks. These are three different responses to the Wisconsin wasteland, and the old man's and Terrie's seem more commendable—even though unsatisfactory because of their own human limitations—than Young Riley's plodding industry.

"Adolescence" and "In a Thicket," both concern adolescents, one a boy in the city, the other a girl in the country. The region is entirely unimportant; both are initiation stories, or, more specifically, stories of transition from innocence to experience, concerned with the beginnings of mature sensibility and knowledge. The concentration is on evoking the quality of the experience of the transition, and the means, in "In a Thicket," is through a symbolic texture of light and dark giving a rich and functional quality to the prose.

The thickets in the story are literally those which obscure the world from the cottage in which the fifteen-year-old Lily and her aged grandfather live, and figuratively the thicket of childhood from which Lily is emerging. The grandfather, in contrast to Lily, withdraws from existence, aging, back through innocence. In a half-waking state the previous night Lily had been aware of a prowler. Even after a neighbor woman, with oblique glances at Lily, comes to inform the old man that a Negro convict has escaped the previous night from the nearby prison, Lily tells her grandfather nothing, but waits in the dark for the prowler's approach that night with a sense that "the unknown, the difficult, the hypnotic, were likely to be revealed at any moment." When she hears the noises indicating his presence, she is, in a compound of terror and hope, drawn, yet transfixed in a spellbound state, toward the mysterious force beyond the screen door. She stops short of it, listening to the sounds suggesting violence and sensuality, and at last sees the prowler, his blackness glimmering in the moonlight: then the two remain poised opposite each other, momentarily transfixed. Finally he walks away, and Lily wakes the next day aware of "clots of color and vortices of movement she had never seen," to find a three inch gash in the screen door. Underneath every detail of the event lies sexuality — the symbolic black man (who has committed a crime of violence), the symbolic white girl, and perhaps too obviously, the gash in the screen door. The qualities of mystery and of darkness, and the elusive rhythm of sexuality, passion and love as the bio-psychological center of life are convincing because all is rendered as the experience from innocence to knowledge.

In "Adolescence," sensitive and effeminate thirteen-year-old country-boy Phillip is taken to a masquerade party by fifteen-year-old brash, dominant and ordinary city-boy Carl, in the costume of a girl provided by Carl's female cousins. The masquerade and costume as a disguise are metaphors for the experience of youth, which is puzzling and painful and colored by sexuality. Carl enjoys in Phillip "qualities he would later enjoy in women;" and Carl is to Phillip the possible future self. Uncomfortable and isolated as a "strange girl," insecure and afraid of his coming maturity, but excited by the games and the clumsy pairing off, Phillip's disguise and still-feminine-like qualities attract a clumsy approach and kiss from another boy; no one but Phillip himself discovers his real identity, for the disguise of pre-adolescence for him is torn away, and soon there would be "no more disguises, nor need to be taken care of, nor harm in being neglected." He is no longer, he feels, an imitation girl, although he has fears his masculinity may not be sufficient. On the way home he plans his first venture into the masculine world of the pool hall; and afterwards his landlady's "Who's that?" as he goes to his room signifies his transitional stage. Although well-conceived, the story is uninteresting. Although Phillip's feeling and thought are communicated he comes through as a kind of dull Penrod; his excitement seems academic, and his conception of himself is mundane.

In "Like a Lover," the hypnotic, spellbinding quality of love, and the relationship of love and death, become the central issue.

The isolated, bewitched girl again appears, as the nineteen-year-old Alice Murray, who is fascinated by a much older man named Hurst. He is uncommunicative and ominous and possesses strange yellow eyes. Defying her mother's frantic prohibitions she marries him and goes to live on his farm, where the atmosphere becomes for her electric with fear. Awake or sleeping she is surrounded by clubs, whips and sharp instruments. Her fear reaches its culmination in an unrevealed incident that drives her, trembling, back to her mother, where she stays for seven years in another spell of isolation until she learns that Hurst is to marry again. Shaken awake, she tries to warn the woman, a widow named Mrs. Clayburn, that Hurst will kill her. Mrs. Clayburn at last believes her, but reveals that she is "powerless" and "paralyzed;" she does marry Hurst. After two months of nightmares foreshadowing the woman's death, Alice one day sees her friend Mary Clifford coming down the road from the Hurst farm. She is nearly standing in her buggy, frantically whipping her lame mare to desperate speed; Alice faints away and falls "backward on the porch."

No one of the stories in this collection is more successful aesthetically, for here form and theme, as they should, fuse, and the theme far transcends any regional setting or detail. In one aspect it is a terror story, and thematically it is about love. Technically it is a symbolic narrative. By a kind of narrative incremental repetition — the changed significant detail being the actual death of Mrs. Clayburn — the same predestined story of love is given twice; as narrative technique it helps to establish a tone of terror, to structure anxiety, suspense, and dénouement; thematically the pattern repeated implies its universal validity and establishes its quality of predestination.

As for the love theme, Rueckert has this to say:

> Love, as the story attempts to make clear, destroys all theories, renders knowledge useless and the will powerless; it is deeply, essentially irrational, a kind of madness; it is more powerful than any parental authority; it is fatalistic, cruel, and leads to self-sacrifice. In this story it is everywhere associated with death...with masochism on the part of the women, with sadism on the part of Hurst, and, in the titlephrase, with "God (who is) like a lover, waiting, stepping out of the hazel-bushes in the dark, opening his arms..."

Rueckert sees, quite correctly, the idea of love in this story as identical with the western, Romantic concept of love with its "religious linkages and the love-death association," as traced in history and explained by C. S. Lewis, Denis de Rougemont, and Leslie Fiedler, the "central idea" being contained in the simile likening God to a lover, and "by implication Hurst, or any lover, is likened to God, and finally, by implication love is likened to a god..." Love is a passion and a passion is a kind of madness, no matter in what form it may appear, whether as a man, a woman, or a god. The spell of madness means that rational behavior is replaced by released irrational forces, the result being unpredictable; hence Wescott's view of love as a Daemonic force, which it is useless to resist, "always just below the surface waiting to be released, to take over, whip in hand, and to ride man to his frequently unhappy and almost predestined end. One cannot often throw this rider; one usually outlasts him, lets the passion, whatever form it happens to take, run its course, and hopes for the best."[4] The story contains, Rueckert believes, "the central vision" of the collection. It is more accurate to call it one-half of the central vision of the love theme. The other half deals with love in a wider sense and encompasses within it the above concept of love; it is the vision in "A Guilty Woman."

Again making use of the kind of material exploited by yellow journalism (another murder, but the murderer is the protagonist), Wescott's sensibility, understanding, and art turn this too into one of his finest stories.

Evelyn Crowe,[5] now forty-five as the story opens, has been pardoned after serving only six years of her sentence for the murder of her lover, Bill Fisher. She was a chaste, passionless spinster in her late thirties when she was suddenly "in haste to be corrupted" by the faithless Fisher, who, when she pleaded with him to marry her, refused, writing her that he had thought he would "try old maid's love — see what *that* was like." In her passion she shot him and unsuccessfully attempted to take her own life. She has suffered the trial which revealed her private letters, and the aftermath including imprisonment. Like most of Wescott's lovers, she is a victim of passion as madness, and is made a fool of by love.

Martha Colvin, an old friend, has taken Evelyn in to live with her on her Wisconsin farm. For a while she lives a quiet life, feeling gratefully that nothing else can happen to her, seeing no one but Martha and Martha's longtime bachelor friend, Dr. John Bolton. But soon she and Bolton are in love, and Evelyn finds love a "personal, portable hell," a "cruel, brilliant light within herself" by which to examine herself. Her ability to transcend disasters and defeats (like Mary Harris in *The Grandmothers,* Bad Han, and others) is what saves her. Most of Wescott's other heroines who survive disaster, however, do it by a kind of stoicism and mute suffering. Evelyn is more sensitive, complex, and interesting. It is clear that Wisconsin (or small-town America) does everything to prevent this flexibility which opposes rigidity and ossification; and when she was a school-teacher, it demanded that her morality be public and her way of life be self-sufficiency. Self-sufficiency, Evelyn realizes, is another name for pride, her "besetting sin," the socially-engendered armor which prevented her from having an emotional life, from loving, until her affair with Fisher. That and its termination in violence, no matter how costly, have freed her from deadly repressions. The trial, exposure, and imprisonment have humbled her. Rather than crushing her, such experience has humanized her, given her the flexibility that makes it possible to love.

The story is brilliantly brought to a close. Evelyn feels guilty, cruel, humiliated and ashamed that she has won the love of the man that Martha loves. But Martha is wise and honest. Both women, through their final conversation, come to realizations about themselves not possible before. Martha now knows that with her own kind of selfishness she has bored Bolton for years by being too proud to need him; it is another example of the pride that has so crippled Evelyn, but the latter, having had it smashed, is the more complete woman, ready for love, and consequently she finds it, even in the Indian-summer of her life.

Passion first entered the life of Evelyn as a kind of madness, and true to pattern it makes a fool of her — she murders, and she attempts the ultimate foolishness of suicide; but the story goes beyond this, to make it, thematically, the most complex and rewarding of the group. It drives to what is beneath the outburst of passion to reveal the complicated makeup of pride, which is the outward face of repression socially and personally engendered, and a sin preventing love and a full life; pride causes passion, then "madness" which is not love but the pas-

sion of outrage at finding one cheated of love and the self
violated. It goes beyond even this to the paradox that suffering
— the madness, and the aftermath of punishment and humility —
extends, deepens, and releases man for a mature (a-Romantic)
love, another and superior thing to the passion previously
experienced.

Martha and Evelyn are both at the end able to overcome behavior based on the Romantic view of love which exploits pride,
selfishness, and jealousy. "Guilty Woman" and "Like A Lover," two of Wescott's finest stories, offer in emphasis the two
opposed aspects of love, but "A Guilty Woman" juxtaposes the
two, showing a protagonist who transcends Romantic "love as
madness" for mature love.

"The Dove Came Down" and "The Wedding March" are
clearly the most inferior stories in the collection; they can only
be called failures. In dealing with Protestantism the former has
something in common with "Prohibition," but the methods are
contrasting. Character, action, and details are at a minimum.
The concentration is on the introspection of Arthur Hale, who,
having visited Europe and being what he is, finds his feelings
and attitudes attempting to coalesce as he reacts against the
church service to which he has taken his fiancée, Emily, in order
to escape the presence of his family, whom they are visiting.
The only two characters are Arthur and Emily. Arthur is de-
pressed by the "weakness or mere poverty of temperament" of
the congregation, their singing, and the details of the church
interior, such as the memorial windows. During the communion
he contrasts the "Catholic mystery" he has seen at Lourdes with
the "merely symbolical worship in a progressive Protestant
church." One is concerned with the visible, the other the invisible, need, which he feels is not satisfied by religion. Grace,
the dove, ought to come down. He is revolted at the ideal
eating of the body of God, tracing it in his mind from primitive
rituals to what seems today simply a remnant. He refuses the
sacrament. Emily admires him for it, although her needs, experience, and attitude are in contrast; an orphan, converted by
a revival as a child, she is still subject to fears and mysteries.
In the spiritual realm, Arthur concludes, "however much love
can do, no two humans can agree."

Except for Emily's dialogue, and Arthur's, we are given only
the thoughts about and reaction to Protestantism by Arthur.

These seem bloodless, passionless, as though Arthur himself were incapable of real interest in them, and lead nowhere. His relationship to Emily lacks interest or verisimilitude, and her long speeches, in the last part of the story, are unbelievable, inert exposition.

The symbol of the dove, a revolving symbol, is the central thing that holds, or tries to hold, the story together, and will be commented upon later.

"The Wedding March" is another story concerned with love, but inferior to the others. Hugo Randolph, a bachelor of thirty-four or five, waits in the church for his bride, and during the actual ceremony, he recalls what he thinks of as his first wedding, his initiation into sexual passion by an older woman, the wife of his employer, when he was a nineteen-year-old farm hand. His mind shuttles back and forth from present to past, but most of the story concerns the early affair, the scenes and thoughts of what he as a boy took for love. For a long time he felt dead after the woman broke off the affair to join her husband whom she loved. While he waits for his bride, the ceremony works on his mind "like some rite of more specific magic," and "raises from the dead...love." The juxtaposition of the two "weddings" has produced certain realizations as well, given in a summing up of *truths* about passion, passion as an intoxicant, overlapping passions, pleasureless love as destiny, and the relationship of love and death. The love-death theme is one of the two that is developed with some clarity, the bells that awaken the protagonist that day taking on both connotations; the recognition of the death of the old love and the rebirth from it of the new, the wedding as an "easter," and the church metaphorically evoked as a tomb that signifies the death and rebirth of love are all parts of the development.

The other important theme deals with memory and its powers: concerning the past affair it makes that "idyll like another... mightier in retrospect than while it had taken place; so much more fleeting are all actions, so much more evanescent the body, than illusions and the mind." The other themes that Hugo's memories suggest remain in the chaotic and underdeveloped form as mere temporary half-hearted theorizing on his part. As a character, Hugo remains a kind of means for speculations attributed to a name. And there is no difference in language, no shift of any kind, from the omniscient commentary on him to his thoughts. The first woman remains obscure behind the language and abstractions, and the bride is even less real to Hugo and the reader alike: "A certain amount of white and green foam," an effect that sharply contradicts the death-rebirth theme, for Hugo seems spellbound by the past. The "meaning" or *truths,* in what is a familiar bad habit of Wescott's, are condensed and jammed into the final summing up of his thoughts. And although the action is in the present, as man and wife leave the church, the present comes to an end simultaneously with the end of the evocation of the past. But the present action has been dim and seems of little interest, in spite of what we are told, even to Hugo himself.

Characters

Of course characters in the short story are not expected to equal those of the novel in depth, complexity, and import, but, as in his novels, Wescott ranges all the way from failure to almost unqualified success in characterization. "The Runaways," and "Prohibition," although not among his best stories, have characters that are at least clear-cut. Of course they are treated at some distance, with an irony that, unusual in Wescott, becomes satiric grotesque, and at certain points in "Prohibition" becomes humor.

"In a Thicket" and "Like a Lover," both superior stories, depend on a close attention to, and especially in the former, an impressionistic rendering of, the sensibility of the protagonists. Such characterization when it succeeds as well as it does in these stories results in a closer fusion with other elements in the story.

It is difficult to say why Phillip in "Adolescence" is so uninteresting, why his excitement is not exciting. Phillip is another character of sensibility, and distance and point of view, discussed later, have something to do with it. Although he has something in common with Arthur Hale and Hugo Randolph he is not as much of a failure in characterization as they. All three of them have a certain energyless morose petulance even when they are in the emotional heights or depths. Hugo, of "The Wedding March," Kahn calls "a grey, bloodless thought machine." He is a disorganized one at that; and the themes he mulls over are never drawn together into any cohesion. Wescott is more concerned with ideas here than rendering them into fiction. "The Dove Came Down" is very similar in this respect, the attitude of Arthur Hale toward Protestantism and the Midwest being confused and leading nowhere as he speculates with a kind of fatigued discontent. In "The Dove Came Down," "The Wedding March," and "The Whistling Swan" (particularly in the first two), it is completely unbelievable that the men have any sentiment or even sexual itch for their fiancees whatsoever; this strengthens the contention that the stories are incomplete attempts to use fiction as a device to clarify a melange of ideas.

In "The Sailors," Terrie Riley is seen from some distance and the omniscient narrator interprets his sensibility, but Terrie comes through with clarity and even sympathy, in spite of his being semi-literate, coarse, and with nothing of the alleged fine sensibility of those discussed above. This very distance and the contrast between what the omniscient narrator (and hence the reader) perceives, and what Terrie does, dramatizes his attempt to understand. Even the minor characters emerge with more clarity and interest than the protagonists of "Dove," and "Wedding."

As a character, Evelyn Crowe of "The Guilty Woman" is the most interesting and the most complex — the most successfully rendered of all. This success is intrinsic to that of the whole story. It is not sensational violence that is the means. Wescott wisely de-emphasizes such. The story, with Evelyn's mind, follows through several steps to fresh insight and perception of human behavior that transcends the cliche or the melancholy dead-end. Her guilt and fears, her tears, shame, and humility — all are means to a fuller life and an understanding of it. Such realization she comes to is not achieved by pure speculation or academic thinking, but speculation under pressure, the pressure of finding oneself in love again.

As for the shortcomings that appear in Wescott's first novel and sometimes in his second, particularly lack of dramatization, scenic confrontation, and adequate dialogue, they are again evident, most often in the unsuccessful stories. "The Dove Came Down" and "The Wedding March" have almost no dramatization or scenic confrontation and since characterization is negligible, the entire weight of the performance rests on narration. The dialogue, when least satisfactory, lacks verisimilitude or conviction in this volume. In "The Dove Came Down" it is held to a very few lines — with the exception of an incredibly long speech — and in "The Wedding March" there is none at all, as though an attempt had been made to find a way around dialogue altogether. "Prohibition" and "The Runaways" contain the only attempts to render Wisconsin speech, but only in a few lines. The sparse dialogue in "The Sailor" is plausible idiom, but as is so often the case in these stories, the dialogue does little that has not already been done in some other way.

Symbolism

Wescott's technique of symbology and symbolic texture is nothing different from what he has done in his first two novels, although there is a variation in frequency, quality, and other factors, depending on the story. A single symbol is often at the very center of the story, whether it be a dove, a swan, or a gashed screen door. The bird continues to be Wescott's favorite symbol, appearing rarely in the other stories in minor ways, but figuring prominently in "The Dove Came Down," and "The Whistling Swan." Flora and fauna are used for symbolic atmosphere in some stories, particularly in "The Runaways" (the marsh), "The Thicket," and "Like a Lover." Sometimes, as in "The Dove Came Down," "The Wedding March," and to an extent in "The Whistling Swan," when other elements in the story are weak, the symbols are left to carry most of the meaning and are inadequately conceived or presented. In "The Dove Came Down," the bird is not only central but is used as a revolving symbol, for it has different aspects of meaning to the protagonist as the story proceeds: the "miracle of healing" which the sick demand at Lourdes, the Holy Spirit at Pentecost as it is presented in the conventional sense in religious paintings — but of deeper meaning, divine Grace, to Arthur — and at last a kind of Grace by means of its association with sunshine. Such technique, of course, is not enough to make a story, and the same can be said of the use of the wedding to attempt to bring off the theme of death and rebirth in "The Wedding March."

A case can be made that the swan's appearance in "The Whistling Swan" near the end of the story is a kind of "rigged" symbolism. No preparation is made for its use by a previous meaningful appearance, even in the character's thought. At the crucial moment it is meant to trigger a stock emotional response to the pitiful death cries of the bird, and to resolve forces in the story that have not been associated with the swan. It is therefore a combination of gimmick, and, since the intended emotional response has not been paid for, sentimentality. Another way of looking at it is that it is an example of the breaking into the literal level of the story what should have remained on the metaphorical or symbolic level, in this case, within the character's mind.

Narration and Structure

In "The Dove Came Down" and "The Wedding March," the narrator has certain qualities of the participating narrator that in *The Grandmothers* is Wescott's great technical discovery. A close look at "The Dove Came Down" reveals that the story is really in control of the omniscient narrator; although we follow the thoughts of the protagonist as he ruminates, the distance in sympathy is great, even evidenced by such phrases as "the thoughtful lover," and "the young man," and what is presented is a thin edge of his mentality. In "The Wedding March" the point-of-view is soon that of the protagonist, the language and development of his thought is better rendered, and the result is the third-person participating narrator; but the rumination is not enough, alone, nor successful in drawing together scene and meaning. "The Whistling Swan," another story to use this narrative method, is more successful despite other flaws. More impressive than any of these is "A Guilty Woman," which uses, with the exception of paragraphs at the beginning and end, a third-person point-of-view that focuses closely on the sensibility of the protagonist, with many of the qualities of the participating narrator in "The Whistling Swan." The trio makes one think that Wescott was experimenting here with the third-person participating narrator, with its attributes of rumination and rhetorical voice, as a technique. Whether written before or after *The Grandmothers,* where the voice is so successfully developed, certain adjustments might have had to be made for the short story form and for the particular piece. His two most successful works, *The Grandmothers* and *The Pilgrim Hawk,* use such a narrator. A degree between these successes and the failures of some of the short stories is *The Babe's Bed,* soon to be discussed. Another point to be made about this narrative voice is that so far it seems to be closely related to the author's second self, the mind of the writer in the story, and that when the narrative voice fails, consequently, everything fails.

In "The Wedding March," and "The Dove Came Down" the protagonist is placed in a specific situation and is almost immobile in location (the wedding in a church, the service in a church). Because of the situation, the character ruminates, bringing in experiences of time-past. There is, therefore, at one level his interior monologue dealing with past action, at another there is whatever action takes place externally in time-present, and at another are the symbolism and the generalities developed by the character's rumination and memory. This is, of course, in concept basically the method used in *The Grandmothers.* The events in time-present are few, and in the stories the concentration is on the monologue. One difference between "The Whistling Swan" and the other stories is that in it events taking place in time-present are more fully developed; another is that the swan is externalized rather than developing in the monologue. Although the use of the narrator in *The Grandmothers* is similar in concept to these stories in the novel, each series of incidents in time-past is well developed in concrete terms, and is more likely to carry its own weight of meaning in the development of a biographical portrait. Another difference is that although it is of utmost importance what everything means to the narrator Alwyn Tower, his position in time and place gives him more distance. The protagonists in the three stories, although they may consider the past from the present, are in a present situation in which whatever is gleaned from the meditation seems to ask for some kind of immediate application. Of course, a most important characteristic associated with the use of such a narrator, whether successful or not, is the emphasis it places on certain qualities of Wescott's prose — generalities, aphorisms, epigrams, and rhetorical voice.

"The Runaways" and "Prohibition" are at the other pole in technique. As with Wescott's first novel, the point-of-view is omniscient and the anonymous narrator makes himself felt through voice. They are narratives in straight chronological order. The prose has less involution, lyricism and less rhetoric than in the stories just discussed, and there is some dialect of the region.

"Like a Lover" is a symbolic narrative, the level of meaning and the level of action fusing for artistic success. "In a Thicket," also successful, is the same kind of story technically. "Adolescence" attempts to be in this category too, the girl's disguise and role being the state from which the protagonist emerges. All of them use an omniscient narrator who is sympathetic to the protagonist's subjective experience and capable of rendering it.

The resemblance in structure of "The Sailor" to *The Grandmothers* is of minor importance, a reversal of the protagonist's position, Terrie Riley viewing Europe from the distance of Wisconsin in an attempt to understand it. More important, he does not do the actual narration, although he tells his brother of his adventures. The omniscient narrative voice takes over the function in relating his adventures to the reader, even informing him that there are some things that Terrie didn't tell his brother; in fact we are informed that he is "inexpressive" and that his ideas are lacking in "virility." The distance, therefore, between the character and the voice is very great. One wonders if this very good story could not have been a very fine one if it had been possible to render it through the language of Terrie. The structure is consistent with the theme, depending on the contrast between Wisconsin and France.

"The Guilty Woman" doesn't fall easily into any of the groups technically, though it does resemble closely the three "ruminating" stories in that the protagonist in a specific situation in time-present ruminates on time-past. Present events are much more developed, dramatically functional and important, but so are events in time-past in that they are not ephemeral or elusive. Unlike the other three stories, action at both levels successfully leads to clarification of theme, insight, and development of character.

It is evident in his short stories that Wescott experimented with different forms, especially in structure and point-of-view and narration, with varying degrees of success, only four of them ("The Sailor," "Like a Lover," "In a Thicket," and "The Guilty Woman") without major flaws.

Yet he was to write only six more stories over a period of a dozen years.

The essay "Good-Bye, Wisconsin," written after Wescott had spent three years abroad,[6] was first published in the New York *Herald Tribune*[7] when the author was at the peak of his career after the publication of *The Grandmothers*. It appeared again as a kind of preface and the title work of his only collection of short stories. For some reason, perhaps because of its wide circulation, and the directness of its rejection of Wisconsin, it was the recipient of more critical comments than anything else by Wescott, except, of course, *The Grandmothers*.[8] Wescott, even though writing an essay, does not discard whatever fictional techniques he feels are useful. Like the protagonists of "The Sailor," "The Whistling Swan," and "The Babe's Bed," Wescott himself in the essay is returning from Europe to Wisconsin. Like those stories too, the essay is organized by contrasting America and the Midwest to Europe, and also by Wescott's approach to an arrival in Kewaskum, Wisconsin, his hometown, his visit there, and his departure. It is not organized in terms of argument; in this respect it is haphazard, Wescott commenting on whatever he feels or thinks concerning everything he observes, his comments being the evaluations which lead him again to depart.

A large part of what contributes to Wisconsin's deficiency for Wescott is identical in essence to what his work has indicated before, allowing for some change in time. In many ways it is another rendition of the myth as discussed in chapter 3. Wisconsin is portrayed as a cultural wasteland, materialistic, drab and depressing, provincial, isolated, unimaginative, repressively "Puritan," a milieu in which artistic talent is stifled, a conforming world in which his own brother asks him not to wear his beret on the street. Both he and Wisconsin have changed, Wescott finds. His attitude is ambivalent toward a "progress" which has ended the deprivation but also the poetry of the older life; it is not the "home" he left—and not the one he wrote about. In the town Wescott meets only group-consciousness, and in the fraternity house, the incubation of what we now call the Organization Man. To him the Middle West is an "abstract nowhere," "out of focus, amorphous, a mystery," and he concludes that "there is no Middle West. It is a certain climate, a certain landscape; and beyond that, a state of mind of people born where they do not like to live." But this does not give an idea of the innumerable subjects upon which the author touches at least briefly, all related in some way to American culture. Concluding that America is "still a land of perennial disappointments" Wescott departs again for Europe.

The essay is not a piece of objective social analysis, but an attack, which presents in terms of his personal vision the reasons why Wescott finds the Middle West and America a place that in countless ways prevents the development of the self. Aspects of the same vision appear in "The Sailor," and "The Whistling Swan," but they are responsible to the aesthetic logic of the stories. The attack in the essay consists of one cleverly phrased generality after another, "the truth of which," as Rueckert so aptly remarks, "a man could not know with any certainty even after half a lifetime of study," although, one might add, so typically broad and dogmatic are they that it is impossible to read the essay without a kind of aggressive doubt rising in the mind.

The essay is pontifical, dogmatic, didactic, authoritative, and couched in a tone of nostalgia and lament. The prose style is dominated by aphorism, epigram, and paradoxical statement. In other words, this is the spellbinding narrative voice, the rhetorical voice so highly developed in *The Grandmothers,* which in fiction, after the first novel, has been the voice of the third-person participating narrator. Here first person is used, with no discernible difference in effect. Ruminating, yet persuasive, the voice is concerned with communicating *truth.* Relieved of most of the concerns necessary in fiction, the author indulges in a *tour de force* of the rhetorical voice. There are no symbols here, for instance, in the sense that they are successfully used in fiction; there is only rhetoric *about* symbols. Even the *images* which give rise to the generalities (the *truth*) or serve as examples are, as is so often the case when encompassed by the narrative voice, vague and general. The following is typical; the subject is the billboards on the local motion-picture theater:

> On the brick wall, on the easels on the sidewalk, samples of what it has to offer: the abnormally large and liquid eyes of a beauty; the ridicule and pity of ill-fitting shoes; distant crystal and iron seas; foreign luxury, fashion shows, garden parties with diamonds and swans.

"Large and liquid eyes" is concrete, but the adverb "abnor-

mally" is not, and the noun "beauty" is a general classification
and hence vague. "Ridicule and pity" are abstractions; "foreign
luxury" and "fashion shows" are vague and general. The
example is an illustration of Wescott's strong impulse toward
generality, even when using images, and toward rhetoric, which
in the essay is brilliant and witty. These impulses, it has been
noticed in previous works, can get out of hand in his fiction.
But he has not forgotten, such a short time after *The Grandmothers,* that the narrative voice can be a powerful and effective
instrument. The question still remains at this point whether he
will be able to control it in the best interests of his fiction.

In the last section of the essay, Wescott boards the train and
announces that he "would like to write a book about ideal
people under ideal circumstances," an "indoor book," and he
describes what might be considered characteristics of the novels
of Henry James. In the last paragraph he describes the kind of
style he would like to develop in a book "out of which myself,
with my origins and my prejudices and my Wisconsin, will seem
to have disappeared." He seems then, genuinely to be saying
good-bye to Wisconsin, and trying to say good-bye to what
there is of Wisconsin in himself. But his description of the style
he hopes for is curious:

> For another book I should like to learn to write in a
> style like those gestures (of the signal flags used by
> sailors): without slang, with precise equivalents instead
> of idioms, a style of rapid grace for the eye instead of
> the ear, in accordance with the ebb and flow of sensa-
> tion instead of intellectual habits, and out of which
> myself, with my origins and my prejudices and my Wis-
> consin, will seem to have disappeared.

Certain of these characteristics are strikingly unliterary. Wescott's weakness in dialogue, idiom and slang is likely to make
one suspect his motives, but no doubt this is unjust. The first
half of the paragraph, however, seems to describe the language
of science. The important thing is to notice Wescott's conscious
desire for a style which he will attempt very late in his career,
and to his detriment.

The Babe's Bed, a somewhat long short story of thirty-five
pages, was written in 1929 and published as a book in a limited
edition in Paris in 1930. It is in part a kind of postscript to the
essay, an extra good-bye to Wisconsin, although the people and

the tensions are more of the twenties than those he has treated before in his fiction. Again we have the expatriate protagonist returning to Wisconsin and comparing it with Europe as a means of coming to conclusions about both. Again, the region and the country is found inimical to the development of the self, but that is only one aspect of the story.

The household that the protagonist, a young nameless bachelor, returns to in Wisconsin is that of his family — his father, mother, and grandfather, his younger sister, an older, ill, married sister, her husband and their baby boy. There is, as before, the familiar three-level pattern: present action, the interior monologue of the protagonist about the past, and the symbolism developing within the monologue from the interaction of the present action and the rumination. The tension grows in the depressing heat as antagonisms and affections in the family break the surface. The "babe's bed" in the story, including the babe himself, is again a revolving symbol, with different facets or concepts revealed by it — but all within the mind of the protagonist. Because the babe is in danger of injuring himself at night during his temper tantrums, the protagonist suggests the making of a harness (quickly accomplished) to provide a discipline for the babe and tranquility for the others.

The central drama in the story, as in others like it, is that of the narrator's mind. It undergoes introspection and involution, and the language and manner in which it is rendered is that of the rhetorical narrative voice, ruminating, turning out generalities, producing layers of meaning as the present action works toward the climax of placing the babe in his harness. This event is the dividing point in the story. For up until this moment the protagonist, as rhetorical narrator, has followed the kind of process such narrators always have in Wescott's fiction. However, he has done exactly what the narrator in "The Dove Came Down" and "The Wedding March" did to contribute to the failure of those stories, and what he did in "Good-Bye, Wisconsin" to make us skeptical, and what to a certain degree Alwyn Tower is guilty of in *The Grandmothers*. Whether it is called excessive generalization, rumination inadequate in drawing together other elements in a story, or something else, the point is that the speculations and conclusions, the generalities the protagonist-narrator produces and the symbolic significance he imagines are *inadequately justified by the concrete events and*

details that take place outside of his mind. Wescott before has
either been unaware of this or unable to do anything about it,
but in *The Babe's Bed* he is not only aware of it, he makes the
protagonist aware of it. In fact, this is the very subject of the
story.

The bachelor sees almost everything as symbolical, or attempts
to make whatever he sees into a symbol or a basis for generalizing—but all of his vision of things is in relation to himself.
The inordinate affection of his older sister and himself for each
other is revealed as an (unconsummated) incestuous relationship.
He uses this, and the existence of the baby, and the events
leading to the baby being put in his bed and harness at dinner,
as the springboard for his imaginings (in a metaphor extension
reminiscent of the convoluted incest metaphor in *The Grandmothers*) which become simply grotesque, absurd; and instead
of enlightening the situation and the human relationships, his
imaginings are a distortion of realities (Wescott might call them
pseudo-truths). Consequently he is disoriented in time, his relationship to the present confused. A crisis develops as the baby
screams at being placed in his harness at dinner. Immersed in
his own mental web, the bachelor flies into a rage at a minor
incident that follows. But suddenly he realizes his anger should
be pointed inward, not outward, that he has constructed fantasies through his involution and rumination, and that they bear
the most tenuous relation to the facts, to reality.

The bachelor then reverses his whole mental process, and the
story consequently reverses itself. Although his mental process
still involves involution and analysis, the layers of meaning which
have been built up are now revealed as unfounded, unjustified,
worse than worthless, mere fantasies. The result is that the
bachelor arrives at a certain knowledge of himself. This is the
first thing that he learns—that he is infatuated with himself,
and that his ambiguous talent and obsession is the making of
fantasies. Consequently, part of his existence he sees as taking
place in his mind only, "in an ephemeral western town in
himself." His attitude then is fatalistic toward this "force."
He looks at it fatalistically as Wescott's lovers look at love, and
he calls it various things, including "nature or destiny or god
or anonym. Maniacal worker, mad about its art." It is, he
feels, his destiny:

Soon he would depart again, to his distant ambitions—

the necessary infatuation with himself, the remorse incessantly attendant upon his faults.... Time could not be depended upon to sweep him safely, normally, onward; but would be forever letting him fall back into what was over and done with, and letting him, enfevered by the unwanted past, leap weakly ahead into what was to come.

This destiny is identical to the very disease that Alwyn Tower in *The Grandmothers* considers his "birthright," and which, by the act of creation, he was seeking to, and did, escape.

Now the bachelor sees that the fantasies he produces are in one sense true to himself, but they are not at all true to external reality. His art then, is not something made in imitation of this objective reality (not in other words *images* of *truth*), and therefore, as a statement about reality they have no validity. Now the bachelor knows that art cannot be solely true to the self but must have a valid relationship to life external to him. Therefore, his insight is bound to be shocking. Reality, he sees, is what happened at dinner, and so complex are even the events contributing to it that this reality is impossible to capture "in print."

Throughout the story, the narration is, of course, by the participating narrator. For the first half the voice carries on its usual functions. The second half reveals the falsity of the symbolizing and generalities which are very characteristic of that voice, and layer by layer, it de-symbolizes and de-generalizes. Yet, incurably, and apparently without the awareness of either character or author, one of the greatest faults of this rhetorical narrator, his profuse capacity for generalizations, particularly in a *summing up* at the end of a story, is indulged in here to a degree beyond any aesthetic justification — an ironic, though unintentional, proof of the validity of the narrator's destructive analysis of himself.

What is especially significant about this story is that Wescott, having developed the participating third-person-narrator, capable of lyricism, but especially of rhetoric, and having failed with it in some stories, having utilized it brilliantly in one of his major works, *The Grandmothers,* now apparently is out to destroy his faith in this method and the psychological sources behind it. And, sadly enough, the story, although important to the understanding of Wescott's art, is a poor example of his use of this

method of narration, so abstract, so continually generalizing, so
dry and devoid of vivid language is the prose. The characters
and present events in the story (the "external reality") are inadequately developed and expositorily presented, and elicit almost no interest whatsoever. There are the same general difficulties of "The Dove Came Down" and "The Wedding March."
It is one of Wescott's most inferior works. One can only assume
that the nameless bachelor, since he is beset by the same problems of narrative art as Wescott himself, is, as artist, his dupli-
cate, and that Wescott is determined to give up what was once
his basic artistic method of narration, or even the writing of
fiction itself. He nearly did just that. With the exception of
three short stories, no fiction appeared from him until ten years
later.

The short stories that were published after the collection in
Good-Bye, Wisconsin are few and inferior. Looking at them, one
hardly needs the clue of *The Babe's Bed* to see that Wescott's
difficulties are to an important degree concerned with point-of-
view and narration. There are only five of them: "Hurt Feelings" (1932), "The Sight of Dead Body" (1936), "The Rescuer"
(1936), "Mr. Auerbach in Paris" (1941-42), and "The Frenchman Six Feet Three" (1942).

"Hurt Feelings" is a rewritten portion of an unfinished novel
Wescott stopped working on in 1931.[9] Unlike any long fiction
before this, it has no "regional" qualities, but its material and
the values that energize it are markedly American. Concerning
John Durn, a multimillionaire of the "self-made" American
species who is on his deathbed, the story reveals what Mrs.
Holly Cleaveland, his divorced, middle-aged daughter, discovers
upon investigating his papers; the secret of her father's success
is simply "hurt feelings," the stupendous rage of a petty man
whose gargantuan ego was violated by jealousy (his wife had
once called his business partner a better business man). His
revenge extends not only to his wife and partner but his daughter and her husband. The ironies are obvious—the contrast of
public image and private fortune to the real man. The prose is
not quite as soporific as that of *The Babe's Bed,* but apparently
is of a style Wescott was trying to develop. The result is a dry,
emasculated prose and the expository method. The omniscient
narrator controls all—a retreat in point-of-view to the first
novel. Although we are told that Mrs. Cleaveland gradually

discovers *all* by going through the papers, Wescott does not do
what might make the story interesting — he does not as he had
done so often let the protagonist's mind become the center of
the story, thus making the reader's and the protagonist's discovery one. Instead he relies on an anonymous omniscient
narrator who remains far removed for a great portion of the
story from the thoughts of Mrs. Cleaveland, and who supplies
us with information and subtleties and details neither she, nor
any one person, could possibly know, and in rhetoric she could
not command.

In the last four sections of the story additional revelations of
her father's destruction of her marriage are rather artificially
contrasted with the complimentary remarks of her father's ex-
partner. Finally, Mrs. Cleaveland comes to a great *truth* — that
the really "great" men are those who simply want to live,
those classified as fools or failures. We are led to presume that
she will get her husband back and save the soul of her son —
as soon as her father expires.

The pattern is familiar. The tying up of everything at the end
so that a *truth* or *truths* may be revealed to apply directly to
the life of the protagonist, the present events juxtaposed against
the past. But the symbol-making and the generalizing occur
both in and outside the mind of the protagonist, and in each
case with distance. The story cries for a Jamesian or Conradian
development that follows the adventure of the central intelligence
— with at least a minimum of social action, more than simply
a perusing of old papers — not condensed exposition about the
material that allowed such an adventure to take place. Emasculated prose, unexciting narration, trite characters and complications, a plot whose dependence on suspense is undermined by
revealing the outcome beforehand — these are other important
reasons for the story's lack of distinction.

"The Rescuer" does not jell aesthetically, and in this respect
is as much a failure as "The Dove Came Down" and "The
Wedding March." The omniscient anonymous voice begins the
story, fades half-way into the view of suddenly-introduced re-
porter Martin Herz, then asserts itself again. The first shift
marks the point where the story divides itself into two fragments. The first part concerns three boys burned to death in the
flames of a "haunted house," the rescue of another boy, a
twin, by a mysterious savior, and the twin's death of grief for

his counterpart. The second half is Herz's attempt to extract some *truth* from these events, but rather than anything being resolved, new complications are introduced, then forgotten. The shift and reshift of narration in the story is only the most glaring evidence of a divided mind on the part of the author. In the last half Herz is an illustration of what the bachelor was trying to avoid in *The Babe's Bed,* only he seems less sane. The detail revealed (by an omniscient voice) when he is first introduced — that he committed suicide later — simply undercuts him and his thwarted investigation.

In "The Sight of a Dead Body," there is a reversion of technique, to no advantage. Even the name and some of the characteristics of the main character, Michael Byron, go back to Wescott's first novel. As a farm hand on a New Jersey farm, Byron one afternoon lazily lolls and speculates haphazardly about love and life, and upon rising to investigate a disturbed bull, finds a nude male corpse on a manure pile. The discovery is the only event in the story. The limited third-person-narrator is Mike Byron, but the use of the narrator does not accomplish much except to allow us to experience the disorganized, thin, half-heartedly symbolic movement of Mike's mind. No attempt is made to load the discovery of the body with meaning, except through obvious contrast with the natural surroundings. The event occurs at the end of the very short story. The story is something like a purely imagistic poem in trying to avoid implication. What it amounts to is "fine-writing" and a poor story.

"Mr. Auerbach in Paris," and "The Frenchman Six Foot-Three" are both didactic, the difference, somewhat important, being a matter of degree. Alwyn Tower appears as narrator in both of them, and, as in *The Pilgrim Hawk,* narrates in first person. The message of both stories is similar, the first emphasizing the shortsightedness of those who had pro-German, anti-French attitudes during World War II; they stand as representative of a certain view of life. The second is concerned with viewing the fall of France in personal-cultural terms. The attempt is to make the single tall Frenchman into a symbol of France and her characteristics at that time, but Alwyn limits his abstracting and generalizing so that in the personal and cultural situation the sad, pitiful, and complex qualities are not ignored. Yet the story falls short of its conception. The fact that the narrator speaks in first person seems neither to add nor detract.

There is too much exposition and rhetoric — the measurement of this shortcoming is that characters and their plight barely emerge from being fixed in language.

As in *The Pilgrim Hawk* and several of the stories, there are two levels of time (three counting the present time of narration), the story held together by the thoughts of the narrator who symbolizes and creates rhetoric in a distinctive voice. With plenty of opportunity for it, there are no really well-realized dramatic situations; everything has the tone and the imaginative deficiency of the "true incident," and the prose, although superior to, say, *The Babe's Bed,* achieves only a certain dry elegance; even though expressing personal biases and tastes and judgments, it is curiously lacking in vitality.

5

THE PILGRIM HAWK, A LOVE STORY

Published in a small edition as a book in December, 1940, *The Pilgrim Hawk, A Love Story,* had appeared the year before in two parts in the November and December issues of *Harper's Magazine.* It is one of the better known of Wescott's works, probably due to the fact that it has been twice anthologized, in 1946 and 1954, and was republished in 1966. Although one more novel, *An Apartment in Athens,* appeared five years later, this short novel is one of his two finest achievements (the other being, of course, *The Grandmothers*) and it is the culmination of his career as a fiction writer. It is also the key to understanding the development and termination of that career, and to be fully appreciated it has to be considered in relation to his earlier fiction. This does not mean that it will not stand alone as a complete and meaningful work — one of the most distinguished of its genre.

The events of one afternoon in 1928 or 1929, at the home of his friend Alexandra Henry, are related by Alwyn Tower in first person as he looks back on them from America in 1940. He is in a situation geographically the reverse of that in *The Grandmothers,* but essentially the narrative position is similar, for although Tower is now commenting on events that took place in Europe when he was an expatriate, he is, as in the earlier novel, commenting from time-present on events that took place in time-past. And, as in *The Grandmothers,* the important meditations and ruminations which hold the novel together include both those which took place in time-past and those in time-present, the latter including new comments on earlier meditations. There is a close resemblance to *The Babe's Bed* and certain of the stories in this respect, except that the present time of narration is farther removed from the time-past in which the main events take place, and, in addition to being superior in every other respect to *The Babe's Bed,* there is a much more successful use of flashbacks from the position of time-past to events taking place even earlier.

These ruminations, meditations, and evaluations are, as in *The Grandmothers, The Babe's Bed,* and some of the stories, not only what hold the work together, but are, in the familiar pattern, the most important "events" taking place, for Alwyn Tower is the narrator and protagonist as well, and most important is what it all means to him.

The Pilgrim Hawk, unlike any previous fiction by Wescott, does not deal with Wisconsin or America, but entirely with the France of the expatriates. However, as in *The Grandmothers,* the time of the events is just as important as the place, and as in the earlier novel the narrator is looking back from the present on a *particular kind* of past, an era whose special conditions are irrevocably gone, and in a tone of nostalgia and irony. It is an historic past, even though recent, and the second and third paragraphs are concerned with evoking the difference between the twenties and the present of 1940.

> Needless to say the twenties were very different from the thirties and now the forties have begun. In the twenties it was not unusual to meet foreigners in some country as foreign to them as you, your peregrinations just crossing theirs; and you did your best to know them in an afternoon or so; and perhaps you called that little lightning knowledge friendship. And vagaries of character, and the various war and peace that goes on in the psyche, seemed of the greatest interest and even importance.

The time-present is a kind of historical corridor (and there is some visionary sense of this in the opening), after the beginning of World War II, before America's entry into the war, and after the long, arid decade of depression and loss of confidence that was the thirties — so much a contrast to the twenties. The crossing of paths, the lightning friendships, the optimistic curiosity, and the word *peregrinations* further imply that the narrator and the "foreigners" are, figuratively, hunters, pilgrims, and wanderers — thereby linking the expatriates and their time to the central symbol — "Lucy was a perfect example of her species, *Falco peregrinus,* Pilgrim Hawk."

The nostalgic irony of the first paragraph is directed toward the undesirable present, and continues in the next:

> Chancellet must be a painful place in the forties, although one of the least changed in France, I suppose, because it is unimportant. As I remember, there was a school of what is now romantically called celestial navigation, with a modest flying field and a few hangars, two or three kilometers away, at Pelors; but if that is in use now the foreigners must have it. In our day, day in and day out, the old Duchesse de Challot and her poor relations and friends in tight coats on windbroken mounts used to hunt in the forest of Pelors. We could hear their hunting horns which sounded like a picnic of boy sopranos, lost. Meanwhile perhaps there have been anti-aircraft guns for the defense of Paris embedded all amid the earths of foxes: angry radio stammering in the well-kept branches. Now at least the foxes and the thrushes can come back. The old ex-cabinet-minister whose chateau and little park adjoined Alex's garden is dead.

Celestial navigation is a romantic term because of its implications of divinity in a world that denies it. The *war and peace* is no longer of the psyche, no longer personal and internal, but projected on a mass scale, the implication being that war is in terrible form a macrocosmic equivalent of the individual hunt; this is further substantiated by the use of the word *foreigners,* which is applied to the expatriates in the first paragraph, and here applied to the invaders, the Germans (but they are doubly foreign, war being destructive of the individuality associated with the twenties). The guns and voices of modern war are juxtaposed against the hunt of the Duchesse de Challot, an example of an almost extinct form of man's hunting. As the comparison to the lost boy sopranos implies, it now seems merely childish and innocent. Once based on physical hunger, it is ritualized and continued because of man's boredom and psychic hunger — a motif developed later. Now in the forties with the hunt taking the form of international war, the foxes and thrushes are safe, but man is not. The manhunt is organized, mechanized, dehumanized (as indicated by the angry radio's stammer). Therefore the narrator doubts, under these conditions, the value of studying the war and peace of the individual psyche. The ironic tone of the last sentences are not only nostalgic, but tempered by disillusionment. Pre-war politics and attitudes, like the ex-cabinet minister, are dead.

With this introduction the main motifs are sounded, and the personal past, with which the main body of the narrative is concerned, is linked not only to the historical past of the twenties, but through the Cullens, the Duchesse, Europe itself, hunting and the four-thousand-year-old sport of falconry, to a broader historical past. The events are thus placed as remote and of another time, although only a decade away, and the events and characters take on a heightened quality, that of "a lost paradise," "a time and place grown more fabulous than Wisconsin ever could...the France of the expatriates after the first World War."[1] It is in that exciting, optimistic time that the narrator has chosen to end his tale. The irony and nostalgic tone do not discredit that time; on the contrary, for the present of war-time is a chaos. In this sense, the novel might well have been subtitled *Good-Bye, Europe.*

The sequence of main events that occur in time-past appears in straight chronological order, but this narrative flow is continually arrested by the meditations, evaluations, and general comments of the narrator upon everything taking place, on whatever associative thoughts they may call up, and upon himself. It is the narrative sequence of events in time-past that gives the novel its structural framework. Although there is an apparent continuous movement forward, the work falls into seven sections, the transition between one section and another marked by a shift in action, or in deployment of characters, or in location of scene, and each section centers around a major event in the narrative. Within each section there is often very little narrative forward movement while the narrator explores in his mind the subjects that the immediate action stimulates, perhaps to be brought up again later.

Section One. After a brief introduction to the setting — the larger historical one of the twenties in Europe and the personal setting of Alexandra Henry's home in Chancellet, where the narrator, Tower, is visiting — the Cullens, unexpected guests, appear: Madelaine Cullen, her husband Larry, the falcon Lucy (perched on Mrs. Cullen's wrist), and the Cockney chauffeur, Ricketts. The surface action is in large part the conversation that takes place between the four main characters, although certain significant and dramatic actions occur. Another level of the narrative consists of Tower observing and speculating about the two people, their relationship, and about Lucy and falconry, which Mrs. Cullen discusses at length. Mrs. Cullen in conversation, and Tower in both conversation and thought, constantly use the hawk as a source of implied and stated analogies — a process that continues throughout the novel — thus investing it symbolically. The major event of the first section is the "bating" of Lucy, when she throws herself from Madeleine Cullen's wrist in a hopeless attempt to escape. The bating pattern begun here is one of several patterns, actions repeated that serve to thread a motif through the work. The conversation shifts, although still emanating from the hawk, to various other subjects. At the end of the section Alex asks the Cullens to dinner, introducing the subplot and its characters, the servants Jean, Eva, and Ricketts.

Section Two. Tower, Alex and the Cullens take a walk in the park belonging to the Chateau de Chancellet — the second major event. The physical movement from indoors to outdoors is consistent with a pattern of nature and domestication. When the Cullens temporarily split off, Alexandra tells Tower about them, their background and relationship. They rejoin the Cullens, who have talked to the old politician Bidou, occupant of the chateau.

Section Three. In the house everyone waits for Ricketts and Jean to return with a pigeon for Lucy's feeding, and the conversation again radiates from the hawk, with a discussion of her feeding, and introducing another major pattern, that of hunger. Tower, wearing the falconer's glove, holds Lucy on his wrist and meditates on himself. Mrs. Cullen talks about the hawk, with implied references to herself and to Cullen, and then shifts back and forth from the hawk to other subjects. Lucy bates a second time, then defecates. The major event — the feeding of Lucy — takes place; the hunger pattern appears again in conversation and meditation, this time connected with religion, art, and marriage.

Section Four. Lucy is taken to "weather" in the garden. The major event is the long conversation between Tower and Larry

Cullen, during which Cullen drinks two full shakers of Alexanders, and Tower meditates at length, particularly on drunkenness. Cullen's entire subject is himself, his wife and their situation.

Section Five. The major event occurs when Larry Cullen, following the bating pattern, emotionally overcome by jealousy, creeps into the garden and frees Lucy. Tower sees him, and without betraying him, informs Mrs. Cullen, who manages to recapture the bird, which has returned to the garden after a brief flight. Tower has a new insight about Madeleine as she recaptures the hawk. The secondary plot and its development rises to the surface as Jean breaks out in jealousy concerning the flirtation going on between his wife Eva and Ricketts, the chauffeur.

Section Six. Mrs. Cullen announces that she and her husband cannot stay for dinner, but must return to Paris. After some discussion they depart and the sixth major event occurs offstage: Larry Cullen's attempt to shoot someone — whether Lucy, Ricketts, or his wife, no one knows. In a few moments they return, and Madeleine Cullen, alone, enters the house in perfect control of herself. Apparently having taken the gun from her husband, she goes to the garden and throws it into the pool. Lucy, on her arm, bates, or seems to, for the third time. Referring to her husband's action as bating, Madeleine explains to her hosts what happened, then leaves for Paris. Tower, shocked by the violent event, shifts his whole view of the afternoon's events, the Cullens, and himself, and begins to de-symbolize the hawk in mistrust of his meditations.

Section Seven. The foreground action is an intermittent dialogue carried on between Alexandra and Tower over the significance of what has happened tha. afternoon. In the background, but brought forward from time to time, runs the climax and happy reconciliation of the quarrel between Jean and Eva, which as a subplot parallels the Cullen relationship. Most important, however, are the ruminations of Tower, and the major event takes place in his monologue as he first tries to compress a formula or moral from the event, then tries to distinguish the meaning of the Cullens to him and what he means to himself. Failing on both counts, he deflates his own proclivity for abstraction, for what amounts to rumination, which he calls "fruitless vegetation."

Character and Theme

The events indicated above give a sense of the framework of the novel, but little sense of the dense, full-bodied form, which is made up not only of the meditations of Tower on all that takes place, but also the detailed background information in condensed flashback or exchange of dialogue concerning the lives of the characters. From these and the events emerges a design of overlapping love relationships, each of which, during the course of the narrative, reaches a crisis.

The central love relationship is between Madeleine and Larry Cullen, and the two other relationships, those of Eva and Jean, and of Alexandra Henry and Alwyn Tower, work as contrasts to contribute to the love theme.

The Irish Cullens, Tower sees at once, are of the very rich, international sporting leisure class, Madeleine elegant and still retaining much of her beauty, Larry large with a soft bulkiness and a "British complexion" that comes from rich food and drink. They are "outdoor people...self-centered, but without any introspection, strenuous, but emotionally idle." They are "self-absorbed, coldly gregarious, mere passers of time." "But nothing about them," Tower observes, "was authentically sedate or even peaceful." As the Cullens gossip about money, neighbors, and especially the hawk, it becomes apparent that the hawk is in some way symbolic of their relationship and has an active part in it as well. Tower feels it "might have been a baby," and Cullen "a lover; or was it the other way around?" At first Madeleine's strength and serenity are striking, but soon her inner tension is revealed to Tower, not only by her gesture and glance, but by her volubility and its quality; it is as though "she felt welling up in her mind some peculiar imagination, or some trouble impossible to ignore, which she tried to relieve by talking, with a kind of continuous double meaning."

Larry Cullen seems to be "constantly fighting some strange feeling, and to be somehow outwitted by it;" he has little imagination or sense of nuance. His sensuality appears a disguise for gross hunger, whether apparent in licking his lips at the thought of a gourmet's dish or in his appraisal of his wife's breasts. Although now and then unfaithful to his wife, because of his own inner needs he is so devoted to her that he exists in a kind of captive state, which he both detests and is afraid to abjure. He is jealous and capable of violence, and it becomes apparent that he hates Lucy, whether it be a literal jealousy or due to the recognition that the hawk is emblematic of his own captive state.

Madeleine, in her "cunning, instructive and curative" love, her care and meticulous attention to the whims, to the physical, sensual, emotional and psychic needs of hawk and husband, is also in her own way a prisoner of hungers and needs which this very activity satisfies, yet they seem more emotional than sexual or sensual. She is clever, strong and tolerant, but one of her fundamental necessities is to impose her will upon her husband. Her flexibility and imagination in ministering to her husband is after all the means by which she dominates him.

She gives no overt sign of being interested in men other than her husband, but she uses the hawk to form a triangle, to arouse the jealousy of Larry and to maintain a tension that eliminates boredom. And although Larry reveals to Tower that his wife had no sexual interest in the Irish poet, McVoy, Larry also shows he was jealous of him; one wonders if Madeleine is not merely letting her husband, like the hawk, "fly at something he can kill." As for Madeleine herself, when she is stalking the hawk, her shoes off, her "hips wide and back powerful ... impossible to trip as a cat," she reveals herself as the obsessed and superb hunter of her prey. She speaks of her husband as well as the hawk when she says she can prevent its fits by "distraction and stroking" and her allowing the hawk to perch "as high as possible," because "it must frighten her to see things higher than she is" indicates something of her constant attention to Cullen's ego, her provision of such activities as pig-sticking and Irish revolutions. It is also characteristic of her own pride and independence, her preference for hawk over dog.

Larry Cullen's rather surprising and prim outrage at his wife's feeding the bird before others perhaps has deeper roots than his sense of manners. It is probable that he senses what Tower is conscious of — the likeness of the hawk's hunger to "amorous appetite" — and of what his wife points out, that it is the hawk's hunger that leads to its captivity, and perhaps he recognizes that it is his sexual appetite that leads to his; he soon licks his lips at the thought of consuming pigeons and has a large appetite for drink. Snobbish, boastful, indiscreet, sentimental and sadistic, Larry looks upon his wife as a child he has spoiled in many ways, including giving her his money. After relating to Tower in private his marital troubles, he portrays himself as a martyr and reveals his jealousy, but speaks of himself and his wife as "the ideal married couple, so to speak. It's real love. She wouldn't look at another man. ...I understand women." His view of Madeleine as "still the proud ignorant girl," further establishes his lack of perception and addiction to trite attitudes. Then, in his "fine moment" of drunkenness, he reveals his raging desire to do away with Lucy, soon sneaking into the garden and surreptitiously releasing her. He then has the impulse to confess and be forgiven but is thwarted by Madeleine; he seems relieved when the hawk is recovered. But within the hour, in the back seat of their Daimler, Madeleine will struggle to take a revolver away from him.

Madeleine's success in averting catastrophe, her firmness in this violent situation, her words as she reveals Larry has threatened to leave her — "Oh, I'm so afraid he will one day. I don't know what would become of him by himself, the fool, the old darling" — emphasize that this is another in a familiar pattern of love relationships in Wescott's work with Madeleine the strong, dominant woman, and Larry the moody but dominated and dependent male; but never before has Wescott portrayed such a relationship with the complexity and insight of this one.

As in a traditional tragi-comic plot, the second love relationship is that of the servants, but the purpose is not comedy as such. Eva and Jean are compared with and contrasted to the Cullens. Jean, at forty, is no longer as handsome as he was. Despite his different life and contrast in station, the description of him as "broken to harness, but still apt to throw off his emotions, still amorous," invites comparison with Larry Cullen. Jean "had acquired Eva in Morocco," we are told, an echo of Cullen's attitude of acquisition in saying of Madeleine, "I took her without a penny," and in thinking of her as "still the proud, ignorant girl" that he married. Although inclined to fatness Eva is, like Mrs. Cullen, a beauty. The description of Ricketts as "a fine Cockney, bright-eyed and sharp-nosed," is faintly suggestive of the hawk, and certainly he serves the same function in the triangle. Eva, at the end of the afternoon, fearing Jean will return drunk and kill her in his jealousy, explains to Alex that she flirts so that Jean, coming between her and his rival, makes her feel his love, "and to that of course she promptly yielded, and her yielding gave him assurance that she loved him." Her psychology is essentially that of Madeleine Cullen, sheared of its complexity and sophistication. Is is implied that the pattern is a natural one, but that in the Cullens it is refined to the point of decadence. The suggestion is that the difference between the couples is the difference between the "natural" and spontaneous (they are "Latin" — French and Italian-Moorish) and the over-sophisticated. When Lucy lets her mute drop to the floor Mrs. Cullen "cheerfully apologized, and also proudly called our attention to its whiteness," and although she assures them it is "the cleanest wastage in nature," Cullen is offended and grows red. Eva, in contrast to Mrs. Cullen's pride in the mute, is merely amused at wiping it up. Jean, in contrast to Cullen's prudery, is not interested in the mute at all but in tapping his wife as she bends down, causing her to blush.

Although Eva, later, feels that this time she has gone too far in arousing Jean's jealousy in flirting with Ricketts and that he will kill her, nothing of the kind happens. Tower is able to tell that they are reconciled easily from the sound of "make-believe fighting that when all goes well, relaxes and relieves the true struggle of love." Their make-believe fighting and the threat of violence dissipated are both comparison and contrast to the actually violent episode of the Cullens. Both, in this respect, are in contrast to the third couple, Alexandra Henry and Alwyn Tower. It is Tower, hearing the "rustle and scuffle" of love-making between Jean and Eva in the corner of the garden, who reflects that, "The air was as warm as Tangier but one could not lie outdoors, I thought, for the grass would be splashed with dew." The simple passion of Jean and Eva and the complex passion of the Cullens are both different from the Alexandra-Tower relationship, which Morton Zabel calls an "enervating Platonic friendship."[2] Alexandra Henry is described by Tower as "my great friend," and "my dear friend," and although she is wealthy and well-traveled, and lives in an attractive house near Paris, Tower reflects that "she must be lonely here in France with only myself and my cousin and a few other friends rather like us." He is surprised at her enthusiasm for the Cullens because

> One of Alex's obvious characteristics was lack of curiosity; and I think that was chiefly fear of arousing or

authorizing other's inquiry about herself. Perhaps her selfishness reassured her and made her less shy.

She is apparently shocked when Tower tells her what Cullen confessed to him. Tower notes, when she avoids Mrs. Cullen's embrace, that Alex "always" shrinks from "female affection," and that in her

> character and way of life in those days there was a certain passivity; at least abstention from other's lives. Whatever she did not understand about them might, she felt, be more awful than anything she could imagine.

If she thought Mrs. Cullen was going to commit suicide in the garden, Tower says, "she might not have cared to interfere or prevent it." Her withdrawal from close human connection, colored by snobbism, is indicated when, speaking of the love-play of Jean and Eva, she says, "The lower classes have a way of making one ashamed of one's sex," but Tower explains:

> She always had trouble with servants. The trouble really was that her kind of interest in them, if aroused at all, soon went too far. Shrinking from them, but pinned down by them at last, she gave a great deal of warmth that lay in her. But between their demands upon her, she fancied that she had no sympathy for them at all.

During the discussion of freedom, Tower remarks:

> Alex wanted freedom more than anything: and if others as a rule did not, she might have a lonely life. In any case, it would take a better man than Cullen to dispel her young misanthropy. I myself regretted never having been able to decide what to think; how much liberty is a true human motive, and how much is wasteful and foolish?

He later says, "When love itself is at stake, love of liberty as a rule is only fear of captivity."

It is difficult to guess Alexandra's age. Although well-traveled and worldly, she is apparently relatively inexperienced in love. This, plus her reticence, her withdrawing and shy nature, her passivity, and fear of what she does not understand, are behind Tower's remarks as he contrasts Alexandra's lack of experience in love to his own. After some generalities about married life he says:

> When love has given satisfaction, then you discover
> how large a part of the rest of life is only payment for
> it, installment after installment.... That was the one
> definite lesson which these petty scenes with the Cullens
> illustrated. Early in life I had learned it for myself well
> enough. It was on Alex's account that I minded. To see
> the cost of love before one has felt what it is worth, is
> a pity, one may never have the courage to begin.

He laments that

> If your judgement is poor you fall in love with those
> who could not possibly love you. If the romance of
> the past has done you any harm, you will not be able
> to hold on to love when you do attain it. Or pity or
> self-pity may have blunted your hand so that it makes
> no mark. Back you fly to your perch, ashamed as well
> as frustrated.

His insights are based on observation and on personal experience, as he indicates later, when discussing the plight of old bachelors:

> I myself was still young then and had been lucky in
> love. But the little early quarrels and failures warn
> one; and in the confidences of friends and in gossip
> about other men, one discovers the vague beastly
> shape of what to expect. Life goes on after one's luck
> has run out.

Although having been "lucky" in love, he feels he knows the cost of it payment by payment, and as he "foolishly" imagines himself growing old he fears the future, although "still young." The quality of Tower's nature that would contribute to keeping his relationship with Alexandra simply platonic, every clue seems to imply, is his reticence to pay the cost of love, his fear that his hand is "blunted." It is this that, along with Alexandra's withdrawing nature, justifies Zabel's adjective "enervating." Tower worries about the "bad example" the Cullens will set for Alexandra, and although teasing, half means it when he tells her she will never marry. Tower, at this age, looked upon by himself in retrospect, is, of course, faulty in his generalizations. We know from the first paragraph of the novel that later, in America, Alexandra marries Tower's brother. The point is, however, that in the present of the story the relationship of Alexandra and Tower stands as a contrast to the other two, and as a relationship without love between man and woman it does, after all, seem "enervating," pale, negative, perhaps even selfish. The two, through reticent inexperience and wary experience, stand as an example of those at least temporarily incapable of love. The inescapable necessity of love for Alexandra is indicated by two things: her remark at the end — "I envy the Cullens, didn't you know?" — and her later marriage. An inclusive consideration of the character of Tower and its function has to take into account that Tower-as-lover is only one part of it; the other, more closely related to his function as narrator, is that of Tower-as-artist. If Tower has his limitations as a lover, the implication is that they are linked to the habit of mind — abstracting — that he believes plagues him as a thinker and artist. "It is like a useless, fruitless vegetation;" he says, "even the ego disappears under it." After a session of such pale thought he notes:

> Therefore I scarcely noticed how long my dear friend stayed away in her bedroom; and therefore I was glad when she came back. For me, putting a stop to so-called thought is one of the functions of friendship.

Earlier, speaking of the hawk, he says:

> But because my writing had gone badly all spring I could not bear to give her more than a passing thought with reference to that. I began to think of her as an image of amorous desire instead. That is the great relief of weariness of work in any case; the natural consolation for its not going well.... No doubt art is too exceptional to be worth talking about; but sex is not.... it must be the keenest of appetites for a majority of men most of their lives.

One of the functions of friendship is to put a stop to self-obliterating abstracting thought; "amorous desire," however, is a "relief" from work, and when work is not going well, one turns to it for "natural consolation." It is evident that for Tower, his work as an artist is of primary importance, and friendship and love, for him, are given their value as a kind of aid and therapy to the functioning of the artist.

Although Chancellet is a long way from Wisconsin, it is possible to find a relationship between these characters and those of a dozen years before. As indicated earlier, Madeleine Cullen continues the tradition, although she is not American, of the dominating woman; there is the same brusque energy and resilience that were so evident in the women who married Towers in *The Grandmothers*—Mary Harris and Marianne Duff and Rose Harrison. She has a certain masculine and primitive strength made vivid when, her three-inch heels discarded and her dress awry, she stalks the hawk. In Mary, Marianne, and Rose the dominating characteristics were positive, and this is also true of Madeleine; but like so much else in the novel, only partially true, as Tower senses when he reflects upon her "wild Irish sons" hoping that "they were really wild," and "that they did not love their mother much. If they were at all backward or sensitive it was good of her, wise of her, to keep out of Ireland."

Larry Cullen continues the pattern of male submission to the dominant female, so evident among the Tower men, but his submission is with an anguish and resentment evident in what he tells Tower; in this he bears some resemblance to Ira Duff, who tells stories of his wife's behavior. Considering Larry's wife, however, it is not certain that his stories are untrue, but what he reveals of himself, his implied values and attitude, make him unsympathetic.

As for the narrator, he is referred to only as "Tower," and then only long after the narration is underway. There is every reason to assume, as the critics have done, that he is Alwyn Tower—that is, a later version of the character by that name in *The Grandmothers*. Of course, the equivalent character at an earlier stage is known as Dan Strane in *The Apple of the Eye*, and appears as the nameless bachelor, a briefly returned expatriate in *The Babe's Bed*. But if there is any doubt about Tower's identity as Alwyn Tower for the literal-minded, there is the following paragraph, with a reference to the taxidermy of Henry Tower (here not named) of *The Grandmothers*, and even particular incidents including the significant one of the chloroformed owl:

> Alex offered her congratulations upon Lucy's evident peace of mind with me; I would make a good falconer. That reminded me of my father and his magic with animals which filled me with envy and antipathy when I was a boy. He could force a crazy colt to its knees, or castrate a young boar, or chloroform a desperate

trapped owl; and their wretched muscles relaxed and surrendered, their eyes blinked in perfect gentleness in alignment with his eyes. His eyes, or perhaps it was his hands, seemed able to promise them something. Half my life, I said to myself, has been discovering that my character is not the antithesis or the contradiction of his; here was a new kinship. Perhaps I could cope with horse or hog or doomed bird too, if I had to; perhaps even with a wild antipathetic son, disinclined to live— who knows? This was a gratifying thought but not altogether happy; vast vague potentiality of things I did not wish to do in any case.

This paragraph is also one example of the narrator's concern with the self, which is as structurally and thematically important as it is in *The Grandmothers* and *The Babe's Bed*. The theme of the self and characterization of Alwyn Tower as artist are intimately related to the problem and technique of narration and are discussed in a following section.

Wescott's main themes in *The Pilgrim Hawk* are as always related, and are the same as in earlier works, love and the self, the motifs of the artist and expatriatism being aspects of the theme of the self. Previously, Wescott has altogether explored many aspects of love, and always he has presented love as ambiguous, but here the given form, in a different way, makes possible an exploration more multifarious and more concentrated than before. The Western Romantic concept of love is certainly one aspect of it, but Tower the ex-expatriate, nearing forty, is aware there is more to it than either the Alwyn Tower of *The Grandmothers* or the characters of the short stories of the same period had thought. He is helped by other characters who are worldly and articulate, and Alexandra and Madeleine especially stimulate him to form concepts and formulas, to draw analogies and define nuances. Their talk and intellection are either directly or by allusion almost always about love, love as a passion, beyond will or conscious control (although they are willing to attempt such) irrational and subject to ambivalent impulses. But above all it is the convincing ambiguous reality of the Cullen relationship that remains in Tower's mind, the obsessive necessity of love for both of them, their restlessness and conflict, and the fact that not all questions about this antagonistic relationship are answered. The Cullen love-relationship is the most complex and ambiguous of any in Wescott's work; and it and that of the other two couples, with the aid of the symbolic hawk, and the dramatic events, give the narrator a chance to explore or comment upon many aspects of love in the following order: love as jealousy (14, 16), as a vocation (19), as hunting, as hunger, and the lover as a fool (19-21); love as greed, and related to other hungers (22-25), as a compensation for the artist (23); married love and its complexities (25); love as captivity (29 ff.), as diabolic and related to hate and murder (38-39), as hunting again (41-42), as release from boredom (42-43), as related to violence (44-46), as hunger again (47 ff.); love and age, desire, pleasure, and isolation (49 ff.); love and death, love, sentimentality and selfishness (55-57), love and faith (57); the marital and other appetites (63) including the religious (63); love as rapture and sentimentality (99); love as surrender (100); love, liberty and captivity again (101), married love again and the cost of love (106), love as violence again (108 ff.), love as related to suicide and murder (120), and love again as jealousy (124-125).

Manners, Drama, and Prose

In this third novel Wescott, after more than ten years between novels, again showed his ability to adequately present complex, vital and meaningful characters. There is, of course, a significant difference in kind between the two expatriates Alexandra and Alwyn and the international rich, the Cullens. They are alike, however, in that they are far removed in background (Tower the exception in this), interests and culture, from the characters in *The Apple of the Eye* and *The Grandmothers;* since Wescott's material is no longer the Middle West or America, it might be expected that this difference would have some effect upon his technique. The porportion, function, and success of dramatic scenes and dramatic confrontation of character, it was found in the previous novels, were important in the measurement of his aesthetic success. The inadequacy of scene and confrontation contributed to inadequate characterization and thematic development in the first novel. In *The Grandmothers,* among other improvements, there was a higher quality and number of dramatic confrontations and scenes. However, they were always key scenes, highly selected because of the number of characters and the album form. Characteristically they were truncated, and were penetrated and surrounded by summary narrative, the tone and selection of them controlled by the rendering of the character's sensibility through the narrator's sympathetic voice.

At the moment it is sufficient to notice that in *The Pilgrim Hawk,* the only sensibility rendered directly is that of the narrator himself. The other characters are observed by him, and it is his speculation and meditation on what he observes during one afternoon that characterizes them. The incorporation of the talents of the novelist of manners with his other gifts is appropriate to the difference in Wescott's material, and it is consistent with the worldly narrator who has been an expatriate.

One of the results is a new sharpness of focus on character confrontation, achieved with a greater subtlety:

> Now Mrs. Cullen was ready to feed Lucy. But her chauffeur and Jean who had gone to the neighbor's dovecot, had not returned. Foolish Eva felt sure they were in a ditch somewhere, or quarreling, or lost. So we sat down again; and I like a fool inquired what they thought of French and English and German politics. Cullen was out of breath but he sniffed wonderfully and cleared his throat, preliminary to an opinion. "Please, Larry, no politics," his wife requested, smiling at me to make it less impolite.
>
> She was fondling Lucy, gazing at her eye to eye, slowly shaking her head at her; and the wicked beak moved in exact obedience to the tip of her nose as if it were magnetized. "Lucy's hungry," she said solemnly.

The details of Cullen's sniffing "wonderfully," his clearing his throat "preliminary to an opinion," the dramatic timing and insight of the sudden intrusion of his wife's request, the nuance of her smile, her preoccupation with Lucy so carefully recorded and its double implication — that Madeleine and the hawk with its "wicked beak" are somewhat alike, that Madeleine has mesmeric powers and insight into other creatures — nearly all of the qualities of this passage and so many like it (the qualities of the novelist of manners) have been little evident in Wescott's work before. The possibilities of the direction of his focus have been enlarged. So concerned before with rendering the subjective sensibility of different characters, he now turns to rendering details of personality and dramatic action; there is a corresponding flexibility and precision of language in his prose that is new.

The proportion of the novel that is devoted to actual confrontation is large, if one includes all dialogue. The ruminations of the narrator, when not directly generalizing or turning out aphorisms, are very often at one with rendering scenes. There is little summary narrative and there is no exposition that is not made active through dialogue or enlivened by the quality of the narrator's mind as he speculates on it. The actual number of scenes are few if one measures them by situation, character, time and location and discounts the shifting back and forth from the narrator's monologue.

There was, in *The Grandmothers,* a noticeable but certainly limited improvement in dialogue over the first novel, the result being a kind of negative achievement, neither realistic nor unrealistic, but ordinary, with a lack of ear for the vocabulary, syntax and idiom of middle western speech. In *The Pilgrim Hawk* there is a great improvement in dialogue. The authenticity is never in question, nor is it ever awkward or unlikely. There is no doubt that much of the improvement is due to the great difference in material. No longer dealing with the language of rural middle western Americans with whom he grew up, but with English-speaking expatriates from America and the British Isles, Wescott is much more at home.

> Mrs. Cullen then quoted Buffon's famous sentence about falcons: *"L'individu seul est esclave; l'espèce est libre."* Buffon had been her father's second-best author after Scott. Her French accent was incorrect but very pretty. Only the individual hawk is a slave; the species is free....
>
> Then Alex spoke up, in what was a loud voice for her; "Oh dear, it is the opposite of human beings. We are slaves in the mass, aren't we? Only one man can hope to free himself; one at a time, then another, and another."
>
> "Oh, I dare say," Mrs. Cullen assented. "Yes, perhaps." But she smiled patronizingly. I think she was congratulating herself upon knowing a freer and stronger type of humanity than our pampered, subtle, self-questioning American type; and perhaps she did: Irish republicans, wild Hungarians with hawks, Germans during their defeat.

"But it is true, isn't it?" Alex insisted. "The man who really loves freedom is the exception."

"Oh quite. How right you are," our lady falconer dubiously murmured.

But her husband disagreed. "No, Alex! What a disgusting idea! Love of liberty is the deepest instinct we have — if you will excuse my saying so."[3]

These characters, more likely than not, speak more than one language. Although the Cullens in particular, in European terms, are certainly not literary or intellectual, they as well as Tower and Alexandra Henry, in contrast to Bad Han, Jule Bier, Leander and even James Tower, are highly articulate, with background and experience providing fluent discussion as a matter of course. As for idiom and syntax, there is the discernible difference between British and American, which is quite appropriately under-emphasized, and both British and American speech seem well observed and accurately rendered.

A discernible difference allied to the enlargement of the author's field of focus, his rendering of manners, appears not only in dialogue but in prose. Wescott's talent for the carefully turned aphorism and the memorably stated generality reaches a new level of achievement. There is not the faulty or strained expression or turn of phrase as is sometimes the case in previous work, nor the vague metaphor of excessive involution. Examples can be found on every page. Below is a rather typical paragraph:

> And highly sexed men, unless they give in and get married, more or less starve to death. I myself was still young then and I had been lucky in love. But little early quarrels and failures warn one; and in the confidences of friends and in gossip about other men, one discovers the vague beastly shape of what to expect. Life goes on and on after one's luck has run out. Youthfulness persists, alas, long after one has ceased to be young. Love-life goes on indefinitely, with less and less likelihood of being loved, less and less ability to love, and the stomach-ache of love as sharp as ever. The old bachelor is like an old hawk.

The passage depends upon a comparison to the hawk, and is part of the process of the symbolic loading of it, but what is beneath the prose and what helps maintain a consistent tone throughout, whether or not one agrees as to the validity of the generalities, is the quality of mind: calm, worldly-wise, sensitive, and disillusioned, capable of subtlety, paradox, and nuance. These qualities, of course, appear also as part of the flexibility and precision of language in rendering manners, and necessarily help characterize the narrator, as well as giving a new dimension to the narrative voice.

Symbolism, Self, and Narrator

The use of a cumulative and revolving symbol first appeared in Wescott's work with his use of the marsh in *The Apple of the Eye,* and there, too, appeared his first use of bird symbology. *The Pilgrim Hawk* is the culmination of these symbolic methods which have appeared in all his novels and many of his short stories up to this time. The hawk is *cumulative* in taking on additional meaning with each reference, and it is *revolving* in that as the narrative progresses, the symbol is turned, so to speak, to reveal the many facets of meaning depending on the context. It is consistent with previous bird-symbology in that its implications are related to love or the inner life. But in this novel, the symbol as never before is in its revolving not only a primary principle upon which the structure depends, but the very turning of it for every aspect of meaning by the narrator is the action from which the themes of the self and the artist emerge.

Shortly after the introduction of the bird by Madeleine Cullen, she, in her conversation, and Tower, in conversation but extensively in thought, begin using the hawk as a source of implied and stated analogies — investing it symbolically, a process that continues throughout the narrative up to the point where the process is reversed. The hawk becomes a symbol in two ways. There is the symbology created by conversation and by Tower's meditation, and there is the symbology aided by conversation and meditation that is dramatic — that forms a pattern of action with symbolic meaning. These are the bating pattern beginning at the end of section one, the hunger pattern beginning in section three, and the act of defecation in the same section. Lucy bates twice, and perhaps a third time. Actions of Larry Cullen in particular are interpreted in the light of the hawk pattern as bating on two occasions, once when he releases the hawk, and once in the end as he attempts violence with the revolver. As for the defecation, the only thing equivalent seems to be the long monologue of Cullen as he confesses so much of his private life to Tower. If so it is a reversal of pattern, for it occurs just before he releases Lucy in the garden. The actions, of course, whether it is the hawk eating, or hawk or man bating, cause fresh speculations and add to the symbolic cluster around the bird.

There is a careful introduction and meticulous preparation for the hawk as a major symbol, step by step, beginning with its dramatic entrance on Madeleine Cullen's wrist, the introduction of the bird to Tower and the second introduction to Alex, who is told that she is named Lucy, "'for Lucy Ashton, Lucy of Lammermoor... Don't you remember her song? *Easy live and quiet die, Vacant hand and heart and eye.'*" At that moment the implications of the name and the song are not clear, but become so as the story progresses, for Lucy Ashton, in Scott's *The Bride of Lammermoor,* is, like the hawk, cruelly kept captive. Unable to marry her lover, she pretends to submit, but goes mad (Larry's humming of the "Mad Scene from 'Lucia'" fortifies the point). The hawk too only seems to submit, but for it "There is no real acceptance or inheritance of the state of surrender;" it does not breed in captivity, has a mad gleam in its eye highly suggestive to the narrator, and is subject to "fits of insanity," or bating. It is Larry Cullen, however, who most parallels Scott's heroine in this respect in his final attempt at violence—for the mad Lucy Ashton stabbed her husband. Early preparation includes Tower's immediate susceptibility to the symbolic potential of the hawk:

> For one thing, the bird charmed me so that nothing else mattered much. And it served as an embodiment or emblem for me of all the truly interesting subjects of conversation that these very sociable, traveling, sporting people leave out as a rule: illness, poverty, sex, religion, art. Whenever I began to be bored, a solemn glance of its maniacal eyes helped me to stop listening and to think concentratedly of myself instead, or for myself.

The paragraph ends with an indication that the theme of the self will be important. Mrs. Cullen's insistence on talking of "the dear theme of the hawk, which meant all the world to her," and her "peculiar imagination, or some trouble impossible to ignore, which she tried to relieve by talking with a kind of double meaning," further stimulate Tower's imaginative meditation.

The movement in symbolizing is the movement of the narrator's mind, and therefore continually illustrative of the theme of the self. Generally his thoughts move from the hawk itself — its action, appearance, or as a subject of conversation — to abstractions and generalities and aphorisms, then by implication or statement and application to the characters and situation, or to himself. Here is Tower's comment after a paragraph of description of the hawk:

> But her chief beauty was that of expression. It was like a little flame; it caught and compelled your attention like that, although it did not flicker and there was nothing bright about it nor any great warmth in it. It is the look that men sometimes have; men of great energy, whose appetite or vocation has kept them absorbed every instant all their lives. They may be good men but they are often mistaken for evil men, and vice versa . . . .

The passage also serves as a hint of the motif of hunger and theme of the artist, for a page later Mrs. Cullen at some length describes how hawks starve to death because of the failing of their hunting powers, at least "philosophically, letting themselves die," and compares the hawk to the mad, sounding again lightly that motif. Then the hunger of the hawk as a subject leads in conversation to the discussion of the literal hunger of man between Mr. and Mrs. Cullen, while Tower meditates:

> And I thought — as the relatively well-fed do think — of other human hungers, mental and sentimental and so on. For example, my own undertaking in early manhood to be a literary artist. No one warned me that I did not really have talent enough. Therefore my hope of becoming a very good artist turned bitter, hot and nerve-wracking; and it would get worse as I grew older. The unsuccessful artist also ends in apathy, too proud and vexed to fly again, waiting upon withheld inspiration, bored to death.

The first sentence refers to "other human hungers," and is

followed up by an exploration of the hunger of the self as artist, and of artists in general; it moves on later to "amorous desire" as a hunger, and so on.

The hawk is compared, and more often than once, to each of the four major characters, and the characters, of course, constantly illustrate and carry through the various themes that the hawk has suggested. The movement of the narrator's mind from hawk to speculation on symbolic meanings, or generalities, back to character, and often again to generalities carries the thread of first one theme, then another in repetition with variation. Thus spun from the revolving symbol of the hawk, the facets of meaning become motifs which are patterned through the work. The process continues until on the level of action, or plot, there is the sudden violent and dangerous event — Cullen's attempt to shoot someone — revealed by Madeleine Cullen when she momentarily returns to the house, by the white lips of Ricketts and the pallor of Larry Cullen. The hawk, trying to maintain its perch on Madeleine's agitated arm, at once strikes Tower as "absurd" and he begins to laugh:

> It struck me as the completion of the cycle of the afternoon, an end of the sequence of meanings I had been reading into everything, especially Lucy. The all-embracing symbolic bird; primitive image with iron wings and rusty tassels and enameled feet; airy murderess like an angel; young predatory sanguinary de luxe hen — now she was funny; she had not seemed funny before.

The cycle of symbolizing by Tower completed by his sudden awareness of the gap between the generalities, the symbolic significance he has read "into everything" and "reality," he begins to see a different, factual, side to things. Madeleine tosses the revolver into the garden pool, and Tower sees the realistic situation of the moment:

> The important gesture was too much for her. Off the dear wrist she went, hung in a paroxysm once more. But this time it was not bating, not mystical dread or symbolic love of liberty; it was just ordinary loss of balance. Symbol or no symbol, I said to myself, if I were busy getting rid of a suicidal or murderous weapon I should hate to have a heavy hysterical bird tied to me, yanking my wrist, flapping in my face.

Mrs. Cullen without her high heels is "beautiful," with her "somewhat bulky body — motherly torso and round neck," as she helps Lucy recover her balance. Tower turns to Lucy again and pities her as a bird, considers her "position in fact," being handled like a "handkerchief or a muff, or a hat." He is again amused at himself "to think how often the great issues which I had taken this bird to augur, come down in fact to undignified appearance, petty neurasthenic anecdote; bring one in fact at last to a poor domestication like Lucy's."

Thus the narrator's mind reverses its direction and turns in effect to destroying the layers of meaning it has built around the falcon. With this transformation, Tower has slowly begun to see that the situation and people involved are not all that he has made of them. Even the "facts" are often not clear. There are certain clues to Tower's difficulty, although no reference is made to some of them. Mrs. Cullen is called Irish by Tower, for instance, but her husband, in anger perhaps, refers to her as English; both overgeneralize if we accept what Alexandra tells Tower, that she has "Ulster blood and English blood." Madeleine, according to Alexandra, has "money of her own," but fact remains obscure, for Cullen says of his wife "I took her without a penny," and "I've let her have all my money." Tower finds himself as he generalizes, "like a fool.... thinking of Mrs. Cullen as a childless woman" and forgetting her "wild Irish sons." Earlier, as Mrs. Cullen is talking about "avian haberdashers" in India and Persian handbooks of falconry, Tower says of himself, "I wanted to know all this. Yet I failed to pay attention." He is too busy with his characteristic exercises of mind.

As Mrs. Cullen leaves for the second and last time, Tower refers to Larry Cullen's act as attempted murder, but is brought up short by Alex, who says, "But it was suicide, surely, not murder." Tower hedges in what he calls "my quibbling way," saying suicide is for lovers often the result of the desire to murder, but Alex is skeptical and replies that Cullen "wasn't really very drunk." Tower, surprised, reminds her that Cullen had "two shakersfull of pre-war vodka," but is told, "That's not much for those immense Irishmen." She has seen Cullen really drunk, Alex says, and perhaps this time he was pretending. Alex reminds Tower that he's "such a sober creature," that he tends to "over-estimate other people's intoxication." This series of exchanges serves to further undermine Tower's confidence in his habitual turn of mind:

> Her saying that made me suddenly unhappy. I thought of the wicked way I had watched him as he drank, the grandiose theories of drunkenness I had spun for myself meanwhile; and I blushed. Half the time, I am afraid, my opinion of people is just guessing: cartooning. Again and again I give way to a kind of inexact and vengeful lyricism; I cannot tell what right I have to be avenged, and I am ashamed of it. Sometimes I entirely doubt my judgment in moral matters; and so long as I propose to be a story-teller, that is the whisper of the devil for me.

It is at this point that Alwyn Tower clarifies for himself why his generalities and symbolic layers are unreliable; his addiction to "grandiose theories," his spinning of symbolic meanings, are "for himself" — a kind of self-hypnotic process. He sees also that it is an expression of the self — lyricism — but unfortunately "inexact and vengeful," the motive inexplicable, the results untrustworthy. A short time later he is engaged in another typical habit of mind:

> ...I fell into a form of fatigued stupidity which, while it lasts, often seems to me an important intellectual effort. It was an effort to compress the excessive details of the afternoon into an abstraction or two, formula or moral; in order to store them away in my head for future use, and yet leave room for something new, for the next thing. Morally speaking, those Cullens had crowded me out of myself. I also hoped to distinguish a little more clearly between what the Cullens meant to me and certain fine points of my own meaning to myself which had fascinated me in the midst of their afternoon's performance. Of course, it was not possible.
>
> I have learned — but again and again I forget — that abstraction is a bad thing, innumerable and infinitesimal and tiresome; worse than any amount of petty fact. The emotion that comes blurring my retrospect is warmer and weaker than the excitement of whatever happened, good or bad. It is like a useless, fruitless vegetation, spreading and twining and fading and corrupting; even the ego disappears under it .... [4]

This mental activity has in common with the spinning of "grandiose theories" and symbolic meanings the impulse to abstraction. Here, however, rather than auto-intoxicating self-expression, there is in the beginning at least a conscious critical effort to judge reality and come to conclusions, to abstract a "formula or moral." It is not possible, he finds, because such a process is opposed to reality, to "petty fact," and removed from "excessive details." So far removed is it that even the unreliable self, the ego, is "corrupted" and entwined in "the fruitless vegetation."

Precisely as the bachelor in *The Babe's Bed*, Tower finds the results of his ruminations are unfounded and unjustified and the product of self-infatuation, self-projection. The shock of reality now brings him to ironic laughter as he mentally strips away the symbolic layers that he has built. The destruction of artistic self-confidence is the result of the devil's whisper and is apparently not a new event, as evidenced by the previous remarks in the narrative, in one of the strongest of which, previously quoted, he refers to himself as an unsuccessful artist.

Even more precise in *The Pilgrim Hawk* than in the earlier work is the recognition of the two aspects of Wescott's talent and technique which developed from the first novel through the short stories to the achievement in *The Grandmothers* and *The Pilgrim Hawk*. These are qualities which became evident as the double nature of Wescott's most important aesthetic discovery, the participating narrator, the success of which is inextricable from his highest achievements. The two qualities are those stressed in the chapter on *The Grandmothers* — the *lyrical* (which Tower here calls "vengeful lyricism"), associated with the expression of the self, the expression of the emotion of the narrator, the imagistic quality of the language, the lyric creation of moods; and the *rhetorical*, in tone and function the quality that makes itself evident in tone and voice through image, metaphor and especially aphorism and generality. Its purpose is to investigate, communicate, and to persuade the reader "not only of the actuality and importance of fictional events, but with *truths*, with abstractly stated concepts."

These are the positive qualities of the narrator. The negative qualities are just what Tower calls attention to in the final parts of *The Pilgrim Hawk*. The narrator here despairs of his habit of abstracting, of his research for formula and moral. The habit is, of course, one with Wescott's concept, discussed in the chapter on *The Grandmothers,* of *images* and *truth, images* being facts, or what passes for them in fiction, and *truth* being abstract, and as with Wescott previously, the very justification of fiction itself, hence his excess of generalities and his tendency to didacticism. In *The Pilgrim Hawk,* Wescott, through the narrator, seems to recognize by implication the fallacy of such an idea, and that the truth is in the image and not derived from it, yet there are strong indications that if he does he is like Alwyn Tower and "again and again" forgets it.

The recognition that is most important for him, however, is that his habit of mind seems incurable. Whereas the Alwyn Tower of *The Grandmothers* was able, with the help of his aesthetic distance (or tower) in Europe, to give form and meaning to his material in America, and Alwyn Tower of *The Pilgrim Hawk,* again distanced in time and geography, again succeeds, he has decided nevertheless that his vision is no longer reliable, that he will descend, and that to be concerned with "petty facts" is the only way to escape the "spreading and twining and fading and corrupting" of the abstracting mind. He destroys what he has created in *The Pilgrim Hawk* because the "whisper of the devil" tells him it is only a projection of the self.

The major theme of the work is that of the self, the self as artist, for the entire aesthetic construct is pointed toward self-examination, and the characteristic impulse of the mind of that self is the primary propulsion of the novel; it is the force that revolves the symbol and moves the narrative; it is the continual effort of Tower to push his insights toward solving the mysterious nature of the Cullens' relationship in order to draw conclusions about their lives and apply these results to himself, and it is the impulse of that mind that terminates in the conclusion that the mental effort is all lyricism and abstraction and must be rejected. Thus the very success of Alwyn Tower as narrator proves his failure as an artist, and the very success of *The Pilgrim Hawk* depends on Wescott convincing himself, apparently, of his failure as an artist. Nothing could be truer than Rueckert's summing up: "Without absurdity, it can be said that Wescott slays himself as an artist in this work." It should be emphasized that the flaws that lead him to this destruction appear to be intrinsic characteristics of his most successful and important means of narration, the participating narrator, never to be used again.

One of the ironies is that *The Pilgrim Hawk* is one of the author's finest works of fiction, unique in form and finely wrought. Some critics have objected to the amount of symbolic meaning the narrator insists on creating about the hawk, revealing that they have not understood what the novel is about, ignoring Alwyn Tower's destruction of the layers of meaning, and his discounting of them as *truth*.

In his brief but fine criticism of the novel, Morton Zabel cites the paragraph which ends with "that is the whisper of the devil...," saying that Wescott "can define his personal difficulty and yet overshoot the mark of creative humility."

> Such lucidity of scruple produces a laudable alertness in the conscience of a writer, but its insistence over and above the volition of his drama soon involves him in a radical difficulty; it leads not only to a serious enervation of the tone, force, and unity of his story and the exaggerated preciosity which is the major weakness of the particular book, but to something more dangerous still — an enervation of his imaginative substance itself and of the impulse that must be counted upon to project it as drama and reality.

If we are to accept Tower's judgment of himself as narrator (and Wescott's as writer), must we not accept the destruction of the very formal beauty we have enjoyed and the attributes of its parts? The judgment of Alwyn Tower on everything is then in doubt, his portrayal of people probably inaccurate, his generalities and aphorisms at best only half-truths. But even though there are clues here and there that such might be the case, the characters presented are among his most fascinating; never has Wescott's style been more admirable, his prose so satisfying to the ear and sense of phrasing; his generalities and aphorisms have the appearance, in context, of being true, and the continual accumulation of the symbolic layers around the hawk is exciting in its complexity and structure.

The point would seem to be that since this is after all fiction, an art form, it is possible to admire the beauty of the artistic object even if its theme denies that such beauty exists. The theme, after all, is one element, and, as Alwyn Tower himself might point out, an abstraction. The reality is the total form, not a statement that can be abstracted about what it means.

Zabel says that the novel suggests rather than "a love story," a fable, "a prepossession of contemporary novelists," and one that "has always been . . . of great appeal to Americans."

> The radical problem of the art exists in its necessary quality of ambiguity and symbolic tension—in the degree to which symbolic or allegorical purpose must remain implicit in the experience or rooted in the matter of the genre as against the degree to which that purpose may derive from the conscious intention or moral intelligence of the author.

Although he finds *The Pilgrim Hawk* "one of the most remarkable works of its kind in recent American fiction," he nevertheless believes it out of balance because "the dramatic substance of his scenes and characters does not succeed in sustaining the elaborate commentary and moral deliberation he has imposed upon it. The annotation of the situation becomes too elaborate, ingenious, and uncomfortably self-conscious."

Zabel is of course making a criticism about essentially the same problem that concerns Tower, but it is not clear whether Zabel sees where the true center of the story lies. Since he quotes a long paragraph on married love as "expressing the story's motive," perhaps not. In any case, one can only repeat that the true dramatic substance is the movement of the narrator's mind, and that the necessary elaborate commentary and moral deliberation must be large for it is both the subject and the means. If, by the "experience," Zabel means the triangle of love relationships, and especially the Cullen relationship, it must offer substantial material for commentary to show the narrator's mind at work, but not as much as if it were the single subject and center of the novel.

There is no question that *The Pilgrim Hawk* is more powerful to those who know something of Wescott's previous work. For the self of this novel unquestionably, as in *The Babe's Bed,* is Wescott's artistic self, and it is looking back on the self of the expatriate-artist that produced *The Grandmothers* particularly, and that attempted without success to produce something worthwhile in the thirties. There is even more of a confessional quality—partly due to the use of first person rather than third—than before, yet there is no morbidity, but rather honesty at the expense of anguish. Wescott states his problem, or at least what he thinks it is. Apparently he has not fully seen the contribution to it of his concept of the dichotomy of *image* and *truth*, for he has said in essence that he can no longer produce the truth from the images, or from the "facts," and that he will therefore produce nothing at all.

It seems to escape Wescott that *if* it is valid that the artist may abstract truth from images, then the way to make the images true is to inject, in the act of creation, the truth back into them. If this sounds too much like a formula for reconstituted rice, it should be noticed that although Wescott's rhetoric has been essentially an analyzing, ruminating, *abstracting* rhetoric, as he is aware, its purpose has been rather to convince, and along with his lyricism, to create mood and to spellbind — that is, it has not been *primarily* concerned with aiding the creation — with aiding the creating of characters, scenes, and dramatic situations through the elements of concrete detail, or images. This may seem to state something of what Alwyn Tower recognizes in *The Pilgrim Hawk*, but it is doubtful if the recognition is in these terms.

Wescott, as Alwyn Tower, apparently meant what he said. Yet he was to produce one more novel, which was to prove, unfortunately, that he still held to one of his favorite theories.

6
APARTMENT IN ATHENS

Although it appeared over twenty-five years ago, *Apartment in Athens* (1945) is quite probably the final novel of Glenway Wescott. Through narrator Alwyn Tower, identical with the author's second self, Wescott had announced his intentions in *The Pilgrim Hawk*, five years before, to write no more fiction. However, the stories "Mr. Auerbach in Paris" (1941-1942) and "The Frenchman Six Feet Three" (1942) appeared during the years of World War II, strongly marked by the events of the time. As for Wescott himself, he referred to his new novel as his war work, and strongly felt that what he had to say about the war, the issues, the Germans themselves, was a truth that must be told.[1] The result of such motivation is very evident in the book itself.

The setting of the novel is neither Wisconsin nor the Europe of the expatriates, but Athens, Greece, during the occupation of that country by the Germans in World War II. The action involving the five main characters takes place during a few months, and almost entirely in the four-room apartment of the Helianos family. Four of the central characters are members of the Greek family; the other is Captain Ernst Kalter of the German Quartermaster Corps. Critic Sy Kahn has said:

> Wescott has fashioned a story which does nothing less
> than explore the psychological effects of occupation on
> both victor and vanquished, the unspectacular heroism
> that tyranny engenders in the defeated, and the suffering

of their spirit as well as their flesh. Slowly and inexor-
ably the novel enmeshes the characters in a design of
suspicion, fear, despair, anger and hatred and presents
in microcosm the dilemmas of not only the Greeks but
all peoples who find themselves under Nazi domination.

Such, at least, is the intention.

Nicholas Helianos, the head of the small family, was, until
the German occupation ended his business, "part-owner and editor of a reputable publishing house in Athens." A mild, rotund
man of middle-age with a scholarly mind, he attempts to survive
the tyranny of Kalter by passive submission. It is his means to
avoid what amounts to extinction on every level, and in the end
it fails. His recognition of this is stated in the letter he writes
in prison, which is revealed at the book's end.

Mrs. Helianos, "indolent and stout," a sufferer of heart
trouble and mild hypochondria, has been spoiled most of her life.
The weaknesses of her character show up in the first year of the
defeat, and as the occupation and Kalter's tyranny continue, the
frequency of her heart attacks increases. Through Kalter's sudden shift of character and her husband's imprisonment, however,
her inner resistance forms and takes on increasing strength until
finally, at the novel's end, her narrow concern with immediate
existence, her moodiness and her ego are purged by the catastrophe of her husband's death. She now hates the Germans as
never before, and is able to give her son, herself, and daughter
to the struggle for freedom.

The two Helianos children are Alex, twelve, and Leda, ten.
Frail and stunted by undernourishment, Alex feeds his imagination with childish dreams of desperate vengeance for his older
brother, Cimon, who has died earler in the war at the Battle
of Mount Olympus. Leda, in contrast, has suffered mental and
spiritual, rather than physical, stunting. It shows in her "sensitive but passive face that made one shiver." Already drained of
resistance by shock, she is robbed of speech after seeing demonstrating Greeks murdered in the streets by the Germans. The
name Leda is intended to call up mythical overtones; there is
no doubt that Wescott intends her as a symbol of Greece, deprived of all reason by Germany's violation, but still alive in
her sensitiveness to the emotional atmosphere.

Thinking over the horrifying atrocities committed by the Germans, Helianos reflects that Captain Kalter is not as bad as he

could be, not one of those who imagines himself "in some barbaric poetic drama or terrible opera, from morning to night, year in and year out." Yet his characteristics are intended to be representative; his ambition and ideals, his brand of discipline, his manner of applying a certain kind of power — all are presented as typical of German mentality and character. As his name implies, his emotional response to others is frozen. The Nazi myth of race and conquest and German militarism are the components of his religion, of which he is an arrogant and fanatic worshiper. His treatment of the Helianos family is, in miniature, Germany's treatment of the subject nations and their populace.

There is nothing complex about the narrative sequence and structure of the novel. The anonymous and omniscient narrator reveals the main events and most of the minor ones in straight chronological order, and the structure is centered around five main events.

In the first section the characters are briefly introduced, then set in motion psychologically as Kalter moves into the apartment and establishes his command over the family — the first major event. Kalter's first act is to requisition over half of the apartment and its furnishings (including the bathroom and toilet) for himself, leaving the family only the kitchen, one bedroom, and a useless foyer. The children are given the bedroom, and the aging couple spend their entire nights together on a narrow folding cot in the kitchen. They find that not only their days but part of their nights too are spent providing, in one way or another, for the Captain. Methodically, almost meticulously, and with a certain pleasure, Kalter attends to subjugating the Helianos. The old family servant, Evridiki, is dismissed, a cruelty to all involved; in the middle of the cold night either Mr. or Mrs. Helianos are often called to wait upon Kalter with a chamberpot, so that he will not have to leave his warm bed. The Captain inspects the food supplies, and the starving family is able to get little from the leftovers of his table, for he either litters them with cigar ashes or has them sent by Alex to a fellow officer for his pet bulldog. Alex is unjustly accused of stealing some of the food, and is whipped. Mr. Helianos gets an occasional kick, and Mrs. Helianos is covered with bruises from falling, from knocking herself against objects as she leaps aside in panic at Kalter's gestures, or in her fear of not pleasing him.

From the first section onward, the physical and psychological suffering of the family is delineated in day-to-day detail, leading in muted drama from tension to tension. Mr. Helianos accepts humiliation as unavoidable and part of the given condition of being defeated, convinced that their only choice is to submit, to serve the master well, in the hope that he will soften somewhat in time. But famine is everywhere in Greece, and their hope is as useless as the instinctive act of the neighbor's baby who feeds itself from an open wound in its own hand. By gratifying Kalter's every whim at all hours, the Helianos are reduced to something lower than personal servants. In the first section they are portrayed as making every adjustment to a situation that would seem unendurable. But as a family they are at the same time drawn together as they suffer and passively endure; and, surprisingly, the love that Nikolas and his wife have let atrophy for the most part, in what is no longer "the autumn of their love," but its "winter," is rejuvenated with a difference as a result of their new hardship. The new relationship is neither erotic nor sensual, for Helianos imagines himself impotent and "Mrs. Helianos' menopause had come early," yet they have the "extraordinary intimacy" and "double eccentricity of lovers, confusion of two in one." They are intended to illustrate, as the story unfolds, those simple humanistic virtues represented by the Greek way of life.

In contrast are the habits and characteristics of Kalter. Helianos observes him with intense curiosity, considering the clues which the Nazi's behavior affords. He is aware that Kalter's purpose is to break their morale, and that it is part of a general plan. At the same time Kalter's apparent intellectual discipline, his study of "military history and the science of war, a topographical atlas, meteorology and a treatise on the diet of armies," is impressive, as are his notebooks which reveal practice at both some "unknown language" and "arithmetic of some sort." His personal life seems confined to study, as dutifully rigid as his working day. Like other German officers, Kalter is in behavior "self-conscious and methodical," as if instructed in it "according to some new historic theory or psychological science." Accompanying this behavior is the "unnerving thing... the great Prussian manner, serene and abstract, almost a mannerism, with insincerity in it somehow, but combined with conviction." Helianos compares the manner to those of priests who are in being more than human, to actors in a great drama, and to madmen who have sublime dreams.

In the second section (chapters 5-10), Kalter takes a two-week leave in Germany. During that time the Greek family finds its temporary release from tyranny a disappointment, demonstrating that they are self-indulgent, and that even the memory of the pleasures of the past have been obliterated by day-to-day hardship. Kalter, now a major, returns a changed man—the second major event—taking an interest in the Helianos as fellow creatures, showing a certain studied pity for them, rejecting his studies for cheap French novels, and even becoming friendly enough to share his evenings and the sitting-room with Mr. Helianos.

Mrs. Helianos is suspicious, her husband puzzled and fascinated. The two men talk for hours, the major dominating the conversation which is nearly always on their favorite subject, Germany and the Nazi party, their motives, ideals, and sense of destiny. These discourses set forth clearly the primary thematic conflict of the German and the Greek, or Humanistic, way of life. It is soon revealed that the change in Major Kalter is due to the death of his entire family—his second son in combat, his wife in a Berlin air-raid. His personal life, Kalter admits, is destroyed, but he has his religion in Germany. Fascinated by what he is learning of this German, and believing that the outward change in Kalter means that he can talk freely, Helianos, in a feeling of pity for all men, openly lays the blame for the world-wide tragedy on Hitler and Mussolini— the third major event. Kalter worships the state and its leaders. He beats Helianos in a rage and has him imprisoned.

Mrs. Helianos suffers a heart attack, but in a few days is well enough to be out of bed. At first she hopes only to please the major, in this way bringing about her husband's freedom. Then she finds herself inwardly defiant and at the same time wanting to kill herself; but it is Major Kalter who commits suicide—because he finds that he is human and personal grief leaves him unable any longer to make himself useful to the state. The fourth major event encompasses the results of his leaving behind instructions that his death may be used to convict the Helianos family of his murder, thereby serving Germany as propaganda. Kalter's friend, Major von Roesch, manages to prevent this, with the intention of using his resulting power and influence

over Mrs. Helianos to obtain information about the underground, in which other members of the family are leaders.

It is at this point that the character of Mrs. Helianos begins
its change from weakness to inner strength and her mood alters
to one of inner certainty and determination, indicated in part by
her new awareness of the significance of the Parthenon.

The fifth and most important major event, then, occurs in the
last section. It is the radical change on the part of both Mr.
and Mrs. Helianos from a passive acceptance of their condition
to one of action against the tyranny they have suffered. Nikolas
Helianos' change comes about in prison during the time he
awaits execution; he writes a letter on scraps of paper setting
forth the knowledge he has gained from his ordeal and the
action that must be taken. The letter is smuggled out to his
wife by her cousin Demos, whom she had thought to be a
collaborator. Demos appears a second time to bring her the
news that her husband has been executed. Although she suffers
her most serious heart attack then, and appears to be broken,
she is not. Her great change through knowledge comes through
reading the letter, and through suffering her husband's death.
She survives and endures with a new dedication to Greek
freedom. The ordeal after the death of her father is also the
catalyst that works as a shock-treatment on Leda, curing her
schizophrenia and restoring her speech. It matures Alex almost
overnight as he assumes the family burdens and responsibilities
left by his father; and his imagination and cleverness acquire
new value. In one of the novel's contradictions, Mrs. Helianos,
realizing that Alex, his childhood full of the horror of war, will
never be good for anything except fighting in the underground,
consents to let him join it. Determined to resist the Germans in
any way possible, she intends to put Leda to whatever use she
can, and become part of the movement herself by leading the
Germans to believe she can give them information. In a scene
intended to symbolize that Mrs. Helianos has, in effect, become
a mother again and that Alex is reborn, the novel comes to a
close.

Apartment in Athens can only be ranked as the least successful, artistically, of Wescott's novels. Even the shortcomings of
The Apple of the Eye are those one might expect of the first
novel of a twenty-three-year-old author, and they are absolved
by its promise, which is fulfilled in the mature and admirable

performances of his later work, particularly *The Grandmothers* and *The Pilgrim Hawk*. Certain of the flaws in the last novel resemble — with a difference — those in the first, and one of these which is of major importance in *Apartment in Athens* is its didacticism. Another concerns the prose, and still another the point-of-view and narrator and narrative voice. These flaws permeate every element of the novel, but it is particularly in characterization and structure in relation to theme that Wescott's insistence on getting across his "message," his *truth,* is most evident.

The major themes of love and the self which appear in all of Wescott's major work are here evident again, discernible, but flattened and distorted by the didactic intention. One aspect of the theme of the self, what serves as the major theme of the book, is, as it was in *The Apple of the Eye,* the life-killing, life-distorting effects of Puritanism, as Wescott defined it before publishing his first novel: "the evasion of experience ... evasion by theory, in conduct and thought."[2] Fascism is a secularized, latter-day Puritanism, a theory with a code which effects the denial of experience. It not only stifles but destroys the self, working as a kind of disease in any society in which it is found. The political form presented here is more widely and insidiously destructive of what is of human value than the religious form presented in *The Apple of the Eye.* Theory, or abstraction, rejects the day-to-day concrete reality of the present for the hypothetical abstract future. Kalter, like Rosalia of the first novel, is destroyed by the resulting separation of the spirit and the flesh. Not only the individual, but the family group, the families of Kalter and Helianos, willingly on the one hand and by tyranny on the other, are sacrificed for the theoretical or abstract good of the state. The theme, of course, is not unusual in our time:

> Like Joyce, Lawrence, and E. M. Forster before him, and Orwell as well as many others after him, Wescott sees this conflict as the central problem in the modern world. *Apartment in Athens* is not just the transplanting of Puritanism to Greek soil, or the serving of the old regional wine in new bottles; it is an attempt to present in fictional terms a profound and, as things have turned out, true perception of what was to be won or lost in the war. The positive values — which were

and still are embodied in the novel in the Helianos
family specifically and in the Greek way of life generally; and the negative values — the destroying forces
present then as now — are embodied specifically in such
people as Kalter and von Roesch and generally in the
Nazi German way of life. [3]

The "positive values," include, of course, love — and love, as
in all of Wescott's work, is a major theme. The drive or mo-
mentum of events is, typically, toward knowledge, and as always
in Wescott's important work, it is knowledge of the self, which
when attained, allows the protagonists to "live life." Puritanism
is the enemy of self-discovery. The dramatic conflict is double;
there is the drama of conflict between Helianos and Kalter
(Greek and German, Humanism and Puritanism) and the drama
of everyday life as one lives it, represented by the Helianos. The
very ordeal of living under Nazi tyranny revives both the
atrophied love of Helianos and his wife for each other and their
love for their children.

The major themes of love and the self, however, are not only
de-emphasized by the heavy emphasis on the truth contained in
the letter of Helianos, the themes themselves are set to work to
carry this truth as a message. The final purpose of self-discovery,
seems, after all, to be not an end in itself but something that
can be put to use to fight Nazi tyranny. The letter not only
dominates the last part of the novel, it, rather than self-discovery, becomes the key moment toward which the novel has been
working. In addition, the *truth* about the Nazis is deliberately
set forth as applicable outside the work of fiction. Under the
thin pretension of telling Mrs. Helianos to tell the world, the
letter directs information and a course of action to the reader.
There is even a special appeal aimed at Americans. Helianos
instructs his wife to tell Petros (the cousin who is in the underground) *"to go to America and talk to people there"* since
Americans will be *"most important again when the war is over:"*

>   *"Tell Petros to warn them beyond the sea that it may
>   happen to them too, before the century is over. Nothing
>   is too difficult for these great mystical, scientific, hard-
>   working, self-denying Germans, possessed of the devil as
>   they are, and despising everyone else.*
>   *"I do not suppose that the Americans are indifferent
>   to their fate and danger. I think that their worst mistake*

must lie in their hope of getting peace established for
all time, as if it were a natural law needing no enforce-
ment, so that they can relax and be frivolous and forget
it. When they see that this is not possible then they lose
hope altogether. They give it all up as a bad job and
yield to their cynicism and fatalism. It is what happened
after the other war. I want Petros to speak very strongly
of this, because it is a terrible folly.

The letter concludes with two paragraphs emphasizing that
there is no such thing as "peace forever," and implying that
eternal vigilance is necessary. The remaining two chapters (less
than twenty-four pages) portray Mrs. Helianos receiving the
news of her husband's death, suffering a heart attack, recover-
ing, observing the miraculous change in her two children, and
determining on her course of action.

The Helianos, man and wife are, like Hannah Madoc, represented as secular saints, and *Apartment in Athens* resembles
the first section of the early novel in its intention to portray the
daily existence which stands as a positive example to be emu-
lated. The "Bad Han" section of *The Apple of the Eye* was
quite inadequate to such thematic intentions, and the Helianos,
as fictional creations, suffer from a certain amount of morally
confused intentions. Perhaps the fact that their love is revived
only under Kalter's sadistic tyranny can be accepted as a paradox, but it can only be assumed that the continuing life of these
good examples under freedom would have led to the permanent
death of love. Their ability to endure passive suffering seems
inextricable from some of their humanitarian virtues, yet its
passiveness is shown to be a mistake. Nikolas Helianos' surge
of pity for Kalter and for all men, when expressed, leads to his
death. The point driven home so forcibly by the plot that
emphasizes Kalter's diabolical scheme against the Helianos is
that the slightest entertainment of such sentiments, with respect
to the Germans, are fatal to the individual and the Western
world. Yet such sentiments are part of the "positive values"
that the Helianos represent. Mrs. Helianos intends, if need be,
to sacrifice herself to the struggle to free Greece, and that is
consistent enough. Yet when she arranges to let Alex fight for
the underground her reason is that, as she puts it, he would
not be good for anything else anyway and she considers him as
"the small boy doomed to heroism." In spite of the rebirth of

her mother-love for him, and in spite of all the realistic concrete evidences of tyranny, her attitude and actions are very like those of one dedicating himself to an abstraction and willing to sacrifice himself — and others — to it.

The characters in *Apartment in Athens* are on the whole the least compelling and interesting of any in Wescott's novels. Of the three main characters, Major Kalter is the least adequately characterized. He occupies the central position in the structure for the major portion of the book, for he imposes the conditions under which the Helianos must live and stands as the example of Puritanism that they observe, both of which bring them to knowledge. Serving as it does to illustrate one of the polarities of the work, his characterization is in its own way as unsuccessful as that of Wescott's first victim of Puritanism, Rosalia Bier.

The actions of Kalter which move the plot, and the details of his personal behavior and his habits, as Nikolas Helianos observes them, wonders, and speculates, are obviously placed like one brick after another to add up to the Nazi personality as Wescott conceives it: the stereotype of war-time films and popular fiction.

There is never an attempt to *render* a single thought or feeling of Kalter as experience. He is entirely observed from the outside. Therefore, whatever struggle or anguish there may be must be discerned through what can be observed. Shortly after the change in Kalter's behavior, Helianos examines the sleeping German's face.

> Helianos started to wake him, then thought it kinder and wiser not to, and tiptoed across the room and stood for a few minutes gazing at his slumbering face. In the weakness, unwariness, of slumber it struck him as more lamentable than ever: the bony mask like a great fist, with the flesh drawn loosely, vacuously over the bone; his cheeks long and slack and pallid, the scar on one cheek bright pink. His lips, so willfully pressed together when he was awake, now looked as though they had grown together, like another scar.
>
> Oh, what was the matter with this man? Perhaps, Helianos thought, it was remorse for the various cruelties of the Germans in Greece, cruelties all over Europe for that matter: the rack and boot and the branding-iron, the whip and the club and the thumbscrew and

the wheel; whatever the terms were in up-to-date parlance, whatever the equivalents were in contemporary German practice . . .

   This was an explanation which had not occurred to Helianos before. [4]

Helianos' speculations on Kalter's possible remorse are followed by the thought that the German may be touched by "collective guilt" and he looks at him again:

There was some constant, almost perceptible motion in his face, now in one feature, now in another; as on the surface of even stagnant water, in a leaf or a little stick or a scum, you see or you imagine the life of the water up and down, sinking, swelling.

   Perhaps it was not remorse, perhaps it was fear. Perhaps Germany had begun to lose the war . . . [5]

But Helianos discounts this last thought as wishful thinking. The point here is that even these observations reveal very little about Kalter the man, and even though they may indicate the existence of an inner struggle, such tentative conclusions are for the purpose of tracing the thoughts and feelings of Helianos about, among other things, German cruelty. In fact, it is later clear that Kalter, pointedly, does not feel any kind of remorse or guilt. Even in the climactic scene in chapter 10 in which Kalter tells Helianos of the death of his younger son and of his wife, and of his intentions to commit suicide because he "cannot go on," thereby revealing the division between the flesh and the spirit, his words are so colored by and inextricable from Nazi thought that he is an observable phenomenon rather than a sympathetic being. Even his tears seem grotesque:

Suddenly his face all twisted into the ugliness of grief, and not one muscle in it moved after that: only the tearducts were alive and active, and his tears were not drops but a little inundation down his cheeks, all the way down to his chin. It was like seeing sculpture weep, not Greek sculpture of course; Gothic sculpture . . . [6]

Finally Helianos is able to feel pity, and "struck by the realization" that Kalter was "sincere at last," makes his fatal blunder of asking Kalter:

. . . "is it not intolerable? To think that two men, two men with too much power, fatal tragic men, should have brought all this tragedy upon us other men?"

Since Kalter's answer is to beat Helianos and have him sent to prison, where he is later executed, it can only be concluded that pity, though an admirable human trait, is not to be applied to Germans.

Wescott's method of showing Kalter entirely from outside is one that is easily turned to presenting only somewhat believable characters as devoid of sympathy. Yet there is nothing in such a method that prohibits the rendition of anything but a flat character, or precludes characters of depth and complexity. The author has shown himself to be in command of the techniques of a novelist of manners in *The Pilgrim Hawk;* but in this last novel there is none of the insight and rendering of selected detail *of the kind* that would make Kalter interesting as a person. Neither does Wescott call upon the resources of the prose that he had developed to render sensibility. Kalter seems only a specimen, and although he suffers the death of all he loves and kills himself, the ironic point remains an abstract one, without pathos, or without any genuine recognition of his suffering as a human, because no attempt is made to show it. On the contrary, the purpose seems to be to elicit a stock response, one that does not require sympathetic understanding through which would come the recognition of the cost to those who would live as Puritans. In attempting to present his concept of German temperament, character, and ideals, Wescott fails to present human temperament and character. There is no probing into the nature of man and his situation — be it ever so special — for that which makes him into a Kalter.

Although Kalter stands at the center of the novel in structure and theme, he does not succeed as an effective symbol. A character, object, or action, even if it be successfully typical or representative, is not necessarily symbolic. Kalter stands as an example, a blueprint carefully labeled, with detailed instructions for handling. The meaning one gains from him is not cumulative, but the result of logical arrangement and progression; he does not radiate meaning. Kalter is no Pilgrim Hawk. Although the Helianos speculate about him and learn, there is here no powerful rhetorical voice to speculate, ruminate, and invest him with symbolic meaning by Wescott's proven method.

If Kalter is an example of the self destroyed by Puritanism, the more positive aspect of the self is represented by Mr. and Mrs. Helianos, who each, like Wescott's previous heroes, have to go through a series of ordeals to find the self. It is there too, such as it is, that the love motif is to be found, as the very core of the "positive values" represented by the Helianos.

The numerous details of the everyday life of the Greek couple, and the meticulous following of the vacillation and change of their emotions and thoughts, are in the long run not engaging nor effective in the intention of gaining sympathy, at least not the kind of sympathy necessary to thoroughly affirm the values that these characters are intended to represent. They arouse curiosity, interest, and a kind of clinically sympathetic under- standing as the plot so clearly proceeds to reveal what the villain, Kalter, will do next, and how he will trick them, and what they will learn from that. Alex and Leda are not more than one-dimensional, nor fully emerged from the conception they are intended to represent. A major portion of these failures in characterization can be attributed to the prose, point-of-view and narrator, which are discussed in the following section.

Symbolism, Prose and Narrator

"There are none of Alwyn Tower's tricks in this novel;" says Rueckert of *Apartment in Athens,* "it is all written on the ground as objectively as possible in a traditional but powerful way. In style and in other matters of technique it is a kind of plain chant in praise of the private, homely virtues." It is true that there are not the complex time levels and structure of *The Grandmothers* and *The Pilgrim Hawk,* nor the entwining and involuting of metaphors intrinsic to theme and structure, nor the symbolic texture, certainly, found in the prose of those works. Yet such a statement hardly describes the actual quality of the novel, particularly the use of symbol, prose, and narrator.

There is an attempt to evoke a reminiscence of classical Greek drama and myth. There is a certain unity of time, place and action in that the setting is almost entirely confined to the small apartment over a period of a few months, and the cast is small. The names of characters seem obvious enough in intent, the Helianos family standing as the inheritors of the Hellenic in culture, thought and ideals. Although the given name of Mrs. Helianos is never revealed, her husband's name, Nikolas, perhaps recalls Nicolaus, the philosopher of Syracuse, who failed in his attempt to prevent violence being done to Athenian prisoners of war.[7] Cimon, the son killed in the battle of Mt. Olympus, has the name of the famous Athenian military hero, "the last of the Greeks whose spirit and boldness defeated the armies of the barbarians."[8] The old and pathetic family servant dismissed by Kalter is named Evridiki, and the narrator is careful to inform the reader that in English the name is *Euridice,* perhaps intending to imply that such a dismissal is a profanation of the past, for there seems little other association. The name of Alex, the son, recalls Alexander the Great, and the name of the daughter, Leda, has already been commented on. Kalter is certainly a cold one, and the clever cousin who pretends to side with the Nazis is named Demos, meaning, of course, "the people." Yet he seems no more representative than any other Greek. He has no character attributes, either, that would suggest that the Greeks, as the saying goes, invented Democracy. No doubt Wescott intends that his characters will be thought of as humble equivalents of their namesakes of a glorious age, but the contrast, perhaps, is too great, the names too obvious; the hoped-for association or emotional response is unearned.

The dialogue is again, as in *The Grandmothers,* generally of a quality that can only be called ordinary or, at best, adequate. There is no attempt to imitate or create speech with overtones of the modern Greek and German language, but that is not the issue. As so often with Wescott, summary narration, rather than direct scenes, allows for a minimum of direct dialogue. It is Kalter's dialogue that calls the most attention to itself. His most memorable utterings, even though conversation addressed to a Helianos for the most part, are speeches. They are, as Kahn says, "more precisely orations," which "locate Wescott's analysis of German temperament, motive and destiny." Quite so, but they are not, as Kahn insists, therefore justified. They are often set speeches, uncomfortably reminiscent of those on Paganism by Mike Byron or Puritanism by Jule Bier. They too were attempts to provide a substitute for what had not been achieved by more difficult means. They too were in result didactic in the attempt to render the thematic polarities in the novel.

The words "traditional" and "powerful" for the method in *Apartment in Athens,* if the contrast of Wescott's best work is kept in mind, seem simply a euphemism. The qualities of technique in the modern tradition of fiction which have been Wescott's from the very first — a patterned, as distinguished from plotted, ordering of events, for design itself or mythic implications; a consistent arrangement of related images for symbolic texture; major symbols; a powerful narrative voice — all are either missing or attenuated and atrophied.

In the essay "Good-Bye, Wisconsin," Wescott had expressed his desire for a prose style "out of which myself, with my origins and my prejudices and my Wisconsin, will seem to have disappeared." In *The Babe's Bed* and in *The Pilgrim Hawk* he objectifies his complete distrust and rejection of the very lyrical and rhetorical qualities that were intrinsic to his most effective means of narration, the participating narrator with a powerful narrative voice. The quality of the prose and the means of the narration in *Apartment in Athens* are apparently the result of such desire and rejection. The participating narrator is abandoned for a third-person omniscient point-of-view much less lyrical or rhetorical than that of *The Apple of the Eye*. It is one of the major reasons for much that is inferior in the novel.

The omniscient narrator makes himself evident from the very first sentence of the novel ("All this happened to a Greek family named Helianos") in terms of voice. Of course it is a very different voice from that of Wescott's participating narrator and from the omniscient voice of the first novel, but its accent and tone, however ineffective, are heard throughout. For the largest portion of the book the narrator focuses on the thoughts and feelings of either Mr. or Mrs. Helianos, never on those of Kalter, and only briefly on those of the two children. Frequently, for brief passages, he suspends his focus for direct comment. Here the focus is on Mr. Helianos. He is thinking about his wife:

> ...but it was hard for him to argue with her about any such thing now, because he was worried about her. She had always had a mind of her own, but of late, he thought, it had gone too far. Agitatedly over and over she would harp on certain subjects all day long, then suddenly shift, and fall into a kind of heavy delirium in which she would not express herself at all for hours. Sometimes she went from the one extreme to the other with a rapidity and apparent lack of sequence that startled him: up and up with her fiery spirit, in some conceited opinion, vain anger, even unexpected mirth;

> then in an instant down, as it were visibly into a pit,
> a soft hopelessness. Often when her spirits fell Helianos
> could see where Leda got her little scowling self-absorp-
> tion, her apathy and loss of self in emotion.
>
> There were days when she talked to herself instead of
> him. He would hear her sometimes quite loud, in the
> kitchen or the children's bedroom, and at first he would
> think that the children were with her; then find her
> alone. She had never done that before, and what he
> heard alarmed him . . .

This particular passage goes on for several pages. It is typical,
except for the few selected scenes that are, relatively speaking,
rendered, of most of the narrative movement of the book. The
narrator has moved to within a certain distance of Helianos to
give us his thoughts. The method is economical, helping to
characterize the thinker and the characters he thinks about. But
there are several points to be noticed. Except for an occasional
turn of phrase ("harp on"), the impression is that these are
neither the actual words of Helianos, nor, upon examination, a
very close equivalent. Although the *focus* is upon the thought
and feeling of Mr. Helianos, there is a steadily maintained
distance between the narrative voice and those thoughts and
feelings of which it gives an account. The language contributes
to this effect in being often abstract when one would expect a
character remembering such details to do so in concrete language.
For example, Mrs. Helianos harps upon "certain subjects," but
there are no samples given of what she says nor are we told
what the specific subjects are. "A heavy daydream in which she
would not *express herself for hours,"* is again language that is
identifiable with the narrator, not Helianos. Much the same
comment can be made about "she went from one extreme to
the other with *a rapidity and a certain lack of sequence."* Such
diction is typical and aids in establishing throughout what is
actually summary — action, thought and feeling viewed in retrospect by the character, but with the aid of the mild narrative
voice and usually from a placement in a rather vague time-
present. Except for key scenes, Nikolas and Mrs. Helianos are
always looking back on what has just happened a very short
time before. As a result, Wescott is able to avoid, as he typically did in *The Grandmothers,* anything but key scenes, but at
the cost of any dramatic immediacy. As for such phrases as

"fiery spirit," "vain anger," "unexpected mirth," and "soft
helplessness," with their echo of 18th century diction, they
further establish the presence of the narrator, but not in a voice
that is vivid, dramatic, or virile.

Without such a narrative voice, and the language or ruminating mind of the participating narrator, the total effect is a lack
of vitality, a dimming of authenticity. Above all, what can only
be called the emasculated narrative voice fails to render the
sensibility of the characters—a talent Wescott had from the
very beginning of his career—to the extent that they are anything more than rather complicated examples.

There are, here and there, occasional reminders of what voice
and prose are in Wescott's best work. There is an echo of the
old lyric quality at the moment the Helianos experience a re-
awakening of their love:

> To be sure, there was nothing erotic or sensual or
> even sensuous about it. Helianos was, or fancied that he
> was, impotent; and Mrs. Helianos' menopause had
> come early, in keeping with her poor health in general.
> Yet in the dead of night they pursued an extraordinary
> intimacy, as they lay wearily in a heap of one body al-
> most on top of the other on the folding cot. They
> knew once more the double egocentricity of lovers,
> confusion of two in one. Everyone else and everything
> else in the world might have been shed away in the
> forgotten sky over Athens, and the dark turning of the
> earth toward next day, purposeless except to rock
> them, on the formless mattress and sagging springs.

Such passages are infrequent. Even here the attempted "objectivity" of the beginning sentences and the rather tepid reminders
in the remainder of the metaphysical poets seem to pull against
each other, as well as maintaining distance. Yet it is one of the
few passages in which the themes of love and the self emerge, if
only briefly, with any power.

In the following passage Helianos is suffering from Kalter's
suggestion that Leda be taken to a Nazi psychologist to be
given treatment:

> He relaxed, he smiled again, he forgave, he stayed
> his impulse to kill, such as it was, he voided his
> indignation. It was an event in his soul. As a rule the

soul cannot relax by halves; one way of yielding
gradually induces another. It is a kind of goodness that
may act as a weakness. If you forgive more than you
can afford, you may find yourself impoverished in
emotion afterward, with a lowered resistance to whatever happens after that.

This passage in particular is more reminiscent of the prose of
The Pilgrim Hawk than any other in the book. The echoes are
strong of the narrative voice of old, with its aphoristic, generalizing, abstracting characteristics that Wescott had hoped to get
rid of. For the most part he has, but almost everything that
made his prose distinctive went along with it.

The only attempt to employ anything like a major symbol
first appears in the last half of the novel, in chapter 11, immediately after Helianos has been taken to prison, with the following
passage:

In spite of her narrow mind and emotional intensity,
Mrs. Helianos was not the simple, Balkan type of
Greek woman; not at all. She sometimes reminded
herself of this distinction, proudly. She had European
culture enough to know in what esteem ancient Greece,
ancient Athens, was held everywhere; how everyone in
the world was indebted to it for something, and ac-
knowledged the indebtedness. Up there, over modern
Athens, there it stood; the chief national treasure that
foreign sightseers by the thousands (including Germans)
came to see — Parthenon on Acropolis; a building that
no amount of warfare had been able to obliterate so
far, in the cloudless blue, on the timeless rock that
even the might of the Germans could not alter; remnant
of past upon portion of eternity. Looking at it in-
spired in her a certain grandiloquence and blissful
stubbornness.

Inability to render sensibility here contributes to the failure of
the passage to establish an effective symbol. The introductory
phrase is in distance very far from the feeling or thought of
Mrs. Helianos. The main clause is ambiguous. Is this the narrator's evaluation, or is it intended to show how Mrs. Helianos
thought of herself? The second sentence and the rest of the
paragraph is intended, apparently, to render essentially what
Mrs. Helianos thinks in the kind of language she thinks it. Yet

"European culture enough," and "chief national treasure," do not seem phrases appropriate to Mrs. Helianos. The diction of the last sentence, of course, can be nothing but the narrator commenting on her condition. The long sentence before that, although it attempts to establish a tone equivalent to Mrs. Helianos' emotion about the symbol, is certainly not presented in the kind of language she would use. The whole passage suffers from the contradictory intentions of conveying the feeling and thought of Mrs. Helianos and of rhetoric directed toward the reader. It is a heavy-handed insistence approaching the language and mentality of American travelogue films, particularly in the implication that the symbol must be powerful because it is a "chief national treasure," and because thousands of "foreign sightseers" come to see it; the narrator is condescending. With such awkwardness Wescott tries to invest his symbol with life and set it going. Here are the next two paragraphs:

> Then as she stood and looked, she assumed an atti-
> tude which in physical sensation corresponded to her
> thought, her spirit. It was an attitude prompted perhaps
> by unconscious memory of ancient sculpture that she
> had seen all her life (although without caring for it
> especially), or perhaps merely exemplifying a racial
> habit of body from which that style of sculpture derived
> in the first place — a classical attitude, her fatigued
> thickened torso drawn up straight from her heels and
> from her pelvis; her head settled back on her fat but
> still straight neck, her soiled, spoiled hands lifted to her
> loose bosom, through which went just then a little of
> the bad thrill of her palpitations, anginal pain like the
> stitches of an infinitely strong and invisible seamstress.
> "One of the Fates," she said to herself aloud, "the
> frightful trio;" but she did not mind the thought. The
> time of not minding her personal destiny had come.

Again, the distance between narrator and character in the first paragraph is very great as the narrator substitutes exposition for the qualities of prose that could invest Mrs. Helianos and her action with symbolic implications. Having sheared his narrator of most of his lyricism and rhetoric, Wescott leaves him with only mediocre capabilities. There is a kind of desperate insistence on what is the author's intention in presenting the character's action: " ... she assumed an attitude which in physical sensation corresponded to her thought, her spirit." There are other things wrong with the passage: the somewhat coy speculation ("perhaps by unconscious memory...perhaps merely exemplifying...") which again is a disguise of an explanation of what the action is intended to symbolize; and there is the condescending label ("a classical attitude"). Mrs. Helianos' action and speech in the next paragraph, after this, border on parody. This is due in part, at least, to the extreme distance between narrator and character.

The other appearances of the Parthenon and Acropolis are few, and of questionable effectiveness. The next is in chapter 12, and takes place during a period of low morale for Mrs. Helianos:

> Lonely, lonely, lonely for Helianos she tried to look up to the dessicated flat-topped rock and the indestructible old temple once more, because they were what he loved — the national treasure of Greece, Athen's trademark, the tourist's delight as well as his — but as she had not yet succeeded in not weeping, they were only a phantom and a smudge, which left her lonelier than ever.

Here the attempt is actually not to get the symbol to work on the reader, but to show how it fails to symbolize for a character (with a careful reminder of what it is intended to signify) because of personal grief. Twice more, on the next-to-last page, after Mrs. Helianos has determined to devote herself and her children to underground resistance, the symbol appears again. In each case Mrs. Helianos tries to shut it out of her mind:

> Then if she had cared to, she might have taken another look at the Acropolis, the temple in a blur, the hill in a black veil, her great reminder, her worst keepsake. She constantly kept her back turned to the window.

A few lines later she rejects the idea of having a neighbor woman come in to work for her:

> No, if she and Alex were going to work for Petros, they could not have this guileless talkative one so close to them. When she took over the housekeeping again, she meant to keep the curtains drawn close against the Acropolis, and work in a half-light.

The implication seems to be that Mrs. Helianos finds the symbol a too-powerful reminder of her husband and the values he, and Greek culture, represent. It is her "worst keepsake," meaning, apparently, that it is a keepsake of the worst that has happened to her. She wishes to avoid pain by willfully not thinking of her husband's death and Greece suffering under Nazi domination. The symbol is, consequently hidden by a mourning veil. The second passage seems to imply that in working for the underground, which she intends to do by appearing to aid the Nazis, she must keep her true sentiments, symbolized by the veiled Acropolis, hidden. Yet it is not clear that that *is* what is meant. Besides, if she is going to "turn her back" on what the Parthenon and Acropolis have been so carefully intended to mean in the earlier passages, *even when she is alone,* she will be turning her back on the very values it, her husband, and she are supposed to represent.

With such mental labor, insistence and confusion does Wescott attempt to will into effectiveness the only major symbol in his last novel. There are none of the characteristics here of successful symbology evident even in his first novel. Appearing only a few times, the Parthenon-Acropolis hardly merits being called a cumulative symbol, especially since confusion, at last, deflates whatever power it had. It is not a revolving symbol that successfully radiates facets of meaning. There is no texture of symbolic imagery, either, to give complexity and depth to the prose. With minor symbology there is also little success. In the book's last pages Mrs. Helianos sits down next to Alex, "the small boy doomed to heroism."

> She liked to be near him now that she had thought of a way to prove to him that life had taught her to understand and love him. He lay curled up close to the wall with his hands under his chin, his knees drawn up, somewhat in the position of a child unborn in the womb.

With such a hackneyed image, in a thin and powerless prose, and with little more than that, the attempt is made to symbolize that Mrs. Helianos has become a mother again in her love for the boy, and that he is "reborn," with a new maturity. Leda never comes alive as a character, and consequently does not succeed as a symbol for violated Greece. Her fictional existence remains at the level of a rather poorly imagined metaphor.

It is evident from the discussion in this chapter that the most positive attributes of Wescott's most successful fictional techniques which reached their perfection in *The Grandmothers* and *The Pilgrim Hawk* are either absent in his last novel or evident only in ineffective and weakened form.

The many shortcomings of the novel — in structure, characterization, dramatic confrontation and dialogue, in lack of richness in imagery and in failure to create adequate symbols — are traceable to an important degree to Westcott's rejection of the participating narrative voice and his inability to reject his concept of *image* and *truth*.

Alwyn Tower, the participating narrator identifiable with the author's artistic self in *The Pilgrim Hawk,* despairs of his incurable habits of "vengeful lyricism, abstracting, and constantly searching for a formula of a moral," because they lead not to the *truth,* but a projection of the self. It is evident that Wescott identified these negative qualities as inseparable from his participating narrator, and that this is one, if not the only, reason for his not using such a narrator in *Apartment in Athens.* Yet the participating narrator was not only his greatest technical discovery, but, with the exception of a few short stories, his only successful means of narration. Having discarded such a narrator, Wescott in effect discarded for the most part the positive qualities of the voice that was inseparable from it: the *lyrical,* associated with the expression of self, the expression of the emotion of the narrator, the imagistic quality of the language, and the lyric creation of moods; and the *rhetorical,* which made itself evident in the tone and voice of the narrator by means of image and metaphor, by aphorism and generality, and which was the means to investigate, to communicate, and to persuade the reader of the actuality of events *(images)* and of *truths.* These qualities, of course, made possible an effective symbology.

An omniscient, anonymous narrator can, in theory, retain many of these qualities, but Wescott has emasculated the narrator and fatally weakened his voice in *Apartment in Athens.* What remains of the voice is simply incapable of the performance of the voice of the participating narrator. Nevertheless, although the voice is weak, and devoid of much of the lyrical and rhetorical qualities evident even in Wescott's first novel, it is, as in *The Apple of the Eye,* inescapable; and, as in that novel, the voice always maintains a distinct *distance* even though the *focus* may vary. The result is that, with such distance, artistic success will be impossible without the success of the narrative voice — a principle proved in Wescott's first novel and his last.

It seemed possible that the fallacy of the concept of *images* and *truth* was recognized by Alwyn Tower, and consequently Wescott, in *The Pilgrim Hawk*. But in *Apartment in Athens* the concept is applied without any attempted justification as part of the rumination of a participating narrator, resulting in didacticism and a form and structure which splits the novel into two parts, the *images* of the daily life of the Helianos and Kalter, and the *truth* contained in the letter of Nikolas Helianos.

Two of the qualities of *The Apple of the Eye* that kept it from being anything more than promising were first, the disparity between the narrator and other elements in the novel and second, and allied to it, its didacticism. In the works that followed, Wescott was able for the most part to solve these fundamental problems, mainly through the development and use of a complex narrator, consequently producing, at least twice, fiction of the highest quality. In *Apartment in Athens,* his work in an unfortunate way comes full circle and the novel repeats, fundamentally, the same aesthetic errors as the first.

7
CONCLUSION

Images of Truth (1964), a collection of eight essays, the majority of which appeared from 1939 to 1962 in various publications, indicates by its title that one of Wescott's most fundamental ideas is, at that date, still with him. William Rueckert's discussion of the work is excellent, although he far overrates the intrinsic value of the essays. His taking the publication of them (along with a projected anthology which never appeared) as an indication that "a new period of growth had apparently begun,"[1] when they consist of eight essays written during a period of over twenty years, is, on the face of it, unjustified.

The essays are, as Rueckert points out, only "ostensibly about prose fiction, but actually about the truths and images of reality" that Wescott has found in his favorite works of fiction. These pieces are not literary criticism but "lyric" essays, written "in a personal voice" in which "details from Wescott's private life...are used as instruments of criticism, and direct applications to the life of the self (are made) as a test of value." The two "centers" of the book are the self and the concept of the ideal novel that Wescott "thought he ought to write and partially achieved in *Apartment in Athens*."[2] It is apparent, it is true, in the following paragraph from the first essay in the book, "Fiction Writing in a Time of Troubles," that Wescott, as he did in *The Pilgrim Hawk,* is rejecting the very qualities that Alwyn Tower found "the whisper of the devil":

My conclusion is that brilliancy of ego, headstrong

and headlong display of intellect, powers of elaboration, poetical afflatus, and that frenzied and exalted artistry which is like drunkenness, play an important part in literature; but as regularly as clockwork, most of the time, everything of that sort has to give way to a prosaic simplicity, to brevity and explicitness, and to traditional themes and immemorial symbols and images.

Throughout the work Wescott admires "the concrete universals of art" for conveying the *truth,* having in mind a "truthful narrative" whose means are the rather traditional ones more likely to be found in the nineteenth century novel than the twentieth. In the second essay, "Katherine Ann Porter Personally," it is clear he finds exemplary the "objectivity" of Miss Porter's fiction; he praises her for being capable of projecting herself into the interior life of those who are unlike herself, and he finds her work devoid of the "narcissism and subjectivity of many modern novelists." The evidence of the essays, Rueckert says, shows of Wescott that "the embodiment of his own vision in narrative art — in short, his vocation as a novelist — were all transmuted and finally transferred to another mode of expression." The result of his ideal of the objective novel is "a profound self-denial for the sake of a fixed idea which ultimately is not worth one page of *The Pilgrim Hawk.*" That Wescott, unable to write the objective novel, "transmuted and finally transferred" such vision and talent into eight essays over a period of more than twenty years seems tenuous; but Rueckert asserts in his final chapter that there was a decrease in Wescott's "source of power."[3] "Like most authors... Wescott was clearly on a double quest at least through *The Pilgrim Hawk;* in addition to an organic form he was also in search of a self and all that this implies." Both quests, "endemic among modern writers, appeared to have been completed in *The Pilgrim Hawk,* but time has now shown that Wescott did not have the same kind of certainty about the form of that work as he did about the truths which it expressed." The search for the form has continued, although the self which "became fixed in its values... became less and less creative," and "contrary to what almost everyone has said, the search for the self rather than the regional material was the motivating creative force.... Read in order, the fictional works present a completed search, the last stages of which can be found in *The Pilgrim Hawk,* with *Apartment in Athens* as a kind of rounding out or amplification of the values arrived at in *The Pilgrim Hawk*." Plausible as this explanation is, Rueckert himself does not seem quite satisfied with it as a final answer. Certainly the ultimate reasons are deeply buried in the personality; yet what has been revealed in this study offers a clarification of the relationship of Wescott's personal self to his creative self, and that in turn to his fictional technique, and some reasonable conclusions on his literary silence can be made.

The most positive and promising aspects of Wescott's art in *The Apple of the Eye* were those associated with the omniscient narrator and those attributes — including the rhetorical and lyrical quality of the prose — inseparable from that narrator's voice. Yet the positive qualities of that voice were at the expense of other techniques of fiction that make for a successful work: characterization, dramatic realization and confrontation, confrontation of thematic polarities that would take the form of believable life, a moral vision complex enough and realized enough to justify what the narrator insisted was the theme, this insistence being embodied in aphorism, generalized statement, and didactic dialogue.

The disparity between the narrative voice and other qualities of technique are discernible, in some form or another, in greater or lesser degree, throughout nearly all of Wescott's work. *The Pilgrim Hawk* is the noticeable exception. In *The Grandmothers* Wescott developed the participating narrator with his many capabilities, including an even more powerful and more flexible voice. Many of the flaws or shortcomings of technique that appeared in the first novel are, in the second, for the most part, justified by its distinctive form in which the narrator oversees all with his ruminating, involuting mind and colors it with the quality of his voice. Nevertheless, examination reveals that often, and significantly, technical flaws are not so much overcome by practice as circumnavigated, camouflaged, and avoided by the adoption of the participating narrator and the particular form intrinsic to him.

A major flaw in *The Apple of the Eye* was the detrimental insistence upon certain *truths* as theme; it appears not only in the didactic dialogue but by means of the narrator. In this first novel the commitment to the idea of *images and truth* is already evident, and the means of abstracting *image* from *truth* is the narrative voice. In *The Grandmothers* the abstraction of *truths* from the *images* that are the family of stories is justified in principle because it is, to a high degree, functional; intrinsic to the very theme of the self and the form is the concluding rumination and analysis for a synthesis of what the narrator has learned. The lyrical and rhetorical voice with its symbol-making and abstracting and generalizing becomes inseparable from the overseeing mind that must draw conclusions, for that mind is the book's subject.

The technique of the participating narrator and his voice, the concept of *image and truth*, the theme of the self — each of these is in *The Grandmothers* dependent upon the others, and their interrelation is necessary. The dangers of slighting other techniques, by depending too much on the powers of the narrative voice, of over-generalizing and over-abstracting, of becoming didactic — these too are all perceivable in the novel in spite of its aesthetic success. The very fact that it does succeed as well as it does and seems perfectly suited in form to Wescott's talents and to his weaknesses and shortcomings powerfully suggest — in retrospect — that for the writer, the new narrator, the concept of *image and truth,* and the theme of the self are strongly fused in the crucible of the creative imagination; and what is more, the relationship of this particular form to the writer's personal self is very close. The thematic self in this novel is Alwyn Tower, the participating narrator; and the participating narrator is identical to Wescott's second or artistic self, the mind of the artist in his work. The fact that in *The Grandmothers,* for example, the author drew on material so near to him personally — his own family history and his relationship to his family [4] — emphasizes that the distance between Alwyn Tower and Glenway Wescott, between the second self as objectified in the novel and the autobiographical, or personal self, is not great. In *The Grandmothers* the thematic self, Alwyn Tower, performs his artistic act of composing the family of stories in order to realize the self, just as Wescott performs the same task in writing the novel. By means of the participating narrator-character, Wescott is able to give at least the minimum distance to his material to perform his task. The closeness of the personal and second self suggests that in *The Grandmothers* and *The Pilgrim Hawk* (but apparently not in *The Babe's Bed*) the distance between the narrator and the rest of the material in geography and time provided an additional and necessary gap. There is, therefore, not only a strong fusion of participating narrator, concept of *image* and *truth,* and theme of self, but a close relationship of the artistic self, which is integral to that fusion, and the personal self.

Wescott's strong commitment to the form that represents this complex of relationships is evident when it is realized that throughout his work the great and major theme is that of the self, and that his only truly and consistently successful form of narration is by means of the participating narrator.

Nevertheless, in the essay, "Good-Bye, Wisconsin," appearing a year after *The Grandmothers,* Wescott announced his desire for another kind of "style." The paragraph is pertinent enough to quote again:

> For another book I should like to learn to write in a style like those gestures (of the signal flags used by sailors): without slang, with precise equivalents instead of idioms, a style of rapid grace for the eye instead of the ear, in accordance with the ebb and flow of sensation instead of intellectual habits, and out of which myself, with my origins and my prejudices and my Wisconsin, will seem to have disappeared.

For whatever personal reasons, Wescott's desire here, it is apparent, is not simply to say good-bye to his Wisconsin, his regional material. It has been previously stated that the first half of the paragraph seems to describe the language of science. In any event the "style" here described is not only a matter of language; it shows Wescott's desire for the "objective" fiction that from then on he began to think he should write. The terms in which he describes it make it obvious it is a form very different from that intrinsic to the participating narrator. The absence of "idioms," and "slang," of "intellectual habits," and especially of "grace...of the ear," would make impossible a ruminating, involuting, generalizing participating narrator with a predominate voice. "Precise equivalents" would mean the virtual elimination of image and rhetoric. Just what the "ebb and flow of sensation," especially if given in "precise equivalents," meant to Wescott is difficult to say, but there is no doubt that what he seeks to avoid is the form with which he has had so much success, and that he is aware of the close connection of the personal self to the artistic self embodied in the participating narrator, and consequently the form to which it is integral. It is his "origins" "intellectual habits," "prejudices" and "Wisconsin" which he hopes will *seem* to have disappeared. What he seeks to find in the new form is a greater distance between the personal self ("myself") and that artistic self as it appears in his work. Rather than having completed the search for a self with which he wants no more to do, he hopes that the personal self will not be *apparent* in his work. He was successful in *The Grandmothers* with Alwyn Tower as a means of objectifying the self, but now, it seems, such a narrator is too close to him.

The Katherine Ann Porter essay, although written years later, makes the same point in different terms:

> ...Whereas in fiction she has been free of herself. In fiction she has maintained a maximum impersonality, a disengagement from any sort of autobiographical point of view, a distinctness between her own ego, her sensitiveness and compulsions and illusions, and those of all the alter-egos that she writes about, and an abstention from fantasy and lyricism and rhetoric, of which most novelists, indeed many journalists and historians, are incapable.

It is the lack of evidence in Miss Porter's work of the personal self that Wescott admires, the "distinctness" and "disengagement" of the personal self from the artistic self. He goes on to apply to Miss Porter "Coleridge's famous formula," saying she is capable of "sending herself out of herself," of "thinking herself into" the interior life of those who are unlike her, and she is devoid of "a good deal of that pride and willfulness and narcissism and excitability by which the life work of most modern fiction writers has often been beclouded, enfeebled, and blemished." The kind of fiction that Wescott denigrates here and in the above paragraph for its lack of artistic discipline has as its artistic attributes the techniques of his own best work, and reveals his deep distaste for it because of its closeness to the personal self ("pride and willfulness and narcissism"). The scarcity of published fiction between 1928 and 1940 and the appearance of only two stories and a very inferior novel since the publication of *The Pilgrim Hawk* are the proof of the inability of Wescott to solve this problem. Kahn has documented remarks by Wescott that show he attempted all through the thirties different techniques of narration, but with results that were never satisfactory to him.[5]

In *The Babe's Bed* (1930), the problem itself is the subject of the story, and the method itself is the problem. The participating narrator finds his own involuting, ruminating, symbol-making, generalizing mind produces fantasies which are in a sense true to himself, but not true to external reality, and hence not valid as *truths*. The story is evidence of Wescott's determination to destroy his own faith in the method of the participating narrator and the psychological necessity behind it. It re-emphasizes that the author felt that such a method was inadequately disengaged from the personal self. Another revelation is intrinsic to the irony of the story's failure. Apparently neither narrator nor author are aware that one of the greatest faults of the rhetorical narrator, his profuse capacity for generalizations, particularly in a *summing up* of *truths* learned by the narrator, is indulged in to a degree beyond any aesthetic justification. As in the short stories "The Dove Came Down" and "The Wedding March," the method of the participating narrator generally fails, showing that even Wescott's most brilliant method was not always reliable, not even for the purpose of proving its own unreliability.

Unlike *The Babe's Bed, The Pilgrim Hawk,* written ten years later, is by every consideration an artistic success. It is in one way, however, a brilliant, superb rewrite of *The Babe's Bed.* The theme of the self as artist, Wescott's artistic problem, is again the central subject and the method illustrates it. Again the narrator (this time Alwyn Tower) concludes that the results of his abstracting, generalizing mind are unjustified and are simply self-infatuation and self-projection, the personal self too close to or identical with the artistic self. This knowledge is the "whisper of the devil" that destroys his artistic self-confidence. Again, even though Alwyn Tower despairs of his abstracting and his search for a formula and a moral (and "again and again" forgets that it is "bad"), neither Tower nor Wescott seem to recognize that such a "habit" is one with the concept of the dichotomy of *image and truth,* for Wescott announces through Tower that since he can no longer produce the *truth* from *images* he will write no more fiction.

It is curious that Wescott wished to reject every quality of the participating narrator and the intrinsic form of which it is a part with the one exception of the concept of *images and truth,* especially when it is this fixed idea that is the rationale that leads to discernible flaws in *The Grandmothers*. It leads to even more damaging shortcomings in other works — to, precisely, the excessive generalizing, abstracting, and insisting on formula and moral that Wescott recognizes as fatal.

In his attempt to write an objective novel in *Apartment in Athens,* this is the only aspect of his former technique that Wescott consciously and deliberately retains, and it is the most obvious cause of making it a didactic novel and a failure. One wishes that the problem were simply a matter of acceptance and rejection and that Wescott had done just the opposite: rejected the concept of *images and truth* and retained all of the other qualities intrinsic to the participating narrator; for one other significant characteristic of *Apartment in Athens* is that the author does not succeed in narrating objectively. The voice and some other qualities of narrator (now omniscient) are still apparent, but so deliberately suppressed and limited that the resulting weakness of narration debilitates the entire work.

Wescott's strong commitment to the idea of *images and truth,* his failure to recognize it as inseparable in practice from the method of the participating narrator and the characteristics he desired to eliminate — these factors and his failure to completely do away with the narrative voice in his last novel suggest that Wescott, despite his conscious desire and apparent distaste for the results of such narration, was powerfully drawn to it, and that this may account for his failure to succeed with what he thought of as the opposite kind of form. This seems all the more reasonable when it is recalled that the narrator in *The Babe's Bed* learns that the habit of mind which is in practice the action of the participating narrator is inescapable. He sees his ambiguous talent and obsession as the making of "fantasies" and his attitude is fatalistic toward this "force." He calls it "nature or destiny or god or anonym. Maniacal worker, mad about its art." In *The Pilgrim Hawk,* similarly, the artist-narrator finds his habit of mind incurable, and that is why he decides to write no more. It is this, certainly, that Alwyn Tower, Wescott's spokesman, has in mind when he says:

> ...No one warned me that I did not really have talent enough. Therefore my only hope of becoming a very good artist turned bitter, hot and nerve-wracking; and it would get worse as I grew older. The unsuccessful

artist also ends in apathy, too proud and vexed to fly again, waiting upon withheld inspiration, bored to death.

If the "hope of becoming a very good artist" has been so disappointing, then "the quest for the self" cannot be thought of as completed, nor the expression of it satisfied, even in the achievement of *The Pilgrim Hawk,* which insists upon the hopeless anguish of the attempt.

The above passages from *The Babe's Bed* and *The Pilgrim Hawk* and the two following quotations from the essays in *Images of Truth* further substantiate the contention that Wescott is still drawn toward the form that he has rejected, that he still habitually thinks of making fiction out of material very close to his personal life, and that he still retains his image-truth obsession:

> In the modern novel the most important thing is individuality, therefore it has to be, above all, explanatory and intimate. The question asked in it as a rule is not *who* but *what*—what is he or she? what are you, the reader? or indeed, as it is often a subterfuge for autobiography, what am I? It is a portraiture or self-portraiture, stepping out of the frame only enough to demonstrate itself in action, or to teach a lesson, or to make a point.

Whether the quotation is accurate as a generality about the modern novel can be argued, but the fact that Wescott so defines the modern novel in terms that sound like a description of his own best work rather than that of others, and that he villifies in other essays what he says are the characteristics of the modern novel, often the very characteristics given here, seems to argue that he is still so emotionally fixed on rejecting the participating narrator form that the very intensity and prolongation of this rejection argue a continuing strong appeal of that very form. The following passage, from the last essay in *Images of Truth*, "Talks with Thornton Wilder," reinforces that impression:

> ...Gide used to say that, even to change the color of the iris of someone's eye, in the transposition from human actuality to the fictitious form of it or substitute for it, falsified the record. Nothing that could ever be

invented or fabricated, he thought — and many of us also think — could compete with what we have seen, heard, touched, enjoyed, embraced or been embraced by, hurt or hurt by. This does not make novel writing easier for us. It seems, sometimes, to make it impossible.

The attachment is to a form close to the personal self and its experience, and one very different from the "objective novel," the process here opposed to "maximum impersonality," the "disengagement from any sort of autobiographical view," and the "distances between" one's "own ego...and those of all the alter egos that" one "writes about," which Wescott so praised in Katherine Ann Porter. It appears likely that Wescott's long fictional silence is due to being immobilized between the pull of two opposing concepts of the novel form: one in which he has done his only significant fiction and which he rejects in spite of it having some deep personal appeal for him, and another which he admires and believes superior but in which he can do only the most inferior kind of work, or none at all, because it is a denial of all his talents and perfected techniques, as well as a denial of the self.

After a long fictional silence of twenty-five years,[6] there seems little chance that Wescott will again publish any important fiction. In a recent review by Wescott of Garson Kanin's *Remembering Mr. Maugham,* there is a passage that, in its comments on the value of memory in affording aesthetic distance, and on the necessary quality and characteristics of the "rememberer's," or narrator's voice, brings to mind both *The Grandmothers* and *The Pilgrim Hawk.* Wescott's certainty about the validity of the qualities of memory and of its inter-relationship to the narrator and his voice suggests the possibility, however slight, that he may someday write again of the theme of the self in the form of his best work. It shows, certainly, no matter how he has tried to rid himself of it, that he is aware of the power of the narrative voice, and his tone is assurance that it still has its appeal for him:

> ...Memory is about the past, the well-digested past, not the hour just ended. It is almost a fictive process; even its lapses create; the proportions in which one recalls things are structural. Recalled (not jotted) conversations, especially, have a third dimension: that of the rememberer's own way of talking, embracing what he quotes.[7]

APPENDIX

PLOT SUMMARIES

The Apple of the Eye

BOOK ONE: Bad Han

Hannah Madoc, a motherless farm-girl of twenty, lives a lonely life with her drunken father on his desolate farm near the marsh. He dies as a consequence of her defending herself when he tries in an alcoholic rage to beat her. Forced to take a job in a village saloon, she succeeds as an attractive but husky barmaid and bouncer. That spring she falls in love with Jule Bier, their love progressing through the summer and winter, when she leaves the saloon to work on a farm near his. Jule's father, however, persuades his son, without much opposition, to seriously court Selma Duncan.

In her anguish Hannah strikes Jule when he breaks the news of his coming marriage, and he responds by again making love to her "in sorrow and desire," while believing himself "still free." Three years later, when she discovers that Han has become a prostitute in nearby Fond du Lac, Mrs. Selma Bier persuades her husband that they must help Han with enough money to allow her to return to her farm on the marsh. "Bad Han" is now physically changed and older, a mystery and an object of gossip. In her early years on the farm she has brief "promiscuous romances" with male visitors, and she becomes the "established mid-wife of the poor" and advisor to the young in trouble. In time she acquires a certain masculine ruggedness, an admirable self-reliance and hardiness that makes her a kind of local saint. She appears to have forgotten loneliness and passion, to be immune to change. Wandering, hunting and trapping in the marsh, she seems to be part of it, and by middle-age she has become an old woman, withdrawn from the community, "in the common mind...legendary" and "an enigma." One day in her forty-first year she falls from her barn-loft, breaking a leg and hip; she is nursed the last two days of her life by Jule, who gleans "from her sunken, unlighted face her wisdom."

BOOK TWO: Rosalia

Many years later, young Mike Byron, who has had various jobs and callings and spent three years at the university in Madison, is hired by Jule Bier as a farm hand. At the funeral of Old Duncan, the grandfather of Rosalia Bier and Dan Strane, Mike finds himself curious about both families. As the sermon of the "hell-fire" preacher Reverend Seazer, continues, Mike fears that Dan will be "crippled" by "this religion of sin," and he soon after begins to initiate Dan into his view of life, in which "our only duty is to be happy." On the same afternoon he sees for the first time in several months the beautiful Rosalia and falls "instantly" in love with her.

When the fifteen-year-old Dan Strane listens to his mother, Theodora, tell the story of her courtship by John Strane, the sheep-shearer, his imagination stops short at the facts of love, and he feels only "disquiet and baffling sorrow," equating his mother with the sheep as victims, and reacting with horror and distaste for his father and things masculine. His mother bends "the sprout before it knew how to grow," demanding a pledge of chastity from him to remain "pure" for his "true mate." A sensitive youth, physically weak but with moral courage, withdrawn from his schoolmates because of superior manners, intellect and sensibility, Dan has a "homesickness for death." He finds animals obscene and cynical, imagining his father's and mother's marriage peopled with "monstrous forms and brutal motions." He turns to his mother's Puritanism, but fears it is an escape from the "carnal and animal."

Nevertheless, he is curous and eager to know, and the morning Mike Byron shows him the grave of Hannah Madoc he welcomes Mike as his initiator. Hannah's story is a "fine" one, because, Mike says, "life is like that." Mike's view is that "Puritanism appeals to the imagination, but it makes people sick," for it "divides the mind from the spirit." Enthralled, Dan is introduced to the facts of sex, Greek myth and Mike's own philosophy of sensuality: "In reality sex is the design, the plan of everything," "not something to be ashamed of." "Be good to each other," Mike tells Dan. "That's the main thing."

Dan's intense mother-fixation diminishes as Mike's "religion" takes opposition to hers. It wakens Dan's "sleeping senses as if with a caress," giving him "an obscure, sweet pleasure which he did not try to understand." In the lushness of summer Dan observes the initial stages of the love of Mike and Rosalia develop, flooded with vicarious happiness, no longer lonely and "shut out."

Love, for Mike and Rosalia, becomes a "bitter conflict." He cannot enlighten her about her religious principles; on the contrary, she tries to convert him. By midsummer, guilt at the consummation of their love results in Rosalia's strange, vacillating behavior and her insistence on their marriage. Mike feels trapped by a passion that flourishes on his unhappiness. Then, Jule Bier, with surprising understanding and no moral righteousness, takes Mike aside; he doesn't want them "to get into trouble." Is Rosalia, who is like her mother, the right girl for him? Jule briefly alludes to Bad Han as a very different kind of woman. Mike, who feels himself a wandering man, knows what he must do.

The news of Mike's impending departure comes without warning to Dan, for Mike has not taken him into his confidence about the misery or unhappiness of the affair. The youth has thought of it as a permanent thing — Ideal Love — and believes Mike incapable of suffering. In his unreal world Dan has imagined "the magnificence of love in the flesh," of life "conceived of as a paradise." Now, again, he feels "shut out," and assumes that Mike is leaving because of parental objections and will send for Rosalia later. As the young man and the boy part regretfully, Dan, measuring his maturing summer, feels that Mike is now part of him.

Now that Mike is gone, Rosalia views her mother as a jailer and her cousin Dan as a spy whom she fears and hates, for he may know her secret. At the same time she feels numb to the

world outside, and, although this doesn't prevent her from
deceiving her mother as to her interior life, it obliterates for a
time even her conscious memory of Mike. Her clouded emotion
soon lifts, however, when she imagines herself pregnant. Ophelia-
like, she gathers leaves and blossoms for her hair and sings to
herself.

Dan learns from his aunt and uncle Guildford that Rosalia
has told them she is going to leave home to join Mike, and
that they have decided not to reveal it to her parents. On the
night of a great winter storm, Rosalia flees along the familiar
marsh path until, her mind filled with images of child-birth,
obsessed, in anguish and terror, she does not even know she
has lost her way. She imagines in her delirium and agony that
she is about to give birth. Stunned, injured, and finally crawling,
she sinks down. "A powerful voice" announces that the child is
born, and she knows she is going to die. "She had given birth
to nothing." Her parents, like Dan, have assumed she ran away
to marry Mike, and they now prejudge Dan as gravely wrong
not to have informed them.

BOOK THREE: Dan Alone

In the burgeoning spring Dan broods over his Swinburne and
Shelley, ready for love, but finding the local girls "coarse."
The memory of Mike urges him to seek the embodiment of
Ideal Love, but he hardly notices the crudeness of his schoolmates because his pride and timidity have isolated him from all
but Phyllis Dunham and her mother, a kind, witty, and sophisticated woman standing in sharp contrast to Selma Duncan, who
no longer sees even her neighbors and never speaks of Rosalia.
Blaming Dan and his aunt and uncle for not preventing Rosalia's flight, Selma weeps and mourns her daughter's moral
death.

Bitter at hearing nothing from Mike, Dan goes out with
Phyllis Dunham, and tries to feign sexual interest, only to be
startled by the girl's kindness, sophistication, and understanding.
One Sunday in Milwaukee Dan is picked up by a prostitute,
but his very excitement and dismay makes him unable "to do
anything about" her insistence. Thinking of Mike, he rejects her
because of his wish to be alone.

Rosalia's body, torn by dogs, is discovered in the swamp. Dan is convulsed with horror at the sight, but recovers enough to help in the burial. At the grave Jule kneels in an attitude of prayer with wide-open eyes that shift "violently, hopelessly, over the ground."

Dan's first reaction is to hate Mike, and he dreams of killing him. But he is soon obsessed by sin and guilt, losing all belief and despising life. He finishes the school year at the "stagnant" town of Rockhill, avoiding the Dunhams, whom he associates with "worldliness and evil." That summer on the farm he tries to numb himself with physical labor until he reaches a state of enervation. Selma Bier dies during the August harvest, leaving Jule with a "clear, strange expression of relief." At the funeral the minister sermonizes on "the rewards of a saintly life."

With the aid of Jule's "grim tranquility," Dan is helped to an understanding and grows out of his sickness. In retrospect, Jule and Dan conclude that if Rosalia was pregnant Mike was ignorant of it; "... religion and morals and so on, are mostly to blame," says Jule. "Most people do as well as they can."

Jule then tells Dan the story of Bad Han "as though to reclaim his own youth by the retelling ... as if at that moment he were taking possession of something he had lost and not expected to regain." Dan realizes Han had not died "the death of despair and dismay" and that her life is "like one of Mike's Greek myths." But he realizes more — the compelling power and mysterious strength of the story's beauty, "its teaching ... inseparable from its narrative." "Everybody," Jule says, "all you children, could learn a lot from Hannah." If Hannah had been his wife, he tells Dan, Rosalia would have been their daughter and would not have been afraid "to tell her mother what was the matter" — and would not be dead. Nevertheless, Jule does not blame Selma, saying he loved her. "But Hannah understood better: she knew how life is; that's all." "I've lost all I've got," he concludes. "They're dead, that's all. And all for nothing. I think it was all for nothing." Jule then sums up in his own words Wescott's theme concerning religion and the meaning of Han's story:

> "The trouble is, you all want something better than what there is. That's religion. Nothing on earth satisfies you. You think there is something finer. Religious people are always like that. They're never satisfied.

Life's not perfect; it's everything altogether; we've got
to make the best of it. They're all right when things
go the way they like to have them; but they can't
stand trouble. When they don't get what they want,
they want to die. Selma was like that; your mother's
like that, I guess; Rosalia was like that; maybe you
are too.

"Hannah was different. She took what came. She
never worried about what she'd done that she hadn't
ought to. She never blamed anybody; she knew everybody did what they had to. She never thought things
ought to be better than they were. When things went
wrong, she stood it. She was always satisfied.

"Now she wouldn't have gone like Rosalia. And
d'you know why Selma got sick and died? Because she
couldn't stand to have her girl run away with Mike.
You know where Rosalia was. And if Rosalia hadn't
been brought up so strict, she wouldn't have been there.
What made her think it was such a disgrace that she
had to run away and die.

"Maybe the old people were all more like Hannah.
Maybe they're more like her in the old country. I don't
know. I never was as good as Selma and your mother;
I'm a German, and I'm not educated. Hannah was just
a common woman; she never went to school. But I see
all the fine people, the people with brains — they all go
to pieces. I guess it's the kind of religion they've got
here. Something's wrong; such things don't have to
be.''

To Mrs. Dunham, Dan retells the story of Bad Han, and finds
an appreciative auditor. Once of Chicago, she reminds him of
the world beyond the one he has known, "to which he believed
he belonged." The act of telling the story has given him a new
conception of himself. "He thought of his whole life and tried
to make of it a legend of Han; but it was not long enough."

The significance of her life and legend, and of her relationship
to the marsh he knows, and he feels it strongly:

She had never had a son; but he felt toward her as
if she were a mother — somehow, in a way that he did
not understand... ...He thought, every man has a
mother; and many men together have a mother. He did
not know who the men were who would then be his
brothers; but Han was their mother together.

Life, like Hannah, has as its purpose "to go on, just to go on."

Speculating on life, Dan thinks that "the best of it is a blessedness. ...there had been his mother, and then Mike, and then Jule. Blessedness as purity, blessedness as sensuous joy, blessedness in the form of an old, dead woman. He had felt love alone, and after that love with a sense of awakening, and at last awe taking the place of love." As to his future life: "His business was to go on, just to go on. He did not understand how; he did not care if he never understood."

But he is disappointed that he cannot go away to college. His father denounces him for shirking his duties, for not informing them of the romance of Rosalia and Mike, for his college ambitions and for being the kind of person he is. His father seems to Dan to stand for his total environment, and he replies with the classic answer: "I didn't ask to be born. I didn't ask to have you for a father." Dan is ordered out of the house, but there is a reconciliation, and he is to go to college after all. Before leaving he is given three chrysanthemums by Mrs. Dunham; "one for each of your mothers: one for your own mother, one for that magnificent Han, and one — for me." "In his imagination there were three other flowers — for his uncle and for his father, and for Mike." On parting he is moved and saddened as his mother asks him to "form a church connection," to "make friends among good, clean boys and girls."

The Grandmothers

The following summaries are of the twelve central chapters only: the family portraits.

CHAPTER THREE: Henry Tower

The title of the chapter ("His grandfather Tower's Character. A Fragment of Autobiography. The Rest of His Life") labels the method; a similar approach is used in other chapters. To Alwyn's boyhood memories and impressions of his grandfather are added the fragment of biography written by the eighty-year-old man just before his death, and then a concise summary of the life left uncompleted in the fragment.

To his grandson, Henry's alpaca jacket symbolizes his "body and soul," his "poverty and indifference," "fatigue," and "pride." He seems "an old and powerful magician" and a "ghost of another epoch," who fought in the Civil War, and who now retains from it only his hatred of war, his drumsticks, his flutes, his trumpet without a mouthpiece, and a bad stomach that can be relieved only by teaspoons of whiskey. To his children who fear him he tells few stories and nothing of his "more important experiences," "brooding" on "his plans which had failed to materialize, his dreams which had given him no rest ... too ill to idealize and too proud to regret anything." The manuscript of the fragmentary autobiography he writes at 80 is given in full. It consists of facts, the exterior life. Here is the pioneering move west from New York State to Wisconsin, full of accurate details and generalities about practical problems of that life and time; but of Henry's inner life there are only the trite phrasing and rhetoric of that age in America. The fragment ends, significantly, in 1848, when Henry was eighteen and youthfully anticipating the new state road that was to make "an Oasis in the Desert of Our Loneliness," but which "like most other visions of my early years, with the lapse of time ... vanished."

The rest of his life is briefly sketched: his return from the war to see both his young wife, Serena Cannon, and his son Oliver die; his marriage to Rose Hamilton, who had been jilted by his brother Leander, and by whom he had six children. He is always something of a stranger to them because after Serena's death the "rest of his life seemed unimportant, and the West came to resemble the East — the light went out of it." Alwyn feels at his death that "the world, in one moment, forgot much that it knew and had never been willing to tell."

CHAPTER FOUR: Rose Hamilton Tower

A compliment and contrast to her husband, Alwyn's grandmother Rose is one of the Hamiltons, a family with no aristocratic pretensions, bearded hunters and trappers who intend to move on west when people like the Towers have made Wisconsin "a woman's country." Already introduced in the early chapters as Alwyn's main repository of the past and as his tutor (and at

whose deathbed he will stand watch in the final chapter), Rose
sees the last threat of the Indians pass. Spontaneous, innocent
but bold, she falls in love with the sensitive and withdrawn
Leander who is constantly shadowed by his jealous younger
brother Hilary. There is no indication that she ever suspects that
the relationship has a latent homosexual-incestuous nature.

Rose does not understand the "ideas and ideals" that make
Leander, with his brother Hilary, enlist, but she admires them.
Before he goes, Leander proposes, but when he returns it is to
fall on his knees to his mother, for Hilary has disappeared in
the war. He breaks the engagement to leave for California, but
shortly after that his brother Henry (whose wife Serena has just
died and whose son Oliver needs a mother) proposes to Rose,
and she is brought back to life. Twenty years as mother and
wife teach her to be "strong, serene" (somewhat reminiscent of
Hannah Madoc in Wescott's first novel), to stoically accept
"every disappointment" and expect "nothing for herself." As for
the Towers, she finds that they are "men she could never understand, men she could only love, quite humbly."

CHAPTER FIVE: Mary Harris

Half a century after marrying Harrison Tower and leaving
Hope's Corner, Alwyn's great-aunt Mary Harris, "the most
romantic member of the family," and "the greatest of pioneer
women," returns to Wisconsin to be buried. The ten-year-old
Alwyn has often heard her story from his grandmother Rose,
and "the life if this woman was fixed in Alwyn's memory like
the plot of the first book he had ever read," "a boy's adventure
story with a single female musketeer for a heroine."

The death of her father, the loss of the family farm, the
voyage down the Mississippi and overland to settle on a sterile
Missouri farm, the marriage of her sister Eliza to one of her
own rejected suitors and the return of the couple to Vermont to
be followed soon by all the disillusioned relatives — these things
help form Mary's strong character and give the young woman
courage to remain the last of her family on the frontier, to
marry a cheerful fifty-nine-year-old doctor, to not only survive
his violent death due to his abolitionist views, but to start alone
on her harrowing pilgrimage back to Wisconsin. To survive and

reach her goal she marries a man for protection, but he turns out to be a drunken bully and coward who leaves her shortly after she reaches Wisconsin, and before she gives birth to a still-born child. After the war she falls in love with and marries Harrison Tower. They settle down in Oklahoma to a peaceful and comfortable family existence. When she is left a widow at sixty-six, she takes her sister on a voyage to England, Europe, the Near-East, Palestine and Egypt, and although she comes home because she misses "the birds of the Mississippi valley," she remains a pioneer to the last. Her dying whisper is "still far to go."

CHAPTER SIX: Nancy Tower

Alwyn's great-aunt Nancy is the kind of woman to whom young men pay little attention, yet she marries Jesse Davis, who "forced his love upon her." The ambivalence intrinsic to Nancy's nature is caught in the image of the flowers of love that are offered only by disgusting male sexuality, a hand on the back of which hair "glistened in a fringe;" Nancy is trapped by desire and repulsion. After two years of marriage she flees to her parents with her infant son, Timothy. Somewhat understanding, her brother Henry nevertheless persuades her out of duty to return to her husband. Her house reflects her obsessive passion for order and meticulous feminine cleanliness; husband Jesse is relegated to a bachelor-like existence in the squalor of a back room, a coarse man with black fingernails and tobacco-stained moustache who cannot change. After the death of a premature child Nancy's mind seems to fail, and she is sent for several months to an asylum, but afterwards she is able to persuade Henry never to send her back there nor to her husband. The result is a "miracle" of recovery. Supporting herself and her son with the female accomplishments of that time, she becomes strong and self-sufficient, and after ten years she even permits the lonely father to return and live with them — in a private room. In a reversal of the former situation, she is strong and even cruel, Jesse pitiful and constantly anxious that he will offend. The emasculated husband's isolation and threatened identity leads to his attempt to bribe a local widow to live with him. Henry Tower angrily ruins such plans, and Jesse, deprived of his *raison d'etre,* returns to Iowa, never to be heard from again. But he is mourned by the "confused and disappointed" Nancy, for in her own way she had loved him. She finds sympathy and understanding only from her brother Leander, who has returned after twenty years from California.

CHAPTER SEVEN: Leander Tower

Previous chapters give only sketchy details of climactic events in Leander's life: his attachment to his brother Hilary, his romance with Rose and his brother's disappearance in the war, his jilting of Rose after coming home to his mother, and his return after twenty years in California to become the confidante of Nancy. He now lives a lonely, melancholy existence as a rural postman, cultivating a subtle herb-garden around the little house where he lives alone. His life is dominated by the memory of that night in the Civil War when Hilary disappeared, its prelude and aftermath, and the regret that he tried to understand Hilary too late. For on that evening in 1864 Hilary, in one moment, brings to expression his previous years: he bursts out that he prefers death to seeing Leander return to Rose, and leaves the tent. Leander resents "the understanding which followed," whispering "one word to himself: 'Love...'" A skirmish with the enemy prevents him at first from realizing that Hilary is missing. For Leander it is the hour that divides his life "into two parts." After the war he rejects Rose, and then lives in western mining towns in California until he returns in 1884 to Hope's Corner. He still repeats "that night in his imagination." He is still regarded as strange by Henry and other men and women generally, but he is "universally respected;" and in Mrs. Ursula Duff, his sister Nancy, and Rose, he finds sympathetic spirits.

He is affectionate and "drawn toward little boys of his brother's age," but they avoid him because to be his friend is a "mark of prudery and effeminacy." His family returns his love, but Rose offers him the same affection devoid of understanding that she does Henry. He knows now that it is "satiety," not repentance, that brought to an end his "excesses in California," and realizes that the subject is forbidden even to Nancy. When Nancy dies, he takes in her son Timothy, the handsome indolent sort of adolescent who "would never have to learn, or hesitate, or pity." After adopting Timothy he is happy for three years, even content that Timothy reverses "the family formula, which was to be proud in anticipation, ashamed in retrospect." But the boy, who does "not want to love or be loved," is oppressed by Leander's sensibilities and principles. He acquires a sweetheart who is disapproved of by the family because she comes of Irish-Catholic immigrant stock.

Dramatic events take place in Leander's garden, where a "solitary woodcock" has a nest that Leander asks Timothy to keep secret. The bird's "unusual courage, and the intuition by which it knew itself safe and loved" arouses emotions in Leander which could only have been shared by Hilary. The bird's shyness and secrecy are like Leander's and symbolize his sensitive and difficult capacity to love.

Timothy betrays his uncle by showing the woodcock to his sweetheart, who goads him into killing the bird so that she may make a hat of it. Although Leander suppresses any show of emotion or criticism, the boy quietly announces he can no longer stand living with his uncle, who loves him "too much," and makes him feel "like a brute." Leander quietly frees Timothy, signing over the deed of his now valuable California property, and the nephew packs to go west as Leander in his now-dying garden reflects that "it was perfect now and his heart was broken." He has played both parts; the rejected and the rejector. At the sight of a bloody feather he begins to destroy the garden with his bare hands. Only later in the novel is it revealed that he dies afterwards on his way west to visit Timothy.

CHAPTER EIGHT: "The Dead. His Grandmother's Final Grief. The Photograph Albums."

"The hard bits of experience" that Rose Tower has not been able to communicate with snippets of information and stories are for her contained in "one or two poetic phrases, her favorite being 'Life is like a great county fair.'" Alwyn extends the metaphor in his imagination to encompass the experiences of life as a whole. His grandmother's concern for the past is evidenced in her arrangement of Decoration Day programs to honor the Civil War dead and her upkeep of the cemetery, where Alwyn contemplates the graves of his relatives and ancestors.

To his grandmother, deaths and departures were alike until her daughter Flora's death in 1914. Then, no longer able "to develop new habits and new hopes," she felt "she would not live to see the end of this anguish." Unreconciled to the "final wound" which the "Divine Hand" has dealt, she seeks to avoid thinking of her griefs in calling on her neighbors (about whom she gossips with a "sardonic gaiety") and posing as a rocklike woman. It is in this mood that she considers the many portraits in the two albums and the daguerreotypes in their cases.

They are, for Alwyn then, and especially as narrator later, fragments which can never be complete because of lack of material, partial reconstructions given what form they have by Alwyn's impressionistic rendering and the shards of his grandmother's comments. "But he knew what she knew and tried to forget, that each picture was a tomb where a dead heart (or merely the youth and freshness of a heart which was now old) lay buried — buried with its affections, its apathy, its fury."

There are over a dozen fragments varying from a few lines to a couple of pages, from mere remarks to incidents (such as that of the man who went mad at the sight of a lynching) that nag the mind.

CHAPTER NINE: Uncle Jim as a Young Man.

The male line of the second generation of Towers, Henry's sons, are Ralph (Alwyn's father), Evan, and Jim, the latter chosen to be a minister, the educated son of the family. Although the brothers are alike in their youth, their natures and fates are different. Evan is the restless one, who loves only his uncle Leander. Ralph is the one doomed to "do what his father had done before him — work the land and care for the old people," and Jim is the lucky one, who goes to a provincial little college where "culture seemed to be more highly regarded than religion." But his burden of fulfilling his father's prophecy of "success at last for one of the Towers" is heavy and binding.

When he announces his desire to marry Irene Geiger and tour with her as a concert singer, his outraged father insists on his duty to "bear witness for the Lord;" besides, what of the investment made in his education which would be "wasted"? The proposition of Irene's father to finance them is rejected: he is a brewer. "Singing doesn't count," his brother Ralph points out to him; "it's not much of a man's job." Everyone he loves does not want him to sing. "He had seemed for a few months to be an exception to the family rule of disappointment; there were to be no exceptions." He realizes that he will have to serve his family in recompense, that he will have to "represent their ideals. Perhaps, he thought, that is all it means to be a servant of God." Resigned, he disappoints himself and Irene for the family. Reflecting that he has "only his talents," he gives the prayer "of all men such as he: that he might make use of other people's passion, in his life — he would have need of it; and that those who loved him should have no reason to be ashamed of him; and that he might never be found out." His will is broken, and he feels left with no heart to break.

Word comes that Leander has died on his way west to visit Timothy; Jim enters a theological seminary, returning to see Ralph married to Marianne Duff. Irene Geiger begins her singing career, her voice given new beauty by her sadness.

CHAPTER TEN: Marianne Tower

Alwyn's mother grew up in an "atmosphere of anger and idealism." Her parents, Ira and Ursula Duff, out of "moral fanaticism" and stubbornness of character made their marriage a "bizarre tragedy." Ursula adjusted to her "despotic and malicious" husband with "intelligent malice and courage," hiding her resentment, with the result that even the two sons, running away from home, "muttered that it was their mother who was a demon."

But by the time she is fourteen Marianne begins to perceive the "true nature of the relationship," that her mother is "continually on trial" before others, "like all men and women before God sitting in judgment," and her father is "a half-divine spirit, all malice." It is but "a short step" to "the Protestant faith." Baptised by immersion during a Free Will Baptist Revival, and now "responsible to God" (in contrast to her mother whose religion is a kind of "public duty," and "unhappy poetry''), Marianne believes in happiness "as a duty as well as a miracle."

While away teaching in Milwaukee, she yearns for Ralph Tower, but is courted by Paul Fairchild, son of the local Episcopalian Bishop. Her father instigates the rumor of her engagement, and when Fairchild hears of it he proposes, springing marriage "like a trap beneath her driven feet," for she thinks like her mother, that "her pride is the spirit of God in her heart." The young man is a deceptive romantic who continually tries to seduce her, and after several months, Marianne is so fatigued she finds it difficult to break with him; her tactic is to pretend innocence to avoid his advances. Finally he threatens to ruin her reputation unless she marries him; she slaps him and flees in a high fever to Hope's Corner with an older friend, Evangeline, to whom she confesses her love for Ralph Tower. Evangeline untangles the misunderstanding, the two are married, and "swiftly the wine of passion itself changed for her into the pure water of Christian married life."

CHAPTER ELEVEN: "His Father. His Uncle Jim's Later Life. The Religious Faith of the Family."

This chapter focuses on three characters, placing them in loose juxtaposition. A hunter that kills with a pitiless tenderness, Ralph Tower takes his little son into the woods with him, but Alwyn is afraid of the bleeding birds and the sound of guns. Toward this reaction his father's attitude is embarrassment and finally displeasure. Ralph is a skillful taxidermist who works as though "bringing about a resurrection," for he "loves the lives of animals as well as their death;" good at breaking colts, he is careful and tender as he smothers a snow owl with chloroform. But he cannot make his son "see the charm of it." "There are things that require not sensibility but the lack of it to be felt, and he was still too imaginative to understand them." Ralph never accomplishes his dream of becoming a veterinary surgeon because a father who never changed his mind is, for Ralph, his "fate."

Ralph's "lucky brother," the Rev. James A. Tower, in his middle life and later, is melancholy and complacent. He returns to Hope's Corner several times each year to brood "lovingly

upon their lives, the labor, the poverty, the narrowness of out-
look," thinking of his own life in contrast as "progress."

After his ordination James "preached a cheerful modern
faith," in a fashionable church of a Chicago suburb, and having
forgotten Irene Geiger and his singing ambitions, he married the
rich Caroline Fielding, only to find it did not release her from
"periodical nervous pain." Nor could the marriage release her
from the claims of her two sisters and formidable dowager
mother, claims so pressing the young minister retired to live in
the Chicago mansion of "the late merchant prince Cromwell
Fielding," a "veritable museum of middle western luxuries,"
"where progress and millionaire civilization had been born." In
this jungle of late Victorian style, where "an elaborate worldliness served as a setting for puritan austerities," Caroline's
"vanity merely emphasized her virtue." Childless, James and his
wife "extend their hospitality to Alwyn," thinking they are
"ready to make all the necessary sacrifices for him."

Alwyn discovers the events which take place in the mansion
are "like the episodes of a long symbolic play at which part of
the audience may laugh, while the rest shudders at the secret
meaning." The establishment is an hierarchy dominated by the
mother. Caroline loves her husband and wants him to serve
God, but her mother's house is "a sacred establishment" a
"sumptuous private chapel to the glory of motherhood, which
is the source of the glory of God." Caroline suddenly dies, her
face "at the last moment" assuming "the first look of humility"
that has appeared there, and a suggestion of regret "for everything believed, everything done, everything left undone." Again
aware of his presence after "the horror and despair" of death,
the three women assure James that to return to the ministry
would be selfish and vain, for "charity and idealism begin at
home." Besides, wealth had been "an aspect of Caroline's
character," and leaving it and the mansion would be like suffering her death a second time. James becomes "a perfect son-in-
law and widower," performing "senseless duties invented by the
ladies to discipline him."

He takes over efficiently the place of a dismissed janitor,
marries another Fielding daughter, and not happy but content,
he looks back "indulgently upon his ambitions: love, music, and
the ministry — unwise wishes of a selfish boy."

The third section of the chapter, concerning the religious faith of the family, is highly condensed and aphoristic exposition. The religious atmosphere of Alwyn's childhood is almost entirely that of his mother, Marianne, who revised with originality her mother's, reversing its disillusionment to produce "strong happy beliefs."

> The very principles on which America was founded were the result; and like certain of the Pilgrims, she represented them with the competence and heedless ardor of a woman under enchantment.

She is willing to spread her religion by force, and prefers hypocrisy in others to their lack of shame. Adherence and obedience is required, secrecy being dangerous. To theology she is comparatively indifferent.

> Thus, though Protestantism is a branch of Christianity founded upon faith, Marianne Tower, like most American Protestants in this respect, was entirely concerned with works: with severities, kindnesses, abstinences, successes, which all the world could hear and understand; with sin instead of heresy, reform instead of repentance; with serving more than with loving God.
> ...and she knew no other God but God, in whose veins there was Jewish blood — God of clean and respectable living, innocent thought, and industry.
> Her religion — perhaps, Alwyn thought, American Christianity as a whole — was a religion of ideal prose; all the beauty it had was the elegance of a perfect law, a Napoleonic code. It deified Jesus, but deified him as a social leader and teacher martyred for his virtue....

Money is "the result of ability, and was in itself an ability or talent," "a power for good," but "more of it than could be spent painstakingly, painfully," is suspicious. She believes the human body is sacred, all dissipation sacrilegious, and love, "often as automatic in its influence as a drug, often wasteful of time, health and money, existed only to bring men and women together in marriage." As for country:

> When she spoke of the continent of America to her children it was as another talent.... that the whole race had.... it would always be the principle talent of Americans.... Lent, not given; to be guarded and risked and multiplied and used to the Glory of God, the owner.

Alwyn speculates that his mother might be called an aristo-
crat. In a country where the upper classes serve the country to
"amuse themselves and to gain their ends of vanity and glory,"
the "middle classes serving only themselves, bringing up sons in
the interests of family fortunes," he thinks that perhaps the only
aristocracy is "in poor homes in the country, in the strong,
ignorant imaginations of such women as his mother and grandmothers," who feel responsible to God and nation "before the
family and to the family only before themselves." They are:

> aristocratic because of a vague sense of having actually
> aristocratic grandparents, many times removed, and be-
> cause their religion happened to be public rather than
> private, putting good behavior above the joys and pains
> of faith, judging private virtue by the public good....
> Thus Alwyn began to make his peace with the torment-
> ing sense of having come down in the world, which
> was his birthright as a Tower.

Alwyn feels his mother's religion is "but a jurisprudence of a
moral commonwealth," with intimate emotions substituting for
religious exercises. Therefore she is not "chilled by a faith which
was all ethics....she was the perfect Protestant." His mother's
version of "the faith of his fathers" helps to determine "the beliefs for which eventually he was to desert that faith altogether."
Alwyn does not feel that God is "one and uniform," but
legion, and "he fancied himself in love with them all." God is
the law, but "also the breaking of the law," and Alwyn realizes
"that even to be an outlaw...would require more strength
than, by himself, he would have.... And if his God were Gods?
Would not his life, if he committed himself to them all, be a
sort of Tower of Babel...?"
For his mother, however, "her religion had indeed brought
about a miracle of energy and peace; it was also true that her
marriage had made her religion what it was then." All that is
in religion enigmatic "gradually wrapped itself in the pure shame
and darkness which hid away her marriage bed." Yet her love
for her husband gave her strength and kept her young, and "for
twenty years the farmhouse was electric with it."
Ralph, in contrast, draws his religious strength from physical
experience, heat and cold, the animals and the land. His wife's
optimism cures his melancholy and pessimism, aiding his natural

obedience and love. The two are beautifully opposite, each finding completion in the other.

From the parents the children inherit "as if it were a religion, a theory of love...which, changing its form but keeping its vitality—as in transmigration a vast, vague soul, typically American—would probably be heard of for some time to come."

The annual Methodist camp meeting with which the chapter closes presents a declining uninspired evangelism that both moves and repells Alwyn. When his father rises to give testimony to his faith, Alwyn feels it is because of the living religion of his marriage, which is one with love and the family.

CHAPTER TWELVE: Uncle Evan (John Craig)

During Alwyn's boyhood a stranger named John Craig visits the Tower family, the second time just before the death of Alwyn's grandfather—although the old man will not see him. Only then does Alwyn learn that the stranger is his uncle Evan Tower, and it is years later before he has the full story and understands it, his uncle by then becoming a friend closer to him than his own father, a parallel to the relationship between Leander and Evan himself.

Hating the war, feeling it unjustified, observing Americans as oppressors, coming "as a soldier to a foreign land, he learned, as soldiers often do, how little he loved his own." A British soldier named Marbury (who gives Evan the name John Craig) one night smuggles a drunken Evan onto a freighter. Reminded of his uncle Hilary's disappearance during another war, Evan writes his mother that he has deserted. "But it was something more than homesickness which hurt him; it was the keenest of regrets, that of a young man who has made his choice, for the infinite possibilities he has given up, when at last it is too late to change his mind."

In London he deserts the ship and his friend Marbury. Alone in "the great beast of a city," "in the yellow fog where everyone, not only himself, had a secret," he feels safe, and the derelicts are "his countrymen." He is cold and hungry when he meets the Italian-French Suzanne Orfeo, who runs her father's antique shop in Soho. Taken in as a helper, he is allowed to do nothing. Well fed and clean, he is happier than he has ever been, unaware of the subtleties of European courtship that Suzanne and his sister are subjecting him to.

> He wanted never to have a home again, or to be surrounded by a family. People of his own kind provoked him to be unlike them — that is, unlike himself; but among those whom he might never understand, he understood himself and was his own best friend.... His only ambition was to escape the ambitions which others might have for him and oblige him to fulfill.

But he does not escape them. He falls in love with Suzanne, proposes and is rejected, then finds to his dismay that he has been accepted, even after confessing he is a deserter. For Suzanne is determined to go to America, and he finds himself promising to take her there and grow rich. He realizes now he loves his country but did not know it. In a moment of profound insight and melancholy he knows his life is over before it has begun, that love has "run its course." He regrets his decision for he knows it means that he will be leaving his self behind. He knows that in his future life he will have to conform more than ever before to keep from being discovered. Aware of a number of other ironies, and that he will always be a deserter, tired of being young, he thinks of Leander's warnings as those of an old man who never grew up. Soon "the total disappearance of Evan Tower" will take place. "So, with the passage of time, the soul of a man loses itself in his life."

The rest of that life is very much as he expected it to be. With Suzanne he settles near Taos, New Mexico, gradually growing fairly wealthy and influential, raising a son, Leander Orfeo Craig. Suzanne and her sister live in one corner of the house and Evan in the other with his gang of tough cowboys, although he never loves another woman. He wishes that he might die if his soul could pass into Orfeo's life "and Evan Tower, the deserter, be disguised by nothing more than fearless childhood, and begin all over again..." Twice in his later life he returns to Wisconsin to find that his father will not see him and his mother is no longer interested in his treason, marriage, or life. He finds that only Leander and Evan are "his real family, and their souls had passed into his life — that is, John Craig's life. He had thought that he was tired of it; but he was a strong man, and had no other life to live."

CHAPTER THIRTEEN: Aunt Flora

To Alwyn as a child, his Aunt Flora seemed "a girl nearly thirty years old." Two men "had troubled five years of her life," the first being Richard Wallace, a local Don Juan who drives "the most violent and shining horses in the country." Flora intends to be "the first to enjoy his wooing and resist his charm." But she soon loses her ignorance, though not her innocence. She is so busy protecting it, in fact, that "she could not study her heart to know whether she loved him." Timid, fearful of temptation, prudish, strictly brought up, her ability to love is sapped, but not those defenses which cause Wallace to capitulate, to propose "merely for relief from pain."

Marianne, another perfectionist, is her only confidante, but Flora, unlike her, finds her own ideals conflict with her wishes and shadowy desires. Undecided as to what she wants or what she should sacrifice, she refuses the proposal—to her mother's dismay.

> For in fact Flora resembled them all, beginning with her father (his fastidious, idealistic melancholy), and her mother (her lack of cunning, her willingness to wait and give in); preventing herself from doing things, just as they had prevented one another.

Then she wants Richard back, but it is too late. Next she is courted by Herbert Ruhl, the new local doctor, but a Catholic. She is no longer broken-hearted over Richard, but the sexual battle repeats itself, with a difference. Ruhl is delighted to be repulsed, for it assures him of her purity. She refuses him on religious grounds, for her father has told her on his deathbed never to marry a Catholic.

> There was a part of herself which would always be closed until the very wall of life was destroyed. The faith of her family was part of this wall.

To her, Catholicism is mysterious and ominous. She overhears her brother John Craig say she should have been a Catholic nun, that she has "the proper spirit" for it. This and the maliciousness of the community about a Tower marrying a Catholic increases her determination. Her love, "what there was of it," sinks "into a quicksand of impossibility," and her singing is something done "bravely throughout the last years of her life." Alwyn, the adolescent, listens in envy of "the secret experience," without caring "how much of it was misery, how much love, and how much homesickness of a spirit which had not felt at home anywhere."

Flora falls ill at twenty-nine, and is treated by Dr. Ruhl, to whom she explains that she had foreknowledge of her early death, and that this was the reason for her indecision. Unable to endure her weeping, Dr. Ruhl calls in a substitute, who diagnoses the case as hopeless. She peacefully dies lifting her hands for the good angel she believes has come for her. Her mother is broken by Flora's death, life never to have any importance for her after that.

CHAPTER FOURTEEN: Ira and Ursula Duff

Alwyn's grandmother Ursula never lighted the lamps until the shades were drawn, he remembers, because she thought it "indecent" to be observed as though one were an actor in a play, an ironic comment on the roles that she and her husband have played throughout life.

Pressured in her youth by two younger sisters to marry Ira Duff, a handsome heavy-drinker, Ursula sets about to reform him, and accomplishes it in four years, complete with a signed pledge, conversion, and church-work. Her twins Ferris and Forrest die of a sickness caused by their father's taking them through a snowstorm to a cattlemarket. to show them off. She makes her accusations of her husband with perfect composure, and they are true, Alwyn learns. Yet her sexual modesty in later life becomes a sort of madness.

Duff is "the greatest talker in the country," addicted to absurd diction and malapropisms. He is constantly wounded by his wife's honesty, and in revenge he insists upon cooking, washing the dishes and playing the martyr, with malice masked as pity and affection, but out of sincere belief in his own goodness. His untrue stories, many of them about his wife, are accepted as the truth by most people, although he fears their disbelief. His wife is not believed, and although her daughter and her grandson love her, her sons do not even pretend pity. In their old age, the couple pray together. He is her "enemy and priest;" she

never speaks of religion or connects it with love. She tells Alwyn that Leander Tower is the only gentleman she ever knew.

In spite of all, she praises her husband for being virtuous,
God-fearing, and church-going. Through old age they battle each
other "as if they lay on one deathbed — the dying hands interlaced by habit, by hatred of each other and love of God, the
dying mouths murmuring truths without pity and complaining
still." As a result, Alwyn is afraid of old age, and tries to
ignore hate, yet understand love. Symbolic of the relationship
is the pair of locked stag-antlers shown by Ira to Alwyn. Ira
claims they are his, but Ursula, as she lovingly dusts them, says
he gave them to her. To her daughter her repeated advice is
never to cry. On her deathbed she gives Alwyn a Begonia leaf
and tells him, "You're my sweetheart, you know."

NOTES

CHAPTER 1: *INTRODUCTION*

1. The term "second" or "artistic" self refers in this study to the mind of the author as it appears in his work, as defined and discussed by Wayne C. Booth in *The Rhetoric of Fiction,* Chicago, 1961, pp. 70 ff. *et passim.*

CHAPTER 2: *THE APPLE OF THE EYE*

1. "The Two Dollar Novel," *New Republic,* XXXV (1923), pp. 158-159.
2. C. E. Shorer, "The Maturing of Glenway Wescott," *College English,* XVIII (1957), p. 321.
3. The title of Wescott's first book of poems is *The Bitterns,* in which the predominant mood is melancholy.
4. Kenneth Burke, "Delight and Tears," *The Dial,* LXXVII (1924), pp. 513-515.

CHAPTER 3: *THE GRANDMOTHERS*

1. Fred B. Millet, "Introduction," *The Grandmothers: A Family Portrait,* Harper's Modern Classics Edition (New York, 1950), p. xl. (All page numbers refer to this edition).
2. William H. Rueckert, *Glenway Wescott* (New York, 1965), p. 60.
3. The second ellipses marks are Wescott's.
4. The first ellipses marks are Wescott's.
5. The last ellipses marks are Wescott's.
6. Joseph Warren Beach, *The Twentieth Century Novel* (New York, 1932), p. 479.
7. Ellipses marks are Wescott's.
8. The concept of *image* and *truth* can be found as well in Wescott's poems and essays of the twenties. See Rueckert, chapter one.
9. *The Bitterns, A Book of Twelve Poems* (Evanston, Illinois, 1920).

CHAPTER 4: *GOOD-BYE, WISCONSIN; THE BABE'S BED; AND OTHER STORIES*

1. Rueckert, pp. 61-62.
2. Kahn, p. 127.
3. Kenneth Burke, "A Decade of American Fiction," *Bookman,* LXIX (1929), p. 566.
4. Rueckert, pp. 66-67.
5. The name is consistent with the bird symbology in *The Apple of the Eye,* where crows signify death.
6. Kahn, p. 120.
7. Rueckert, p. 69.
8. Kahn, p. 120.
9. Rueckert, p. 93.

CHAPTER 5: *THE PILGRIM HAWK*

1. Morton Dauwen Zabel, "The Whisper of the Devil," *Craft and Character in Modern Fiction,* p. 504.
2. *Ibid.,* p. 305.
3. The ellipses marks are Wescott's.
4. The last ellipses marks are Wescott's.

CHAPTER 6: *APARTMENT IN ATHENS*

1. *Twentieth Century Authors,* eds. S. J. Kunitz and Howard Haycraft (New York, 1942), pp. 1498-1500.
2. "The Two Dollar Novel," pp. 158-159.
3. Rueckert, p. 117.
4. The ellipses marks are Wescott's.
5. The ellipses marks are Wescott's.
6. The ellipses marks are Wescott's.
7. *Lempriere's Classical Dictionary,* ed. F. A. Wright (London, 1951), p. 407.
8. *Ibid.,* p. 149.

CHAPTER 7: *CONCLUSION*

1. Rueckert, "Preface," n.p.
2. *Ibid.,* pp. 132-134.
3. *Ibid.,* p. 152.
4. Kahn, pp. 191-192.
5. See Kahn's chapters on the thirties and the personal letters of Wescott in Kahn's appendix.
6. The exceptions are two inferior short stories.
7. "A Record of Friendship," New York *Times Book Review* (October 9, 1966), pp. 1, 26.

BIBLIOGRAPHY

PRIMARY SOURCES

I. *Books*

The Bitterns, A Book of Twelve Poems. Evanston, Illinois: Monroe Wheeler, 1920.

The Apple of the Eye. New York: The Dial Press, 1924.

Natives of Rock: XX Poems: 1921-1922. Decorations by Pamela Bianco. New York: Francesco Bianco, 1925.

The Grandmothers, A Family Portrait. New York: Harper & Brothers, 1927; Harper's Modern Classics Edition, 1950; Atheneum Paperback Edition, 1962.

Good-Bye, Wisconsin. New York: Harper & Brothers, 1928; Signet Edition, 1964.

The Babe's Bed. Paris: Harrison of Paris, 1930.

Fear and Trembling. New York: Harper & Brothers, 1932.

A Calendar of Saints for Unbelievers. Paris: Harrison of Paris, 1932; New York: Harper & Brothers, 1933.

The Pilgrim Hawk, A Love Story. New York: Harper & Brothers, 1940; Harper & Row, 1966. Included in *Great American Short Novels,* edited by William Phillips, New York: Dial Press, 1946; and in *Six Great Modern Short Novels,* New York: Dell First Edition, 1954.

Apartment in Athens. New York: Harper & Brothers, 1945.

Twelve Fables of Aesop. Newly narrated by Glenway Wescott. Linoleum Blocks by Antonio Frasconi. New York: The Museum of Modern Art, 1954; Paperback Edition, n.d. (1964).

Images of Truth: Remembrances and Criticism. New York: Harper & Row, 1962; Harper Colophon Edition, 1964.

II. *Essays, Poems, Reviews and Stories*

"Classics in English" (Review of *Sappho* by H. T. Wharton, *The Golden Treasury of the Greeks,* by A. L. Lothian, *Medallions in Clay* by R. Aldington, and *The Poet's Translation Series: Second Set), Poetry,* XIX (1921), 47-51.

"Still Hunt" (Six Poems), *Poetry* XVIII (1921), 303-307.

"New Fire" (Review of *A Canopic Jar* by Leonora Speyer), *Poetry,* XIX (1921), 47-51.

"Alexander Blok" (Review of *The Twelve* by Alexander Blok), *Poetry,* XIX (1921), 149-151.

"A Sonneteer" (Review of *Poems* by Steward Mitchell), *Poetry,* XX (1922), 49-51.

"The Crocodile's Tears" (Review of *Neighbors Henceforth* by Owen Wister), *New Republic,* XXXIII (1923), 206-208.

"The Two-Dollar Novel" (Omnibus Review of fiction), *New Republic,* XXXV (1923), 158-159.

"The Gift Horse" (Review of *Futility* by William Gerhardi), *New Republic,* XXXV (1923), 214.

"Sense and Sensibility" (Review of *One Hundred Best Books* and *Samphire* by John Cowper Powys), *New Republic,* XXXVI (1923), 26-27.

"Men Like Birds" (Poem), *Contact,* No. 5 (June, 1923).

"Named Flamingo" (Poem), *The Dial,* LXXV (1923), 264.

"The First Book of Mary Butts" (Review of *Speed the Plough and Other Stories* by Mary Butts), *The Dial,* LXXV (1923), 282-284.

"Impure Splendor" (Review of *Escapade* by Evelyn Scott), *Broom,* V (1923), 233-235.

"Old Style of Garden" (Poem), *The Little Review,* Spring, 1924.

"Concerning Miss Moore's Observations" (Review of *Observations* by Marianne Moore), *The Dial,* LXXVIII (1925), 1-4.

"A Historian of Conquests" (Review of *Hernando De Soto* by R. B. Cunningham Graham), *The Dial,* LXXVIII (1925), 417-419.

"Mr. Osbert Sitwell's Fiction" (Review of *Triple Fugue* by Osbert Sitwell), *The Dial,* LXXXVIII (1925), 506-507.

"The Quarter's Books" (Essay-Review), *The Transatlantic Review,* II (1925), 446-448.

"A Monument" (Review of *The Spanish Farm* by R. H. Mottram), *The Dial,* LXXIX (1925), 246-247.

"A Courtly Poet" (Review of *A Draft of Sixteen Cantos* by Ezra Pound), *The Dial,* LXXIX, 501-503.

"Miss Robert's First Novel" (Review of *The Time of Man* by E. M. Roberts), *The Dial,* LXXXIII (1927), 73-75.

"Elizabeth Maddox Roberts: A Personal Note" (Essay), *The Bookman,* LXXI (1930), 12-15.

"Hurt Feelings" (Story), *The North American Review,* CCXXXIV (1932), 223-240.

"A Sentimental Contribution" (Essay on Henry James), *Hound and Horn,* VII (1933-1934), 523-534.

"Poor Grueze" (Art Criticism), *Wadsworth Atheneum,* XIII (1935), 2-8.

"The Rescuer" (Story), *Life and Letters Today,* XV (Autumn, 1936), 150-156.

"The Sight of a Dead Body" (Story), *Signatures,* I (1936), 135-136.

"Biography and Impression," Leaflet by Julien Levy Gallery Concerning the Painter Kristian Tonny, 23 February 1937-15 March 1937.

"A Commentary," Leaflet for the Julien Levy Gallery Announcing the Exhibition of the Murals of Jared French, 24 January 1939-7 February 1939.

"The Summer Ending" (Poem), *Poetry,* LIV (1939), 306-307.

"The Dream of Audubon, Libretto of a Ballet in Three Scenes," *The Best One-Act Plays of 1940.* Ed. by Margaret Mayorga. New York: Dodd, Mead & Company, 1941, 361-374.

"Personal and Otherwise" (Autobiographical Note), *Harper's Magazine,* CLXXXI (November, 1940), n.p.

"The Moral of F. Scott Fitzgerald" (Essay originally published in 1941), *The Crack-Up.* Ed. by Edmund Wilson. New York: *New Directions,* 1945, 323-327.

"Mr. Auerbach in Paris" (Story), *Harper's Magazine,* CLXXXIV (1941-1942), 469-473.

"Personal and Otherwise" (Autobiographical Note), *Harper's Magazine,* CLXXXIV (April, 1942), n.p.

"The Frenchman Six Feet Three" (Story), *Harper's Magazine,* CLXXXV (1942), 131-140.

(Autobiographical Essay), *Twentieth Century Authors.* Ed. by S. J. Kunitz and Howard Haycraft. New York: The H. W. Wilson Company, 1942. 1498-1500.

"Erich Maria Remarque," Leaflet for the Knoedler Galleries Announcing the Showing of the Remarque Collection of Paintings, 19 October 1943 - 18 November 1943.

"I Love New York" (Essay), *Harper's Bazaar,* LXXVII, Part 2 (December, 1943), 53, 55, 58, 104, 106, 108, 111.

"Stories by a Writer's Writer" (Review of *The Leaning Tower* by K. A. Porter), New York *Times Book Review,* 17 September 1944, 1.

"A Day in the Country" (Essay), *Tomorrow,* IX (July, 1947), 35-37.

"Love for a Traitor" (Review of *The Heat of the Day* by Elizabeth Bowen), *The Saturday Review,* XXXII (19 February 1949), 9-10.

"In Praise of Edith Sitwell," *Proceedings of the American Academy of Arts and Letters, and the National Institute of Arts and Letters,* Second Series, No. 1, 1951, 49-52.

"Presentation to Marianne Moore of the Gold Medal for Poetry," *Proceedings of the American Academy of Arts and Letters and the National Institute of Arts and Letters,* Second Series, No. 4, 1954, 11-13.

(Autobiographical Essay), *Twentieth Century Authors.* Ed. by S. J. Kunitz and Howard Haycraft. New York: The H. W. Wilson Company, 1955, 1067.

"The Old and the New" (Opening Remarks for an exhibit of paintings), *Proceedings of the American Academy of Arts and Letters, and the National Institute of Arts and Letters,* Second Series, No. 5, 1955, 69-71.

"Introduction to a Reading by Robert Frost, 11 December 1955," *Proceedings of the American Academy of Arts and Letters, and the National Institute of Arts and Letters,* Second Series, No. 6, 1956, 67-68.

(A Reading, with Louise Bogan, of their favorite poems by contemporary poets), *Proceedings of the American Academy of Arts and Letters, and the National Institute of Arts and Letters,* Second Series, No. 6, 1956, 71-72.

"Presentation to Lincoln Kirstein of the Award for Distinguished Service to the Arts," *Proceedings of the American Academy of Arts and Letters, and the National Institute of Arts and Letters,* Second Series, No. 9, 1959, 266.

"The Best of All Possible Worlds" (Essay), *Proceedings of the American Academy of Arts and Letters, and the National Institute of Arts and Letters,* Second Series, No. 9, 1959, 277-289.

"Presentation of Grants and Awards," *Proceedings of the American Academy of Arts and Letters, and the National Institute of Arts and Letters,* Second Series, No. 10, 1960, 324-325.

"Presentation of Grants and Awards," *Proceedings of the American Academy of Arts and Letters, and the National Institute of Arts and Letters,* Second Series, No. 11, 1961, 29-30.

"Statement (on censorship) Read at the Council Meeting February 3, 1959," *Proceedings of the American Academy of Arts and Letters, and the National Institute of Arts and Letters,* Second Series, No. 11, 1961, 71-73.

"Not a Proper Englishman" (Review of *The Fifth Queen* by Ford Madox Ford), *Book Week,* 27 October 1963, 1, 10.

"A Surpassing Sequel" (Review of *The Wapshot Scandal,* by John Cheever), *Book Week,* 5 January 1964, 1, 9.

"All of Us on the Half-Shell" (Review of *The Oysters of Loc- mariaquer* by Eleanor Clark), *Book Week,* 12 July 1964, 1, 14.

"A Record of Friendship" (Review of *Remembering Mr. Maug- ham* by Garson Kanin), New York *Times Book Review,* 9 October 1966, 1, 26.

SECONDARY SOURCES

Beach, Joseph Warren. *The Twentieth Century Novel: Studies in Technique.* New York: D. Appleton-Century Company, 1932.

Brace, Marjorie. "Thematic Problems of the American Novelist," *Accent,* VI (1945), 44-53.

Burke, Kenneth. "Delight and Tears," *The Dial,* LXXVII (1924), 513-515.

———. "A Decade of American Fiction," *Bookman,* LXIX (1929), 561-567.

———. "The Poet and the Passwords," *New Republic,* LXXI (1932), 310-313.

Cowley, Malcolm. *Exile's Return.* New York: The Viking Press, 1951.

Hatcher, Harlan. *Creating the Modern American Novel.* New York: Farrar & Rinehart, 1935.

Hicks, Granville. *The Great Tradition, An Interpretation of American Literature since the Civil War.* New York: The Macmillan Company, 1933.

Hoffman, Frederick J. *The Twenties.* New York: The Viking Press, 1951.

———, Charles Allen, and Carolyn F. Ulrich. *The Little Magazine.* Princeton University Press, 1951.

Kahn, Sy Myron. *Glenway Wescott: A Critical and Biographical Study,* Ann Arbor: University Microfilms, 1957, Publication number 20,631.

———. "Glenway Wescott: A Bibliography," *Bulletin of Bibliography,* XXII (1956-1959), 156-160.

Kohler, Dayton. "Glenway Wescott: Legend Maker," *Bookman,* LXXIII (1931), 142-145.

Millet, Fred. "Introduction," *The Grandmothers.* Harper's Modern Classics Edition. New York: Harper & Brothers, 1950.

Paul, Sherman, "Paul Rosenfeld," *Port of New York.* Urbana: University of Illinois Press, 1961.

Quinn, Patrick R. "The Case History of Glenway Wescott," *Frontier and Midland,* XIX (1938-1939), 11-16.

Rosenfeld, Paul. *Port of New York.* Urbana: University of Illinois Press, 1961.

Rueckert, William H. *Glenway Wescott.* New York: Twayne Publishers, Inc., 1965.

Schorer, C. E. "The Maturing of Glenway Wescott," *College English,* XVIII (1957), 320-326.

Suckow, Ruth. "Middle Western Literature," *The English Journal,* XXI (1932), 175-182.

Zabel, Morton Dauwen. "The Whisper of the Devil," *Craft and Character* in *Modern Fiction.* New York: The Viking Press, 1957.